100 THINGS CRIMSON TIDE FANS SHOULD KNOW & DO BEFORE THEY DIE

100 THINGS CRIMSON TIDE FANS SHOULD KNOW & DO BEFORE THEY DIE

Christopher Walsh

TRIUMPH
BOOKS

Library of Congress has catalogued the previous edition as follows:

Walsh, Christopher J., 1968–
100 things Crimson Tide fans should know & do before they die / Christopher Walsh. — updated BCS championship ed.
p. cm.

1. Alabama Crimson Tide (Football team)—History. 2. University of Alabama—Football—History. 3. Football players—Alabama. I. Title. II. Title: One hundred things Crimson Tide fans should know and do before they die.
GV958.A4W346 2012
796.332'630976184—dc23

2012020650

This book is available in quantity at special discounts for your group or organization. For further information, contact:

Triumph Books LLC
814 North Franklin Street
Chicago, Illinois 60610
(312) 337-0747
www.triumphbooks.com

Printed in U.S.A.
ISBN: 978-1-62937-325-6
Design by Patricia Frey
Photos courtesy of the Paul Bryant Museum unless otherwise indicated

In the spirit of a certain coach,
this one's for "Mama"…again.

Contents

Acknowledgments

When I was writing the original version of this book during the fall of 2007 and spring of 2008, it was in the back of my mind that hopefully someday there would be an opportunity for an update.

I never dreamed the first would occur just four years later, and the second before a decade had passed.

A lot has happened since Nick Saban's first season at the Capstone, and not all on the football field. Barack Obama was elected president of the United States, Chesley Sullenberger landed a plane on the Hudson River, and the Deepwater Horizon oil spill in the Gulf of Mexico filled some of the online headlines as newspapers went more and more digital.

With the Crimson Tide, Saban didn't even wait for his recruits to grow into team leaders, winning the 2009 national championship and then going back and doing it again in 2011, 2012, and 2015. Alabama finally secured its first and second Heisman Trophy, it became the premier spot for National Football League teams to find prospects, and Tuscaloosa endured the gut-wrenching April 27, 2011, tornado that went through the heart of the community that would take years to rebuild.

And I thought I had it tough writing the book the first time.

It probably won't surprise any of you to learn that the hardest thing about doing the original version was coming up with the list of 100 things. It remained a work in progress long after the writing process, well through the editing, and still stuck with me well after publication.

Which should be higher, the 1925 or the 1961 national championship? There doesn't seem to be a wrong answer there. Where does Derrick Thomas fit in Alabama history? Who should be mentioned first, Mark Ingram or Derrick Henry, who changed the way everyone in college football looked at Alabama running backs?

But instead of simply updating the book, I wanted to take it to another level. In the original version I grouped together all the national championships and players inducted in the College Football Hall of Fame, which accounted for one third of the 100 things. I also made a point of making sure that every Alabama player enshrined in the Alabama Sports Hall of Fame was mentioned.

The second time I went with a different approach, mixing everything up and trying to find balance between the top players, championships, things to know, things to do, and biggest games—targeting a minimum of 12 to 15 of each with many more mentioned in the boxes, charts, and even trivia questions.

The third time I had to get out the writing equivalent of a shoehorn.

So if your favorite player isn't mentioned or displayed as prominently as you hoped, consider that not even 40 players from the Crimson Tide's long and rich history have their own listings. I also made the conscious decision not to give entries to players who were still in school and continuing to build their legacies. Maybe for the next update.

In going through this process not just once, but numerous times, I'm well aware that 100 Crimson Tide fans could be polled about the list order and would probably give 100 different answers. So feel free to disagree—in fact, I encourage it. Just know that my intent was not to slight or insult anyone. Far from it. More than anything, this is meant to be a celebration of Alabama football and everything it's about.

For the 2015 edition I've added a checklist of things every Alabama fan should do, but what I invite readers to do is make up their own lists, and include the things that are important to them. Whereas this book might include an entry on a legendary player, fans can seek to get that player's autograph—or, better yet, meet him in person. For the national championships, a fan's to-do list could include something like "Have a recording of the 1992 National Championship Game," or "Own something from the 1979 title team." There are scores of possibilities, from "See Bear Bryant's coaching tower," to "Visit every site, on and off campus, where Alabama played home games." If you don't know where these sites are, read on.

Finally, there are some people who need to be thanked.

Thank you to my family for their love and support, even though you all think I'm a bit crazy for doing what I do. The same goes for my extended family around the nation and world. You all know who you are, and how important you are to me (even when I was ignoring your emails, phone calls, and instant messages while working).

Thank you Tom Bast for green-lighting this project and Noah Amstadter for leading the updated edition.

A very special thanks to everyone I worked with while covering the Crimson Tide including Bleacher Report, BamaOnline and 247Sports, and the *Tuscaloosa News*.

Thanks to Patrick McDonald, Brad Green from the Paul W. Bryant Museum, the person who shall only be mentioned as "He Who Shall Not Be Named" so I don't unnecessarily get him in trouble, and Megan Honeycutt for, well, everything.

And thank you, fans. Without you, this book never would have happened, in any version.

Introduction

[The following was the 2007 A-Day cover story for the Tuscaloosa News' *Game Day special section, and appears courtesy of that publication. With Nick Saban making his debut on the Alabama sideline, attendance that afternoon exceeded the 92,137 capacity of Bryant-Denny Stadium, with thousands more turned away at the gate. It crushed the NCAA record for attendance at a spring game.]*

April 21, 2007

Dear Coach,

There's been a cool wind blowing across Tuscaloosa for the past month or so, keeping area residents from storing away their long-sleeve shirts and prolonging the tease of the heat that's certain to follow. Spring came late to this town that you knew so well, but its regular demands, hopes and expectations remain forever unchanged.

Today is A-Day, that unofficial holiday that captivates so many throughout the state, a significant number of whom will congregate at Bryant-Denny Stadium to see, well, very little. Although more than 50,000 fans are expected for this year's celebration, they'll only get a glimpse of the upcoming season by watching a coordinated practice that will be recorded and repeatedly examined between now and the season opener, September 1 against Western Carolina.

There's a lot to like about what's going on around the University of Alabama. Enrollment is up. Sports are again helping propel the school. Your buddy Mal Moore, now athletic director, recently spearheaded a major upgrade of the athletic facilities at a cost exceeding $100 million.

Softball and gymnastics have become national powers, and one can see the women's rowing team practicing in the early morning hours as the steam rises off the Black Warrior River. On the men's side, basketball and baseball have had their moments too.

But Alabama has always been, and always will be, a football school.

As part of the renovations, which included another expansion of Bryant-Denny Stadium, bumping capacity above 92,000 and signaling the end of games at Legion Field, the Crimson Tide fully embraced its history and tradition.

Statues of the national championship winners were erected, and of the seven head coaches who have come and gone over the past 25 years, only Gene Stallings was able to join your elusive club. They left room in the scenic courtyard for another addition, and Alabama hopes it already knows whom he will be.

In many ways you'd probably really like Nick Saban. After Alabama's 6–7 season last year, he was hired away from the Miami Dolphins—the National Football League team that tried to hire you away, only to land Don Shula from the Baltimore Colts (at the expense of a first-round draft pick)—and received the biggest contract in college football history, averaging $4 million a year.

Yeah, that seems like a lot to me too, but there's so much at stake nowadays. The Southeastern Conference annually distributes more than $100 million among its 12 schools (Arkansas and South Carolina joined in 1992), and considering the financial windfall the university expects to receive from donations and other sources, his salary is expected to easily pay for itself.

But that also gives Saban four million reasons why he'll win every argument about how things should be done, not to mention that's he's already won a national championship. It's amazing how that will get a player's attention and put fans into a frenzy.

"He came in, he told us what he wanted and we knew that's what we're going to do," defensive end Wallace Gilberry said. "Don't ask any questions, you just do it, but know you're doing it for a good reason."

Only I'm getting ahead of myself.

When Saban arrived it was under a cloud—OK, thunderstorm—of controversy. National reporters couldn't fathom why anyone would actually want to leave the Dolphins or South Florida, especially after telling reporters that he wasn't interested in Alabama. A recording of an off-the-record conversation was played by a radio station, during which Saban used the Cajun slang term "coonass." And there was always the issue of the money, even though schools like Notre Dame, Southern California and Oklahoma were already paying their head coaches more than $3 million a year.

Naturally, it all caused many outsiders to overlook anything he said or did.

For example, in his first public appearance, Saban wrote a check for $100,000 to the university's first-generation scholarship fund. After a devastating tornado killed nine people, including eight high school students, in Enterprise on March 1, Saban was one of the first to call and offer help. Consequently, the university, in conjunction with the United Way of West Alabama, will have donation stations set up outside the stadium entrances today with proceeds earmarked for the Enterprise city relief fund.

"I just like having an overall program that is helpful to developing players so that they have a fair chance of being successful in life for having been involved in the program—the character, the attitude, the thought and priorities that they develop, the ability to make commitments to things, invest their time in something worthwhile," Saban said. "Get some positive self-gratification and confidence for it, do it with a lot of pride. I think those things will probably help you be successful in anything you choose to do. I enjoy that part."

After a rigorous month of recruiting prior to National Signing Day, Saban began to put his imprint on the team itself. The first impressions were accurate: Intense, driven and detail-oriented.

"He's really big on doing the little things right," cornerback Simeon Castille said.

No one disagrees with the notion that Saban is an extremely good coach; his record alone attests for that. The two seasons before he arrived at LSU, the Tigers finished 7–15. He quickly turned it around, compiling a 48–16 record with two Southeastern Conference championships and the 2003 national title.

What was surprising around the Capstone was that he didn't necessarily talk or act like a typical coach.

Granted, there's been some coach-speak, like: "One of the things that we harp on with our players is finishing things. Finish plays, finish the game, finish the period, focus on the next play regardless of what the circumstances are. That's something we have not done as well as we need to. You never know when the game-defining play is coming up."

Yet, as spring approached, he didn't bemoan the lack of depth on the defensive line, talk about how new starting linebackers needed to be found, or how the offense had to find ways to score in the red zone after struggling there the previous season. Instead, he discussed the team's intangible qualities, thus immediately changing the focus of the program.

"Discipline, effort, toughness, ability to do your job, be responsible for your own self-determination, know what's expected of you, and be able to see it through," Saban said were the top goals of the 15 spring workouts. "Conditioning is obviously an important part of that. You make mistakes when you get tired, you loaf when you're tired. That part of it is important and I feel like our team has done a good job of making progress in that area in the offseason. We'll continue to work on that in spring practice."

They did. Players said they never would have made it through the rigorous workouts without first enduring the conditioning program. With the coach extremely hands-on during practices, especially with the defensive backs, the messages were drilled into their skulls in both word and deed (does that sound familiar, Coach?)

"Mental conditioning and mental toughness is the ability to deliver at a critical time and a tough time in a game," Saban said as if quoting one of his books, like *"How Good Do You Want to Be? A Champion's Tips on How to Lead and Succeed at Work and in Life."*

"As soon as something goes wrong you have to be the kind of person where you can focus on the next play. I think that's something we can continue to improve on and have more players on the team be able to do that on a consistent basis because that's what helps you win."

There are times when his rhetoric comes across as almost sermon-like. Saban likes to talk with his hands, and if at a podium will increasingly tap it if agitated. In conjunction, his voice might rise and bear down on his subjects no matter what the subject, with a purpose in mind, a reason behind everything he does.

"Really, the bottom line is the team's competitive character is made of up of the individuals, and what kind of competitive character they have, what kind of discipline they have, what kind of effort they give, what kind of toughness they play with, how responsible they are to do their job, what kind of conditioning they're in and if they can sustain that for 60 minutes in a game," Saban said. "That's really what's most important.

"It's all their choice."

As alluded to before, there's also been friction, some behind the scenes at the school, but the most public with the media. Saban closed practices except for a few minutes during individual drills, limited exposure to players and barred reporters from scrimmages.

From the first news conference, he made it clear there would be no "evaluations, predictions and comparisons" type of questions allowed, nor anything hypothetical.

Naturally, fans didn't care, even those starving for any tidbit of information they could get, yet for a position that receives more intense scrutiny than possibly any other job in the state, if not region, it caused immediate resistance. So did what's become known as the "It is what it is" speech after practice on March 31, when a reporter asked Saban to evaluate the first week of spring practice:

"It is what it is, guys. I don't understand why we're asked for expectations, all we're asking for is evaluations, every day we go out there it is what it is. Every player is what he is. We're working hard, the coaches are working hard, the players are working hard, and everyone's trying to improve and get better. So it really doesn't matter what it compares to someplace else. I don't have any [comparison] because I accept it is what it is. So I don't have expectations of what it should have been after five days. It is what it is on the first day, then we take it to the second day, the third day and we take it to the fourth day. We take every day we have until we play a game, and every day through a season we try to improve and get better. Now, I don't have a calendar in there that says OK, the thermometer is supposed to go up to 72 percent of efficiency on this particular day and if it doesn't I'm going to jump off the Mal Moore Building. And it really doesn't matter. Someone gets hurt, it's unfortunate, but you have to get somebody else ready to play. That's what we try and do. I know you want me to evaluate it and make some sort of comparison so you can make a big news story out of it, but I'm not going to do that because it really doesn't matter."

Thus, Saban's manner was being referred to—similar to previous stops in his career—as abrasive, demeaning and condescending, with nicknames like "The Iron Saban," and "Fearless Leader." But when Saban blew off a reporter from *Sports Illustrated*, who in turn called him a "jerk" in his article, Saban called, apologized and gave an extensive interview.

At the same time, Coach, he's also provided copious fodder for reporters, like the line about making pizzas, which was a polite way of saying vomiting, during conditioning. Granted, players weren't wrestling to the point of exhaustion like in the old days in Lower

Gym, but they were running extensively as part of the program that can only be described as brutal.

Although hardly any players quit or left the team after Saban's arrival, there have been some small bumps with them as well.

For example, when asked what he thought of Saban the first time he met him, Gilberry tried to say something like "He's shorter that I expected," like many people experience when they meet a high-profile person for the first time. It instead came out as "short." Still, the effect didn't linger.

"I was star-struck the first couple of days," Gilberry said. "I was, 'This is Coach Saban,' you always see him in the NFL. That's everyone's dream, mine especially. For him to be right there you kind of want to walk up and touch him. Once I got over that, and it didn't take long, I'm just trying to learn as much as possible from him and hopefully can take it to the next level, and throughout life.

"It's his whole personality, the way he carries himself, it's like he's in a league of his own. If you aren't trying to be better, he doesn't want you around. That's what we all strive for, to be the best. He definitely wants the best out of us, and not only that it's more off the field than on the field. He cares about your academics, he cares about your attitude. You just don't find that very often, and from a guy of his caliber."

When asked what the offseason conditioning, called the Fourth Quarter Program, was like, Castille said "pain." He then caught himself and used preferred terminology.

"Mental toughness," he said. "That was the biggest thing. It was a good program, though. It really got you in shape."

Saban also hasn't hesitated to send the team messages through the media, like after suspending first-string running back Jimmy Johns for two days for academic reasons.

"He missed Friday's scrimmage," Saban said at the time, also acknowledging that Johns missed another workout.

"It's wide open. Dependability's part of it. You've got a guy who can't even do what he needs to do to get to practice, that's not saying much for him."

Johns returned the following practice, but was buried on the depth chart. That part I know you would have liked.

But every once in a while, as if he can't help but do so, Saban gives a glimpse into what's underneath the facade, how he sees things around him and how his thought process has emerged over the years.

"Sometimes a little more intensity and vigorous attitude is more than some might feel is appropriate, but I think they all understand that we're just trying to make them better," he said. "It's not personal, and I love the players here and I love their attitude and what they're trying to do, and we're trying to help them do it.

"My wife always tells me, how you think you're perceived relative to how you are perceived, is your blind spot. She tells me mine is many, many miles wide. We all have one, and we're all responsible for that. I get told that one quite often."

In short, there's ruthlessness to the program that it hasn't experienced in quite some time. Probably not since Stallings, perhaps longer.

That, above all else, is what has the fans exceedingly excited. They can sense the potential. It washes over them like that cool breeze, leaving each refreshed and invigorated, as if truly awake for the first time in years.

The momentum is building.

"He has a great philosophy, I know it's going to work," linebacker/defensive end Keith Saunders said.

"It's competition, we love it," cornerback Eric Gray said about the challenging practices.

"You can't describe it," Gilberry said. "You're almost too busy to be excited. You don't have time to sit there and really take anything in. That's how I feel, and once the smoke clears, after the A-Day game, and the summer, and everyone has a chance to reflect on what's happened, it's going to hit me. Coach Saban is a good coach, but that hasn't really hit me yet either."

Years in the making, the buzz has returned to the Crimson Tide. But it all comes down to one thing, winning. You knew that better than anyone.

Sincerely,
Christopher Walsh

Nine years later...

- Four national championships (2009, 2011, 2012, 2015)
- A record of 100–18 (.847)
- Since 2008, Alabama was ranked No. 1 at some point of every season.
- Four Southeastern Conference Championships (2009, 2012, 2014, 2015)
- 25 consensus All-Americans
- After Alabama had no players selected in the 2008 NFL Draft, it had 48 selected including 18 in the first round, from 2009 to 2016.
- The consensus No. 1 recruiting class in the nation from 2011 to 2016
- After stadium expansion, this time beyond the southern end zone to enclose the upper deck, Bryant-Denny Stadium capacity increased to 101,821.
- Alabama extensively renovated its facilities, including a state-of-the-art weight room.
- When Saban arrived, Alabama's enrollment was on an increase up from approximately 20,000 in 2004 to 23,878 in January 2007. It topped 37,000 in the fall of 2015.
- In 2015–16 Saban was still the highest-paid coach in college football, but his base salary was up to approximately $7 million.
- With the addition of the SEC Network, not to mention Missouri and Texas A&M to the league, each league school received record $31.2 million payout ($436.8 million distributed out of an NCAA-record $455.8 million in revenues) in the spring of 2015.

1 See Alabama Win a National Championship

In Nick Saban's words, the 2015 Alabama football team was all but "dead and buried" by media and the rest of the college football world. At least that's what he was portraying to his team after an early season loss that made every subsequent Saturday essentially an elimination game regarding its national title hopes.

Only the Crimson Tide responded. With the defense and running game leading the way, Alabama did what the two previous teams could not, run the table, successfully defending its Southeastern Conference title and then surviving the playoffs for the program's 16th national championship.

"This is my—I hate to say it—favorite team because I love'em all," Saban said. "These guys have come so far and have done so much. Their will, their spirit to compete and do the kind of things they needed to do to be the kind of team they could be, I'm happy for them.

"This is all about winning a game for them. It's great for our fans. It's great for the state of Alabama, but I wanted to win this game for these guys."

With the 45–40 victory against Clemson at the site of the Fiesta Bowl (giving Alabama a grand slam at what used to be the four Bowl Championship Series locations), the debate could really begin on if Saban was the greatest coach in college football history, and if Alabama's ongoing dynasty was the best the game has ever seen.

The crown was Saban's fifth, fourth with the Crimson Tide, which became the first program during the modern era to win four titles over a seven-year span.

Additionally, it was Saban's sixth career victory against a team ranked No. 1, while no one else in college football history had more than four (Lou Holtz, Jimmy Johnson, and Jack Mollenkopf; Paul W. "Bear" Bryant had three), and Alabama extended its streak of being No. 1 at some point in a season to an incredible eight straight years.

Regardless, after both semifinals were blowouts, with Alabama defeating Michigan State 38–0 in the Cotton Bowl, the championship more than made up for it and would be remembered as one of the best title games ever played. The two teams combined for 1,023 yards and it still went down to the very last play.

Junior running back Derrick Henry rushed for 158 yards on 36 carries and scored three touchdowns while becoming Alabama's all-time leading rusher.

Despite being sacked five times, senior quarterback Jake Coker had a career high 335 yards on 16 of 25 attempts, and no turnovers.

Overshadowing both was the game's offensive MVP, junior tight end O.J. Howard, who had a historic performance with five receptions for 208 yards and touchdowns of 51 and 53 yards.

"O.J., quite honestly, should have been more involved all year long," Saban said. "Sometimes he was open and we didn't get him the ball, but I think the last two games have been breakout games for him in terms of what he's capable of and what he can do.

"I would say that it's bad coaching on my part that he didn't have the opportunity to do that all year long."

Alabama also pulled off a jaw-dropping onside kick when the game was tied 24–24 with just under 11 minutes remaining, as kicker Adam Griffth perfectly bounced the football into open space and redshirt freshman Marlon Humphrey made a leaping catch to the dismay of Clemson coach Dabo Swinney (a walk-on receiver on Alabama's 1992 national championship team).

In terms of overall talent, this might have been Saban's best as 18 players were rated a consensus 5-star talent as a recruit. The defensive front seven led by linebacker Reggie Ragland and defensive linemen A'Shawn Robinson and Jarran Reed might have been the deepest anyone had seen since the 85-man scholarship limit was imposed.

However, the offense had to replace nine starters, including quarterback Blake Sims, running back T.J. Yeldon and wide receiver Amari Cooper, the program's first winner of the Biletnikoff Award.

2015: 14–1, National Champions, SEC Champions

Date	Opponent	Location	W/L Score
September 5	Wisconsin	Arlington, Texas	W 35–17
September 12	Middle Tennessee State	Tuscaloosa	W 37–10
September 19	Ole Miss	Tuscaloosa	L 43–37
September 26	Louisiana-Monroe	Tuscaloosa	W 34–0
October 3	Georgia	Athens, Ga.	W 38–10
October 10	Arkansas	Tuscaloosa	W 27–14
October 17	Texas A&M	College Station	W 41–23
October 24	Tennessee	Tuscaloosa	W 19–14
November 7	LSU	Tuscaloosa	W 30–16
November 14	Mississippi State	Starkville, Miss.	W 31–6
November 21	Charleston Southern	Tuscaloosa	W 56–6
November 28	Auburn	Auburn	W 29–13
December 5	Florida	SEC Championship	W 29–15
December 31	Michigan State	Cotton Bowl	W 38–0
January 11	Clemson	National Championship	W 45–40

Coach: Nick Saban
Captains: Reggie Ragland, Ryan Kelly, Jake Coker, and Derrick Henry
Ranking (AP): Preseason—No. 3; Postseason —No. 1
All-American: First team—Derrick Henry, running back; Ryan Kelly, center; A'Shawn Robinson, defensive lineman; Reggie Ragland, linebacker
Second team—Eddie Jackson, safety
All-SEC (first team): Cam Robinson, tackle; Ryan Kelly, center; Derrick Henry, running back; Jonathan Allen, defensive lineman; A'Shawn Robinson, defensive lineman; Reggie Ragland, linebacker; Eddie Jackson, safety
Leaders: Rushing—Derrick Henry (2,219 yards, 395 carries); Passing—Jake Coker (263 of 393, 3,110 yards); Receiving—Calvin Ridley (89 catches, 1,045 yards)

With help from third-year center Ryan Kelly, a co-captain and winner of the Rimington Award, their replacements did fine in their wake. Coker, a graduate transfer who didn't secure the starting job until the Ole Miss game in Week 3, had just one pass intercepted over the second half of the season and none in the post-season. Henry didn't just win Alabama's second Heisman Trophy, but the Maxwell and Walter Camp awards for player of the year, in addition to the Doak Walker Award as best running back.

Freshman Calvin Ridley also stepped in for Cooper and became just the second freshman in Alabama history to notch 1,000 receiving yards. With his rapid development, the Crimson Tide under the direction of coordinator Lane Kiffin was known for its quick-strike ability.

Alabama's run was even more impressive when you consider its brutal schedule that began with a neutral-site game against Wisconsin, and included the top three teams from the SEC East: Florida, Tennessee and Georgia.

Overall, Alabama played nine opponents that were ranked at the time, the most of any national champion. Every team in the division not only finished with a winning record, but at some point of the season was ranked—a first in college football. Combined the SEC West went 31–4 against non-conference opponents, and 13–2 against the SEC East.

"To face 12 straight elimination games after the Ole Miss [loss]," Saban said. "The resiliency, the competitive character that this team showed at being able to do that, and even coming back from behind in the national championship game really shows the spirit that made this team something special."

2 Paul W. "Bear" Bryant

They called him "Bear."

Think about that for a moment, and the words it evokes.

Powerful, gruff, intimidating, and yet with a gentle side. Paul W. Bryant was all of those things and much, much more, and perfectly nicknamed after actually wrestling a bear at a carnival for $1 at the age of 13 (he didn't get the money, and the animal bit his ear).

Today, the name is synonymous with college football, and Bryant has been widely regarded as the game's greatest coach. He compiled an amazing record of 323–85–17, led teams to 29 bowl appearances and 15 conference championships, and won six national championships (1961, 1964, 1965, 1973, 1978, 1979). In the 1960s and 1970s, no team won more games than the Crimson Tide (193–32–5), and a national coach of the year award is named in his honor.

Even though Bryant died January 26, 1983, at the age of 69, hardly a day goes by that most Crimson Tide fans don't mention his name at least once, and half of Tuscaloosa is seemingly named in his honor.

Bryant was born September 11, 1913, the 11th of 12 children, three of whom died as infants. His father was an Arkansas farmer, but after he became ill when Paul was a child, his mother, Ida Mae, took over, with the kids helping out.

After leading the Fordyce High School Redbugs to a state championship, Bryant left home for the University of Alabama, where during his first fall he took high school classes to finish up his diploma. In June 1935 Bryant secretly wed Mary Harmon because it was against team rules for players to marry. Their first of two

The most famous pose of Alabama coach Paul "Bear" Bryant, the SEC's all-time winningest coach, shows him leaning on the goal post while his players go through pregame warm-ups.

children, Mae Martin, was born nine months later. Paul Jr., who would become a prominent businessman, was born in 1944.

After turning down a chance to play in the National Football League, Bryant went straight into coaching and was an assistant at Alabama for four years, and at Vanderbilt for two, before serving in the Navy. Upon leaving the military he was named the head coach at Maryland, but resigned after one season. Next he took over Kentucky and guided the Wildcats to their first Southeastern Conference championship in 1950. In eight seasons, his teams went 60–23–5 and played in four bowl games, including the 1951 Sugar Bowl where Kentucky ended Oklahoma's 31-game winning streak.

After the 1953 season, Bryant signed a 12-year contract extension with the promise from Kentucky officials that football would be the athletic department's top priority, or at least on par with basketball. When it became clear that wouldn't be the case, he quit. Texas A&M signed him to a six-year deal to be coach and athletic director for $25,000 a season and an unprecedented 1 percent of the gate receipts, one day before Southern California made a lucrative offer that almost certainly would have snared Bryant.

That first training camp with the Aggies, Bryant took his players 250 miles west to a barren army base in Junction, Texas,

Crimson Tide Coaching Titles (through 2015)

SEC Championships:
Paul W. "Bear" Bryant 13, Nick Saban 4, Frank Thomas 4, Red Drew 1, Bill Curry 1, Gene Stallings 1, Mike DuBose 1.

National Championships:
Paul W. "Bear" Bryant 6, Nick Saban 5, Wallace Wade 3, Frank Thomas 2, Gene Stallings 1.

Note: Nick Saban also won a national championship (2003) and two SEC titles (2001 and 2003) at LSU.

and put them through the mental and physical equivalent of a meat grinder. More than two-thirds of the players quit, with those who endured dubbed the "Junction Boys," but it also defined the coach's legacy as a hard-nosed disciplinarian.

Bryant's Aggies were closing in on the 1957 national championship when he was lured away by Alabama and made his famous statement: "Mama called, and when Mama calls, then you just have to come running." He agreed to a 10-year contract with an annual salary of $17,000 and a house.

"I ain't never been nothing but a winner."

Four years later, Bryant won his first national championship, and the rest is history.

3 Attend the Iron Bowl

For a Crimson Tide fan, there is no bigger day of the year than the annual Auburn game, although things like birthdays, weddings, and Christmas come close.

Seriously.

Pick a random day of the year, and ask a random person in the state, "Who won the last game?"

Then ask who Van Tiffin is and wait for the reaction. If the person is a Tide fan, his or her face will probably light up, and he or she will say something like, "You don't know who Van Tiffin is? Oh, you poor thing," as if there's something seriously wrong with you.

If he or she is an Auburn supporter, expect the exact opposite reaction, because the 1985 Iron Bowl was decided by a 52-yard field goal by the kicker as time expired, giving Alabama a dramatic

The First Iron Bowl

In February of the 1892–93 academic year, Alabama scheduled one final game to its inaugural season, against Auburn. Like the team's first three contests, the game would be played in Birmingham, but in front of approximately 4,000 fans, who were probably far more curious about the sport than anything else. Auburn won 32–22, and Alabama's first season concluded with 2–2 record.

Auburn won the second meeting as well, 40–16, in Montgomery on November 30 of the same calendar year. With many of its best players from the inaugural season lost to graduation, Alabama finished the 1893 season winless (0–4), including a loss to its first out-of-state opponent, Sewanee, 20–0.

25–23 victory after the lead changed hands four times in the final 15 minutes.

Fans take this game so seriously that they start the countdown to the next one the day after the game. Heavy rains and the threat of a tornado didn't stop the 1983 meeting when running back Bo Jackson had 256 rushing yards and two touchdowns to lead Auburn to a 23–20 victory.

The series actually dates back to February 22, 1893, when the two sides met at Birmingham's Lakeview Park and Auburn claimed a 32–22 victory. Auburn also won the subsequent matchup, 40–16. The following year, Alabama won 18–0, and a football rivalry was well under way. However, following a 6–6 tie in 1907, the schools refused to play again for 41 years due in part to animosity. The series was revived only after the state legislature threatened to get involved.

Yeah, it's that extreme. Scott Brown wrote in his book *The Uncivil War* that he had "never felt anything more intense than the hatred between Alabama and Auburn. Period."

ESPN analyst Beano Cook did it one better by referring to the rivalry as "Gettysburg south."

"I was working the 1995 game at Jordan-Hare [Stadium at Auburn], which had zero championship implication, with a producer from another part of the country," said ESPN's Rece Davis, himself an Alabama graduate. "He said, 'I can't believe how intense this is.' I said, 'You should see it when they're playing for something.'

"Actually, come to think of it, the intensity never changes with the circumstances."

For 50-some years, the two sides met at the neutral site of Legion Field in Birmingham, even though Auburn continually argued that the location provided Alabama with an unfair advantage since it was much closer to the Tuscaloosa campus.

Only once have they played when both were undefeated. That was in 1971. The No. 3 Crimson Tide posted a lopsided 31–7 victory over the No. 4 Tigers as Alabama halfback Johnny Musso outshined Auburn quarterback Pat Sullivan, who went on to win the Heisman Trophy. However, Alabama lost the national championship game to Nebraska at the Orange Bowl, 38–6.

"Any game that causes married couples to divorce, or even worse in some psychotic cases, must be a pretty big deal," said Norm Wood of the *Daily Press* in Virginia.

"I went to Auburn for a basketball game in 1986 shortly after Alabama won the football game, and some Auburn football players told me they hadn't shown themselves in public for three days," John Henderson of *The Denver Post* said. "Enough said."

4 Nick Saban

Although the touchdown occurred at an airport instead of on a football field, it nonetheless was still considered one of the most important in Crimson Tide history.

At approximately 3:45 PM on January 3, 2007, Alabama's private jet landed in Tuscaloosa, where hundreds of fans had gathered in eager anticipation. They didn't even wait for the man wearing a gray suit, lavender shirt, and no tie to emerge from the open door to start celebrating, and they couldn't wait to give him rock-star treatment.

The following day, when Nick Saban was officially announced as the 27th head coach of the Crimson Tide, he didn't hesitate to send a clear and deliberate message to the program's fans, players, and boosters, with what instantly became the latest Alabama mantra.

"Be a champion in everything that we do," Saban said. "Every choice, every decision, everything that we do every day, we want to be a champion."

With that, the Saban era was under way at the Capstone, ending one of the rockiest periods in program history and a tumultuous five weeks after Mike Shula was fired on November 26, 2006, during which interim coach Joe Kines guided the Crimson Tide to the Independence Bowl (a 34–31 loss to Oklahoma State resulting in a 6–7 finish).

"I waited forever to talk with him," Director of Athletics Mal Moore said about not flying down to visit Saban until after his season with the Miami Dolphins concluded. "Once I talked with his wife [Terry], I thought I really had a chance."

So when did Moore know he had a new coach?

"About three hours before I picked him up at his home to come to the airport," he said.

The end result was Saban, who decided that the pro game wasn't all that he hoped and preferred the college version, and culminated when the coach signed the richest contract in college football history, eight years and at least $30 million, plus incentives.

"I realize I was out on the gangplank, so to speak, or out on thin ice, but I felt like I had to do this," Moore said. "I recognized that this was such a crucial hire for the university."

Amazingly, it nearly never happened.

Saban was essentially Moore's top choice throughout the process, but Alabama did briefly turn to West Virginia coach Rich Rodriguez with an offer for roughly half the money Saban eventually received, and flirted with both South Carolina coach Steve Spurrier and Louisville's Bobby Petrino.

With Rodriguez's rejection in early December (a year later he was hired by Michigan, which wasn't a good fit and he subsequently landed at Arizona), Moore decided to roll the dice and wait for his opportunity to make a formal pitch even though other coaching openings were being filled.

Meanwhile, Saban made the mistake of telling reporters in Miami on December 21, "I guess I have to say it. I'm not going to be the Alabama coach," which led to widespread criticism, especially in national circles, even though he was obviously trying to keep his team's focus on the ongoing season. He later expressed regret about the statement, but added that his attention at the time was solely on the Dolphins and no job offer had been extended.

"I can't tell you how pleased and honored I am to be your coach at the University of Alabama," Saban said after being introduced. "The spirit and enthusiasm that have been demonstrated to myself and my family has been phenomenal since we arrived."

While Saban also indicated that he planned on Alabama being his final coaching job, with his next stop retirement at the family

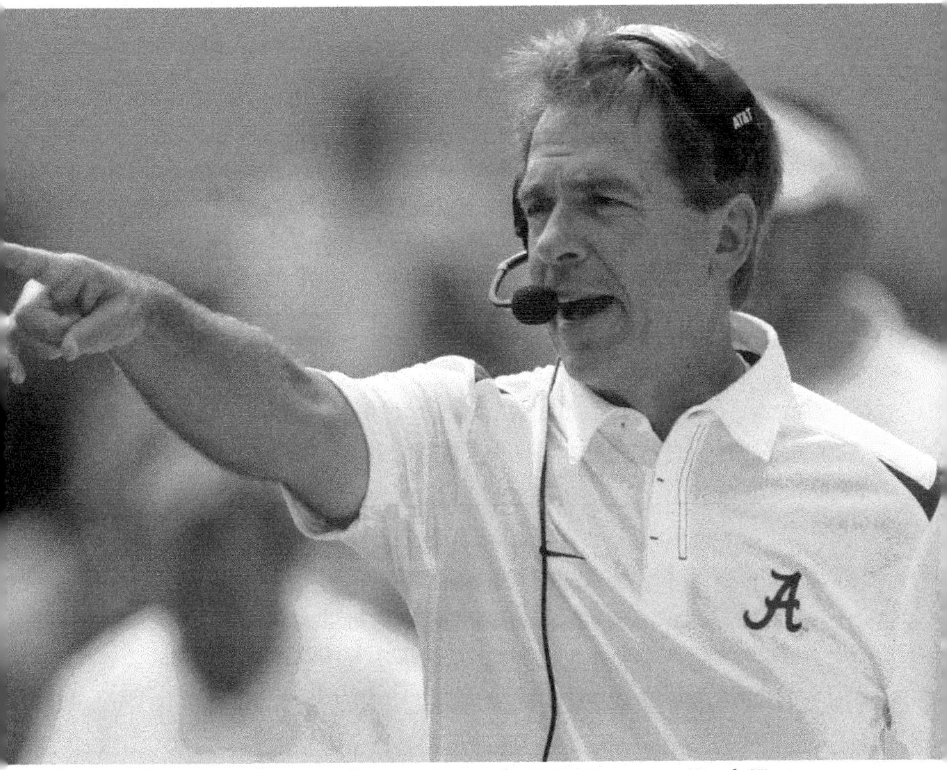

Nick Saban directs his team during a September 2009 win over North Texas. The former Michigan State and LSU head coach left the NFL's Miami Dolphins to take the Alabama job in January 2007. In his first five seasons, he led the Crimson Tide to two national championships. (AP Images)

home in Lake Burton, Georgia ("They don't have a football team there. They do have a pontoon boat, though."), he also didn't back down from the huge expectations of making a serious run at becoming the first coach in college football history to win national championships at two different schools after lifting the crystal football with LSU in 2003.

It took him just three years to do so, and five to become one of a handful of coaches in college football history to win three national championships, joining Bernie Bierman of Minnesota, Frank Leahy of Notre Dame, Robert Neyland of Tennessee, John McKay

The LSU Rivalry

LSU has a traditional rivalry with Tulane and a trophy game with Arkansas, but in 2007 its biggest rival arguably became Alabama. Granted, being in the same division had already caused frequent sparks, but what brought it to new heights was former LSU coach Nick Saban leaving the Miami Dolphins to coach the Crimson Tide.

Media dubbed the subsequent game between the two schools the "Saban Bowl," and LSU fans arrived at Bryant-Denny Stadium early sporting purple-and-gold houndstooth hats, which only reinforced the idea to most people in Tuscaloosa that Tigers fans are pretty much crazy. LSU, with 17 of the 22 offensive and defensive starters having been recruited by Saban, came from behind to win 41–34 and went on to win the national championship.

The rivalry was elevated even further in 2011 when LSU won the first No. 1 vs. No. 2 matchup at Bryant-Denny Stadium, 9–6 in overtime, but Alabama still finished the regular season No. 2 to secure the first rematch in the BCS National Championship Game. Not only did the Tigers lose 21–0 to the former LSU coach and SEC West rival, but the game was also in their back yard at the Mercedes-Benz Superdome in New Orleans.

of Southern California, Woody Hayes at Ohio State, and Barry Switzer and Bud Wilkinson of Oklahoma. Bryant, of course, won six, and Notre Dame's Knute Rockne five, which Saban matched in 2015.

"I learned a lot from him about being accountable, being responsible, working hard to accomplish your goals," center William Vlachos said. "The same stuff he tells y'all he tells us.

"I think his one quote that I've taken to heart the most and tried to apply is 'You either suffer the pain of discipline or the pain of disappointment.' He said that the first day and I think it's so true. You either suffer the pain of discipline or the pain of disappointment. I think that's a great way to live your life, honestly."

5 Joe Namath

When he came to the University of Alabama from Beaver Falls, Pennsylvania, he was simply known as Joe Willie, but became the most famous rogue quarterback in history. When "Broadway Joe" eventually hung up his cleats, he was not only a legend but an icon for both football and America.

"The late '60s and the early '70s were times of compelling social and political upheaval, and Namath, with his antiestablishment shaggy hair, mustache, white shoes, and Life-Is-a-Bacchanal philosophy, became a symbol of inevitable, triumphant change. The antihero," Tony Kornheiser wrote in *Inside Sports*.

After being rejected by Maryland for academic reasons, Namath became Alabama's starting quarterback his sophomore season and led a senior-laden team to a 10–1 record. Even when Lee Roy Jordan had 30 tackles against Oklahoma in the Orange Bowl, Coach Paul W. "Bear" Bryant couldn't stop raving about his quarterback following the 17–0 game.

However, when Namath broke team drinking and curfew rules as a junior, Bryant dropped him from the team for the regular-season finale against Miami, and the Sugar Bowl against Ole Miss (Alabama won both). He returned for his senior season, but during the fourth game against North Carolina State sustained the first of his troublesome knee injuries, which would limit him the rest of the season.

Against Georgia Tech, Namath entered the scoreless game in the second quarter to lead the team to a 24–7 victory. He performed similar heroics against Auburn on Thanksgiving Day. With Notre Dame losing to Southern California, the 10–0 Crimson Tide was named the national champion at the end of the regular season

(Alabama lost to Texas in the Orange Bowl on a controversial play, but Namath was still named the game's MVP).

Namath turned pro football on its ear before even throwing a single pass by ignoring the National Football League's St. Louis Cardinals, who had drafted him, to sign with the New York Jets of the American Football League for a then-staggering $427,000 and a Lincoln Continental.

It triggered a recruiting war between the upstart and older leagues, and with salaries quickly rising they merged with their annual champions meeting to play for one all-encompassing title. That's how the Super Bowl came into existence.

Namath won the starting job in his third game and was named AFL Rookie of the Year in 1965 (incidentally, one of his backups with the Jets was 1964 Heisman Trophy winner John Huarte from

Perhaps the most famous player in Alabama history is quarterback Joe Namath, who helped lead the Crimson Tide to a national championship and went on to guide the New York Jets to a stunning 16–7 victory over the Baltimore Colts in Super Bowl III.

Notre Dame). Two years later, he became the only quarterback to pass for 4,000 yards in a 14-game season.

Namath is best remembered for Super Bowl III and the Jets' stunning 16–7 victory over the Baltimore Colts. At the time, AFL teams were still considered inferior to their NFL counterparts. The Colts were considered huge favorites, and three days before the game Namath answered a heckler at the Miami Touchdown Club dinner by saying, "We're going to win Sunday. I guarantee you."

Few took him seriously. But they should have.

Namath led the Jets on four scoring drives, completing 17 of 28 passes for 206 yards.

Despite chronic knee problems, Namath completed 1,886 passes for 27,663 yards and 173 touchdowns in 12 seasons with the Jets and a final stab with the Los Angeles Rams in 1977, and was enshrined in the Pro Football Hall of Fame (FYI, he's not in the College Football Hall of Fame because he was not a first-team All-American, which is a minimum requirement).

The charismatic quarterback also enjoyed a high-profile life off the field, reflected in the name of his New York bar, Bachelors III, which he opened with singer Bobby Van and teammate Ray Abruzzese at the age of 26. Namath acted in movies, in television shows, and in the theater, and he made well-known ads, including one for panty hose and another in which he shaved off his mustache for $10,000.

In the fall of 2007, Namath returned to the Capstone to receive his degree after finally graduating at the spry age of 64.

Bryant once described Namath as "the greatest athlete I ever coached."

6 Derrick Henry

The play was one that a lot of people probably overlooked, but spoke volumes about the progress that University of Alabama junior running back Derrick Henry made during his career.

It was the 2015 season opener against Wisconsin and Alabama had first down at the Badgers' 32-yard line early in the third quarter. They blitzed up the middle, and with Jake Coker dropping back the senior quarterback could have potentially been in serious trouble...only Henry stepped forward and promptly stonewalled the charging linebacker.

It didn't hurt that the running back was actually bigger than the player he was blocking, T.J. Edwards, who had all of his momentum vanish on impact, but even Henry admitted afterward that it was not a play he would have successfully made a couple of years previous.

"Probably not, because I wasn't experienced," he said. "But like every player, the more you experience the more you learn and the better you get.

"Pass protection is very serious and we take it seriously here. That's what they want me to do—pass protect when I can. I'm glad it worked out."

To say that Henry's Crimson Tide career worked out would be like saying that the Grand Canyon is good-sized ditch. His 2015 season was nothing short of phenomenal.

In addition to taking home Alabama's second Heisman Trophy, he won the two other major national player of the year awards, the Maxwell and Walter Camp, making him the first player in Crimson Tide history to pull off that trifecta. He also won the Doak Walker Award for best running back.

Mark Ingram Jr. had previously been the only Alabama player to win the Heisman. AJ McCarron had been the lone Maxwell winner. No one had ever won the Walter Camp. Trent Richardson was the single Doak Walker winner.

The Southeastern Conference's first 2,000-yard rusher, Henry topped Bo Jackson's numbers and broke some of Herschel Walker's longstanding single-season records including his 1,891 rushing yards on 385 carries set in 1981.

"I'm not the type of person who's going to compare myself to him, Herschel's a great back," Henry said during a Heisman Trophy press conference. "I've still got a lot of things to get better at and work at to be in that same conversation. I still have to get better."

Try telling that to all the players Henry ran over en route to not just accumulating the most rushing yards in any Crimson Tide season, but smashing the mark by 540 yards—almost 25 percent of his total.

Consequently, he has to be considered the best running back in Crimson Tide history.

Even though he wasn't considered Alabama's starting running back until his junior season, he finished as the program's all-time leading rusher. Henry had 3,591 career yards to top Shaun Alexander's 3,565 (1996–99).

His 2,219 single-season rushing yards shattered Trent Richardson's mark of 1,679 (2011).

Henry had 10 100-yard performances in 2015 alone, to set another school record.

His 28 rushing touchdowns shattered the SEC record that was previously 23 (Tim Tebow and Tre Mason). His career mark of 42 tied Mark Ingram (2008–10) atop the Alabama all-time list. The last time Henry failed to score a touchdown in a game was as a sophomore, against LSU in 2014.

The numbers are even more remarkable considering that Alabama's initial approach for 2015 was to use a two-back attack.

"I didn't know who would be more productive, Derrick Henry or Kenyan Drake," Nick Saban said.

But Drake ran into some injury issues and since the only other running backs on the roster were freshmen Henry carried more and more of the offense, especially during the second half of the season.

His 46 carries against Auburn set an Alabama single-game record, and 44 the following week against Florida in the SEC Championship Game totaled 90 a mere seven days apart.

Crimson Tide Records Derrick Henry set in 2015

Alabama (Game)		
Category	***Record***	***Second Best in Alabama History***
Carries	46	Derrick Henry 44
Alabama (Single Season)		
Rushing Yards	2,219	Trent Richardson 1,679
Rushing TDs	28	Richardson 21
Carries	395	Shaun Alexander 302
100-yard Games	10	Mark Ingram Jr./Richardson 9
200-yard Games	4	Bobby Humphrey 3
Points Scored	168	Alexander 144
Touchdowns	28	Alexander/Richardson 24
All-Purpose Yards	2,230	Richardson 2,083
Alabama (Career)		
Rushing Yards	3,591	Alexander 3,565
Rushing TDs	42-*t*	Ingram 42
100-yard Games	16	Three tied with 15
200-Yard Games	4-*t*	Humphrey 4
SEC (Single Season)		
Rushing Yards	2,219	Herschel Walker 1,891
Rushing TDs	28	Tim Tebow/Tre Mason 23
Carries	395	Herschel Walker 385

"I didn't think I would see that ever, 90 carries in seven days—and then I think he could have kept going," offensive coordinator Lane Kiffin said. "He was in the locker room afterward like he just was warming up.

"Somehow he just continues to get stronger, and that goes back to how he works, the way that he practices, the way that we're in the sprints in the practice—and he's not worried about anything else except for getting himself better."

It didn't hurt that those performances were also around the time voters were casting their ballots for awards

On the biggest stage of his career, the National Championship Game against Clemson, he had 158 yards on 36 carries and scored three touchdowns after Tigers coach Dabo Swinney called him "a whole different animal." Henry probably would have been named the offensive MVP of the title game if junior tight end O.J. Howard hadn't recorded 208 receiving yards.

"It's tough to go one-on-one with him," Clemson linebacker Ben Boulware said. "It's like old-school football, if you're not ready to go before he touches the ball, then it won't work out."

Consequently, when it comes to Henry's legacy, he's in very exclusive company, and you're splitting hairs when trying to separate him from the best running backs to ever play the game.

Overall, there have been only four in SEC history to have four 200-yard games in one season: Henry, Walker, Jackson, and LSU's Leonard Fournette—who joined them with his 212-yard performance in the 2015 Texas Bowl.

But none of them led his team to a conference and national title while playing the toughest schedule of any national champion, having faced nine ranked opponents.

Against them Henry ended up rushing for 166.6 yards per game (1,499), exceeding 200 three times. The only one in which Henry didn't get at least 125 yards against was Michigan State in the Cotton Bowl, a 38–0 victory during which the coaches clearly held him back.

Henry was also named a team co-captain by his teammates, in part due to his incredible work ethic that rubbed off.

"I think our team kind of [took] on his persona and physical nature," Alabama defensive coordinator Kirby Smart said.

Perhaps that's Henry's true legacy even though it'll be widely overlooked. He didn't just have more drive and determination as anyone else, but the Crimson Tide did as well.

"That's just the culture that our program and our coaching staff has created here at Alabama," Henry said. "We work as hard as we can and try to get better week after week. It all comes down to hard work."

7 Derrick Thomas

On Tuesday, February 8, 2000, Bill Kenney, a Missouri state senator and former quarterback for the Kansas City Chiefs, made a somber announcement and asked for a moment of silence.

"Derrick Thomas was a true hero," he said. "He will be missed by football fans around the nation, but we will miss him in Kansas City for his attitude and his efforts he put forth in our community."

Thomas was driving an SUV during a snowstorm on January 23 as he and two friends headed to the Kansas City airport to fly to St. Louis for the NFC Championship Game. He lost control of the vehicle and it overturned at least three times, according to police. One of the friends was not wearing a seatbelt and was immediately killed. Thomas sustained a severe spinal injury, resulting in paralysis from the chest down. He died a little more than two weeks later due to a massive blood clot in an artery between his lungs and heart.

The nine-time All-Pro linebacker was just 33.

Derrick Thomas had an incredible 27 sacks in 1988 after shattering the previous school record of 18 the year before.

DeMeco Ryans

During his senior season this linebacker led Alabama with 76 tackles, including 16 for a loss, en route to being named a first-team All-American, the SEC Defensive Player of the Year, and the Lott Trophy winner as college football's best IMPACT defensive player. (IMPACT is actually an acronym for integrity, maturity, performance, academics, community, and tenacity.) After being the first pick in the second round of the 2006 NFL Draft, he led the league with 126 solo tackles and all rookies with 156 tackles, the most tackles by a rookie in the past 20 years. He was also named the NFL Defensive Rookie of the Year—edging out former Tide teammate Mark Anderson with the Chicago Bears—and the Alabama Sports Writers Association Professional Athlete of the Year.

"I just want to thank God for blessing me with some athletic talent and letting me play for the University of Alabama," Thomas said after winning the Butkus Award as the nation's top linebacker his senior season in 1988. He had an amazing 27 sacks that season and finished 10th in voting for the Heisman Trophy.

Thomas once said, "Whenever I see those crimson jerseys and crimson helmets, I feel humbled to have played football for Alabama. Other players in the NFL talk to me about their schools and their traditions. I just smile knowing the immense love Alabama fans have for our school and its football program. I'm proud to be part of that Crimson Tide heritage."

When the Chiefs made him the fourth overall selection in the 1989 National Football League Draft, team president Carl Peterson called it a new "beginning" for the organization. Thomas recorded 10 sacks that initial season and was named the NFL Defensive Rookie of the Year.

For an encore, Thomas had 20 sacks in 1990, the fifth-best single-season total in NFL history, and helped lead the Chiefs to the playoffs. While doing so, Thomas set a league single-game record with seven sacks against the Seattle Seahawks and just missed an eighth when quarterback Dave Krieg was able to slip from his grasp to throw the game-winning touchdown on the final play. Despite the loss on Veterans Day, Thomas dedicated his performance to his father, an Air Force pilot killed in Vietnam during Operation Linebacker II.

"I was on a mission today," Thomas said following the game. "I read in the paper that Derrick Thomas was in a sack slump."

Thomas established franchise career records for sacks (126.5), safeties (three), fumble recoveries (18), and forced fumbles (45). The 126.5 sacks were the fourth-highest total ever by a linebacker at the time of his death.

Additionally, Thomas started the Third and Long Foundation to encourage inner-city reading, received the '93 NFL Man of the Year Award, won the '95 Byron "Whizzer" White Award from the NFL Players Association, and was President George H.W. Bush's "832nd Point of Light." He was inducted into the Pro Football Hall of Fame in 2009, and its college football counterpart in 2014.

"For me, my goals are a lot higher than just being a successful linebacker or being All-Pro," Thomas said after the 1994 season. "When my career is over, I want people to look back and view me as the best, or one of the two best to ever play the position."

8 2009: 'Bama's Back

When the University of Alabama decided to hold a special celebration for the 2009 football season, a parade was nixed along with anything that didn't involve Bryant-Denny Stadium.

Walking through the home tunnel one more time with fans ready to greet them was what the players wanted. So on January 16,

2010, with approximately 38,000 fans in attendance (and ignoring the lousy weather), the Capstone featured fireworks, tributes, speeches, and a whole lot of hardware.

"I want everyone here to know this is not the end," Coach Nick Saban said. "This is the beginning."

Although Tuscaloosa had been waiting a long time for its 13th national title—the first since 1992 and second in 30 years—no one anticipated what would become the most accomplished team in the program's history. Not only did the Crimson Tide become the first Southeastern Conference team to finish 14–0 to win the crystal football known as the Coaches Trophy, but Alabama also landed college football's most prestigious individual award.

"I'm a little overwhelmed right now," sophomore running back Mark Ingram Jr. said. "I'm just so excited to bring Alabama their first Heisman winner."

Adding to the drama was that the vote turned out to be the closest in Heisman Trophy history, with Ingram topping Stanford running back Toby Gerhart by just 28 points.

Meanwhile, junior linebacker Rolando McClain won Alabama's second Butkus Award for linebacker of the year, a record six players were named first-team All-Americans, Saban won the inaugural Bobby Bowden Coach of the Year Award, and defensive coordinator Kirby Smart took home the Broyles Award as the assistant coach of the year.

Numerous records were also set. Ingram set the UA mark for single-season rushing. Kicker Leigh Tiffin took over as the Tide's all-time scoring leader. Javier Arenas finished 10 yards short of becoming the NCAA's career leader in punt-return yards.

"It just shows that when you put in so much hard work and effort that things really do pay off for you," senior guard Mike Johnson said. "I really honestly feel like we worked harder than any other team this year and that's why we came out on top."

Quarterback Greg McElroy waves to the crowd after Alabama topped Texas in the BCS Championship Game on January 7, 2010. The win gave the Crimson Tide its first national championship since 1992. (AP Images)

Alabama captured its 22nd Southeastern Conference title, was the first team in history to beat 10 opponents that finished with a winning record, and it dispatched the three previous national champions along the way. The victims included No. 2 Texas, No. 3 Florida, No. 10 Virginia Tech, No. 17 LSU, and No. 20 Ole Miss, and the Crimson Tide also played South Carolina when it was ranked 22nd.

"What an unbelievable year," athletic director Mal Moore said.

If that wasn't enough, Alabama won the BCS National Championship Game at the site of its first title, the Rose Bowl.

With five turnovers created by the defense, which knocked Texas quarterback Colt McCoy out of the game with a shoulder injury, and both Ingram and freshman running back Trent Richardson tallying more than 100 rushing yards, the Tide celebrated in the same place where it won its first title 84 years previous in similar fashion against Washington.

Ingram was named the game's offensive MVP and defensive lineman Marcell Dareus took home the defensive award despite having just one tackle. He intercepted a shovel pass, made a spin move, and ran over another quarterback en route to the end zone for a 28-yard touchdown with three seconds remaining in the first half.

Although Alabama had scored 24 unanswered points, it didn't seal the 37–21 victory until linebacker Eryk Anders caught Longhorns freshman quarterback Garrett Gilbert from the blind side, with linebacker Courtney Upshaw recovering the fumble at the Texas 3 to set up Ingram's final touchdown.

"We back," Ingram said afterward.

9 The Bear's 315th Victory

In 1981 Paul W. "Bear" Bryant was in the twilight of his career, but the state was abuzz about the coach's date with destiny.

At season's start, he was just eight wins away from Amos Alonzo Stagg's amazing record of 314 wins, which took him 57 years to achieve and which many people thought might never be broken. At Yale, Stagg had been a member of Walter Camp's original All-America team in 1889, and he didn't give up football until the age of 90, after coaching at Springfield College, the University of Chicago, and College of the Pacific.

Considering it had been more than a decade since a Bryant-coached team had failed to achieve eight wins (6–5–1 in 1970, which caused the coach to make drastic changes in the program, including changing to the wishbone offense), it simply appeared to be a matter of time.

"All I know is, I don't want to stop coaching, and I don't want to stop winning, so we're gonna break the record unless I die," Bryant said.

Few knew it at the time, but Bryant's health was indeed beginning to fail and he had coronary heart disease. Over the next year he would begin to develop heart problems that would eventually take his life in 1983.

"My life has been so tied up in football it has flown by," Bryant said. "Practice, recruiting, and games. There hasn't been anything else but football."

A 24–21 upset loss to Georgia Tech and a 13–13 tie to Southern Miss delayed the celebration, but Alabama got on a roll to quickly bring the countdown to its final stages. Bryant was finally in reach of tying the mark on the Tide's first trip to Happy Valley to face Penn State and Coach Joe Paterno (who would eventually surpass the record himself). Similar to the 1979 Sugar Bowl, the defense made a dramatic goal-line stand, and when the players walked off the field the coach tipped his hat to them.

With Walter Lewis leading the offense, Alabama won easily, 31–16.

Fittingly, Bryant would go for No. 315 against the Tide's biggest rival, Auburn, on November 28 at Legion Field. Iron Bowl seats had always been the hardest to secure each year, but this was special. Former players wanted to be there, celebrities flew in from all over, and the nation watched with eager anticipation for history to be made. It might have been the toughest ticket to score in state history, and Alabama wouldn't disappoint.

Major Coaching Awards

National Coach of the Year:*
Paul W. "Bear" Bryant 1961, 1971, 1973; Gene Stallings 1992, Nick Saban 2008.

SEC Coach of the Year (AP):
Paul W. "Bear" Bryant 1959, 1961, 1964, 1965, 1971, 1973, 1978, 1979, 1981; Bill Curry 1989; Gene Stallings 1992, 1994; Mike DuBose 1999; Nick Saban 2008, 2009.

SEC Coach of the Year (Coaches):
Frank Thomas 1945; Harold Drew 1952; Paul W. "Bear" Bryant 1961, 1964, 1971, 1973, 1974, 1977, 1979, 1981; Bill Curry 1989; Gene Stallings 1992; Mike DuBose 1999; Nick Saban 2008, 2009.

Frank Broyles Award (national assistant coach of the year): Kirby Smart 2009.

*There are now numerous national coach of the year awards. For example, Nick Saban won the Amos Alonzo Stagg Coaching Award in 2010 and the Bobby Dodd Coach of the Year Award in 2014.

Although Auburn had a 17–14 lead in the fourth quarter, a touchdown drive led by Lewis had the sellout crowd chanting "315." Heartfelt emotions started to pour out before the game even ended, with many tearing up in spite of themselves.

When Alabama scored again in the closing moments, the celebration could no longer be quelled, and after the clock struck zero players proudly carried Bryant off the field. Two presidents, Ronald Reagan—who had been a sports reporter at the 1935 Rose Bowl that Alabama won—and Jimmy Carter, called to offer congratulations.

Almost completely lost in the festivities was that the Tide had finished as co-champions of the Southeastern Conference with Georgia, led by future Heisman Trophy running back Herschel Walker, giving Bryant his 13th conference title at Alabama.

Unfortunately, it would also be his last.

10 The First Black Players

In terms of pioneers, one would be hard-pressed to find a bigger one in Alabama football history than Wilbur Jackson, the first black athlete to sign a football scholarship to play for the Crimson Tide.

Integration was a hot issue in the South in the 1960s, especially in Alabama, which had endured everything from the bombing of the Sixteenth Street Baptist Church in Birmingham, which killed four young girls, to Governor George Wallace trying to block the University of Alabama's first two black students from entering their classrooms.

Tensions were at an all-time high, and for years Coach Paul W. "Bear" Bryant maintained that the local social and political climate wasn't ready for black football players. During a deposition for an antidiscrimination lawsuit filed against the school, Bryant testified that he had actively been trying to recruit black players for years but had found no takers and had forwarded some on to other coaches.

Alabama finally made history with Jackson. He was followed by Bo Matthews.

What helped ease the transition was the 1970 season, when, in part due to an obvious difference in talent, the Tide finished 6–5–1. In the opener against visiting Southern California, a 42–21 pasting, Trojans halfback Sam Cunningham, who had been recruited by Alabama, rushed for 135 yards and two touchdowns.

Noted assistant coach Jerry Claiborne, "Sam Cunningham did more to integrate Alabama in 60 minutes than Martin Luther King did in 20 years."

The first black player to get into a game for Alabama was John Mitchell, a two-time Junior College All-American defensive end who had transferred in from Eastern Arizona College.

"I wouldn't say everyone accepted me, but Coach Bryant was fair so the players all treated me the same," Mitchell said.

Sylvester Croom

This Tuscaloosa native was one of the first black football players at Alabama, and as a senior captain he was named an All-American in addition to winning the Jacobs Trophy as the Southeastern Conference's best blocker. Before playing center, he was a linebacker, tight end, and tackle.

During his three seasons, Croom helped lead Alabama to a 32–4 record, three straight SEC titles, and the 1973 national championship.

"In my career, I've been around a lot of great leaders," Ozzie Newsome said. "And he led that huddle, trust me. He was impressive at a lot of things, but mostly a leader."

In 2003, Croom became the first black head football coach in the SEC at Mississippi State and in 2007 was named the conference's Coach of the Year.

Mitchell was named an All-American in 1972, and was Alabama's first black co-captain and first black assistant coach. He later became the conference's first black defensive coordinator at LSU.

"I'd do it again in a minute," he said. "If you're a football player, you dream of playing for Coach Bryant."

Meanwhile, during his junior season, Jackson led the Southeastern Conference by averaging 7.1 yards per carry. For his senior year, he switched from halfback to fullback in the new wishbone offense (another important change) and accumulated 752 rushing yards on 95 carries for a 7.9-yard average.

Alabama went 11–1 in 1971, 10–2 the following year, and capped it with an 11–0 regular season in 1973 to be named the United Press International national champion in the final year the coaches' poll was conducted prior to bowl games (it lost to Notre Dame in the Sugar Bowl, 24–23). All three years, the Crimson Tide captured the SEC championship.

Jackson was selected in the first round of the 1974 draft by the San Francisco 49ers and played eight years in the National Football League, including with the 1982 Super Bowl champion Washington Redskins. He accumulated 895 yards his rookie season and was named NFC Rookie of the Year, and for his career he posted 3,852 career rushing yards on 971 carries, with 1,572 receiving yards on 183 catches.

Meanwhile, by the 1973 season, one-third of Alabama's starters were black.

11 Wallace Wade

Wallace Wade was known for being a tough disciplinarian and a perfectionist before Dr. George Hutcheson Denny hired him to take over the team prior to the start of the 1923 season. Not only had he been a star guard at Brown and played in the 1916 Rose Bowl, he was also a cavalry captain during World War I.

"The best you can do is not enough unless it gets the job done," Wade was known for saying.

His first season produced a 7–2–1 record, but one of the losses, a 23–0 pounding at Syracuse, was the game he claimed taught him more about football than any other.

Apparently he learned a lot because Alabama subsequently put Southern football on the map and won its first national championship.

The run began in 1924, when Alabama went 8–1 and captured its first conference title. The Crimson Tide won its first three games by a combined score of 130–0 and didn't yield a point until its seventh game, a 42–7 victory against visiting Kentucky. A week later, a 17–0 loss to Centre College prevented perfection, but a dominating 33–0 Thanksgiving victory against Georgia clinched the Southern Conference championship.

Not only did the Tide defend its league title in 1925, but after outscoring nine regular-season opponents 277–7, it received an invitation to play Washington in the prestigious Rose Bowl. Although Alabama was considered a heavy underdog, it pulled out a 20–19 victory that had long-reaching effects and gave the region a dose of much-needed pride.

With the national championship in tow, Alabama continued its winning ways in 1926, which included a third straight Southern

Conference title, and returned to the Rose Bowl. Although the Tide didn't win, the 7–7 tie against Stanford answered any questions about whether the previous year had been a fluke, and again Alabama could claim at least a share of the national title.

Wade had one more title run in 1930. Even though he had turned in his resignation at the end of the previous season, he agreed to stay on for the final year of his contract before heading to Duke. It was arguably his best team yet, and the only points Alabama yielded that season were seven to Vanderbilt and six to Tennessee, while the offense cranked out 271.

A season-ending 13–0 victory against Georgia meant both a perfect record and fourth Southern Conference championship, resulting in another invitation to the Rose Bowl to play Washington State. This time the game wasn't close, and after winning his third national championship, the coach was carried off the field by his players.

Wade compiled a 61–13–3 record at Alabama, and his teams went 110–36–7 at Duke from 1931 to 1950, though he returned to service during World War II. Many of the losses came in the

The Iron Dukes

Although Wallace Wade never won another national championship after leaving Alabama for Duke, he came extremely close. The 1938 team is the one most bragged about, as the Iron Dukes finished the regular season undefeated, untied, and unscored upon, closing with a 7–0 victory in a snowstorm against No. 4. Pittsburgh. However, that still earned only a No. 3 ranking in the final Associated Press poll, and Duke subsequently lost in the Rose Bowl on a last-minute touchdown by Southern California. The Blue Devils were No. 2 at the end of the 1941 season, but instead of traveling back to California, Duke hosted the Rose Bowl due to West Coast safety concerns following the attack on Pearl Harbor. Although favored, Duke was flat and lost to Oregon State 20–16. It remains the only time the Rose Bowl was not played in California.

years after the war, prompting Wade to say, "I'm no longer tough enough."

Durham Herald writer Jack Horner had a different take: "The truth was that Wade mellowed after seeing 135-pounders die for America as gloriously as 200-pounders."

12 Lee Roy Jordan

There have been numerous Crimson Tide players who have placed high in voting for the Heisman Trophy, including Lee Roy Jordan, who had a fourth-place showing in 1962.

However, what makes Jordan's finish really stand out is that the All-American was primarily known for his defensive play as a linebacker.

Jordan arrived at the Capstone one year after Paul W. "Bear" Bryant returned to coach, and he helped return Alabama to the top of the college football world.

In 1960, Jordan's sophomore year, Alabama went 8–1–2 with a 3–3 tie against Texas in the Bluebonnet Bowl, where he was voted the game's most valuable player.

A year later, the Tide finished a perfect 11–0, including a 10–3 victory against Arkansas in the Sugar Bowl, for Bryant's first national championship. Opponents scored 25 points all season, compared to 297 for Alabama, with North Carolina State, led by quarterback Roman Gabriel, managing the most points, seven. Two others scored six, and two more had just three points.

For his senior season, 1962, Jordan was a unanimous All-America selection, and Alabama went 10–1 with a 17–0 victory over Oklahoma in the Orange Bowl. Jordan made an amazing 30 tackles in the game.

"He was one of the finest football players the world has ever seen," Bryant said. "If runners stayed between the sidelines, he tackled them. He never had a bad day, he was 100 percent every day in practice and in the games."

Alabama finished 10–1 and ranked No. 5. Jordan finished his college career with a 29–2–2 record over his last three seasons. The

In 1961 the Crimson Tide finished its season a perfect 11–0, including a 10–3 victory over Arkansas in the Sugar Bowl, for Bear Bryant's first national championship. Although Alabama had a prolific offense, its defense—led by Lee Roy Jordan—gave up just 25 points all season.

Dallas Cowboys selected him with the sixth-overall pick in the 1963 draft, and he became a key part of the Doomsday Defense. Despite being only 6'1", 215 pounds, he played 14 seasons in the National Football League, became the franchise's all-time leader in solo tackles with 743, helped lead the Cowboys to three Super Bowls (winning one), and was named All-Pro five times (with five Pro Bowls).

"He was a great competitor," said Tom Landry, the Cowboys' Hall of Fame coach. "He was not big for a middle linebacker, but because of his competitiveness, he was able to play the game and play it well. His leadership was there and he demanded a lot out of the people around him, as he did of himself."

In 1989 Jordan received the Cowboys' highest honor when 13 years after his retirement he became the seventh player inducted into the club's Ring of Honor, joining Bob Lilly, Don Meredith, Don Perkins, Chuck Howley, Mel Renfro, and Roger Staubach. A contract dispute late in his career with former Cowboys president Tex Schramm was believed to be the reason for the delay.

"I'd like to thank Jerry Jones, the Dallas Cowboys, my friends, and the fans who remembered me for all these years. You've got a hell of a long memory," Jordan said at the time. "I'm honored to be put on the board with these guys."

1962

One of the teams that doesn't receive the recognition it deserves is the 1962 squad, when Alabama was coming off Coach Paul W. "Bear" Bryant's first national championship. The Crimson Tide had a sophomore quarterback named Joe Namath and All-American linebacker Lee Roy Jordan. After being voted No. 1 in the Associated Press poll for the third time that season, Alabama stumbled at Georgia Tech, 7–6. The Crimson Tide finished 10–1, outscored opponents 289–39, and ranked fifth. Not only did Alabama shut out Auburn for the fourth straight year, but Jordan closed his career with 30 tackles against Oklahoma in the Orange Bowl. He placed fourth in Heisman Trophy voting (won by Terry Baker of Oregon State).

13 Mark Ingram Wins the Heisman Trophy

It was a moment many Tide fans thought they'd never see.

By Alabama football standards it was 117 years in the making, since the first team was organized in 1892. For the Heisman Trophy it was a long overdue addition. A Crimson Tide player had never been honored in the 74-year history of the award.

That is until December, 12, 2009, when sophomore running back Mark Ingram Jr., heard his name called and then couldn't contain the emotions after seeing the tears flood out of his mother's eyes.

"I'm a little overwhelmed right now," he finally said after reaching the stage of the Nokia Theater, where other members of the Heisman fraternity awaited the newest member. "I'm just so excited to bring Alabama their first Heisman winner."

While the roars were heard throughout the New York theater, and back in both Alabama and his hometown of Flint, Michigan, Ingram proceeded to thank everyone he could think of, from his coaches and teammates down to the support staff and teachers. The seemingly impossible had happened and he wasn't going to miss anyone.

"I'm very excited," he said.

Adding to the drama was that the vote turned out to be the closest in Heisman history, with Ingram topping Stanford running back Toby Gerhart by just 28 points.

Previously, the narrowest margin was 1985, when only 45 points separated Auburn running back Bo Jackson from runner-up Chuck Long of Iowa, which was also the last time a Southeastern Conference running back won.

Mark Ingram poses with the Heisman Trophy after becoming the first Crimson Tide ever to win the award on December 12, 2009. (AP Images)

With the Heisman using a 3-2-1 point system (a first-place vote worth three votes, second two points, and third one point), Ingram finished with 1,304 points, just edging Gerhart's 1,276, Texas quarterback Colt McCoy's 1,145, and Nebraska defensive tackle Ndamukong Suh's 815 (the most points ever for a fourth-place finisher).

Ingram had the most first-place votes, 227, compared to Gerhart's 222, and won every region except the West (Gerhart) and Southwest (Suh), where he was third in both. He topped the South with 254 points compared to McCoy's 176 and Gerhart's 165.

With all ballots submitted solely online for the first time and the race obviously close, nearly all voters waited until the last minute to cast their ballots. Of the 904 tabulated (out of a possible 926) 89 percent weren't submitted until the final few days, after Ingram totaled 189 yards from scrimmage and three touchdowns against Florida in the SEC Championship Game.

"I realized that game he's a real dude," said Florida quarterback Tim Tebow, the 2007 winner who finished a distant fifth with just 390 points.

"I was pretty sure I wasn't going to win it, I'm a realist."

That sentiment appeared to be felt by the other finalists as well, with Gerhart going so far as to have a photo taken of his reaching for the trophy and it just out of his grasp.

"It's just an honor to be here," he said. "No disappointment, no hard feelings."

Ingram tallied 1,658 rushing yards to set the Alabama single-season record, and 1,992 all-purpose yards while scoring 20 touchdowns. He had nine 100-yard games, including a season-high and Bryant-Denny Stadium–record 246 yards against No. 22 South Carolina on October 17.

Against the Gamecocks, Ingram handled the ball on every play during the Crimson Tide's game-clinching drive. Also standing out to voters were his one career lost fumble, 1,002 yards after contact (53.7 percent), and 825 rushing yards and six touchdowns in Alabama's five games against Top 25 teams (averaging 165 yards per game against Virginia Tech, Mississippi, South Carolina, LSU, and Florida). In those same games, he averaged 201.1 all-purpose yards.

Previously, David Palmer had the Tide's best Heisman finish, placing third in 1993. The following year Jay Barker placed fifth, the last time Alabama had a finalist invited to New York.

Overall, 16 Tide players had placed in the top 10 since the award's inception in 1935, with Lee Roy Jordan (1962) and

National Honors (Through 2015)

Alabama, 2011 Disney Spirit Award (most inspirational player/team, accepted by Carson Tinker); Alabama offensive line, 2015 Joe Moore Award (best offensive line); Jay Barker, 1994 Johnny Unitas Golden Arm Award (best senior quarterback); Cornelius Bennett, 1986 Vince Lombardi/Rotary Award (outstanding lineman); Amari Cooper, 2014 Fred Biletnikoff Award (best receiver); Derrick Henry, 2015 Heisman Trophy (outstanding player), Maxwell Award (outstanding player), Walter Camp Award (player of the year), Doak Walker Award (best running back), Mark Ingram Jr., 2009 Heisman Trophy (outstanding player); Barrett Jones, 2011 Outland Trophy (best interior lineman) and Wuerffel Trophy (exemplary community service with athletic/academic achievement), 2012 Rimington Trophy (best center) and William V. Cambell Trophy (academic Heisman); Ryan Kelly, 2015 Rimington Trophy (best center); Antonio Langham, 1993 Thorpe Award (outstanding defensive back); AJ McCarron, 2015 Maxwell Award (outstanding player) and Johnny Unitas Golden Arm Award (best senior quarterback); Rolando McClain, 2009 Butkus Award (outstanding linebacker); Trent Richardson, 2011 Doak Walker Award (best running back); DeMeco Ryans, 2005 Lott Trophy (defensive impact player); Chris Samuels, 1999 Outland Trophy (best interior lineman); Derrick Thomas, 1988 Dick Butkus Award (outstanding linebacker).

Johnny Musso (1971) both finishing fourth, and Joe Kilgrow (1937), Harry Gilmer (1945 and 1947), Pat Trammell (1961), Terry Davis (1972), and Jay Barker (1994) all fifth.

"You know I really wasn't aware until Mark was in the thick of all this that that was really the case," said Coach Nick Saban, who never had a Heisman finalist before. "You don't really think about things like that. It made this an even greater opportunity from a big-picture standpoint."

Until Ingram it had been a point of pride that Alabama had won 12 national titles without a Heisman. Paul W. "Bear" Bryant, who had one player win the award, John David Crow at Texas A&M in 1957, even went so far as to say, "At Alabama, our players don't win Heisman Trophies, our teams win national championships."

For an encore, Ingram helped lead the Crimson Tide to a 37–21 victory over Texas in the BCS Championship Game at the Rose Bowl, and subsequently enjoyed Alabama's first visit to the White House to commemorate its national championship.

14 Attend a Game at Bryant-Denny Stadium

Those who haven't experienced a college football game at Bryant-Denny Stadium are missing out on one of the sport's unique experiences.

Football in Tuscaloosa isn't quite like anywhere else. Where else can one:

- See flags for all of the national championships snapping in the wind?
- Watch dressed-up people spend the morning tailgating and pointing out recruits by name like they're long-lost friends?
- Hear a sellout crowd go nuts every time they show Paul W. "Bear" Bryant on the video screens, with the gruff voice of the legendary coach proclaiming "I ain't never been nothing but a winner"?

Prior to the stadium, Alabama played on campus at the Quad, first on the southeast corner with the field running parallel to what's now 6th Avenue. At the turn of the century, the field was turned 90 degrees to the west to run alongside University Boulevard.

In 1915, games were played on University Field, renamed Denny Field in 1920, where the Tide played for 14 years. It was located two blocks east of the current stadium, behind Little Hall. Mallet Hall and Parker-Adams Hall now stand on what used to be the north end zone, and a parking lot covers what was the rest of the field.

Overall, Alabama was 44–9 in those locations, and opponents were scoreless in 35 of the 45 games played at Denny Field.

With university president Dr. George Hutcheson Denny using football as a means to promote and build up the school, upgrading the facilities was an obvious priority even though the team played at least one home game a year in Birmingham.

The stadium opened on September 28, 1929, with a 55–0 victory against Mississippi College, and was officially dedicated a week later during homecoming by Governor Bibb Graves. Initial seating capacity was 12,000. It wasn't until 1975 that the state legislature renamed the facility Bryant-Denny Stadium.

There have been numerous improvements and expansion projects since it opened, including the following:

- 1937: The first stadium expansion added 6,000 seats to the east side.
- 1946: Bleachers were constructed behind both end zones, bringing capacity up to 31,000.
- 1961: Another 12,000 seats were added, along with a press box and elevator. With the lower bowl nearly closed in, capacity reached 43,000.
- 1966: The lower bowl was enclosed with seating expansion, bringing capacity up to 60,000.
- 1988: The western upper deck was completed, adding another 10,000 seats for a total of 70,123.
- 1998: The eastern upper deck was added along with two rows of skyboxes, bringing capacity more in line with that of other Southeastern Conference home stadiums, 83,818. Four additional skyboxes were built in 1999, bringing the total to 85.
- 2006: The north end-zone addition added a club level, skyboxes, upper-deck seating, and a courtyard. The project, which cost approximately $50 million, brought the total number of

skyboxes up to 123 and capacity to 92,138. Additionally, three new video scoreboards were added, along with state-of-the-art ribbon wraparound display boards on the facades of the east and west upper deck.

- 2010: A $65 million expansion of the south end zone filled in the last upper deck and increased seating capacity to 101,821. Along with the 34 added skyboxes, bringing the stadium total to 157, another Zone Club just like the original on the north side was added along with a new Stadium Club. Two new scoreboards were installed in the corners along with a new sound system, and the outside along Bryant Drive was given a brick exterior to better blend in with the rest of campus.

With university enrollment growing from roughly 20,000 to 37,000-plus from 2004–2015, the number of student tickets was increased by 2,000, up to 17,000, giving Alabama the highest percentage of student-available seating among major public school programs at 59 percent.

"We are fortunate to play our home games in one of the finest football facilities in the nation," former director of athletics Mal Moore said. "Our fans enjoy fantastic campus activities prior to the game and then move into a state-of-the-art facility to watch the game. The atmosphere is second-to-none."

15 1961: The Bear's First

When Paul W. "Bear" Bryant was hired in 1958, he told both the incoming recruits and the holdovers from the previous teams—well, those who survived his brutal offseason conditioning program—that if they weren't there to win a national championship, they were in the wrong place.

During his first three seasons, Alabama produced no championships and no All-Americans, but in 1961 the Crimson Tide was coming off an 8–1–2 season, had key players returning, and had increased capacity at Denny Stadium by 12,000 to 43,000.

Led by quarterback Pat Trammell, linebacker/center Lee Roy Jordan, and lineman Billy Neighbors, Alabama simply destroyed the competition, beginning with a 32–6 victory at Georgia. Opponents scored 25 points the entire season, compared to 297 for the Tide.

"They play like it is a sin to give up a point," Bryant commented on his defense.

After Tennessee managed a field goal in a 34–3 loss, Alabama didn't yield another point during its five final games of the regular season, recording shutouts against Houston, Mississippi State, Richmond, Georgia Tech, and Auburn.

"I don't know if that's a great team, but they most certainly were great against us," Auburn coach Shug Jordan said after the 34–0 loss. "I don't guess anybody has ever hit us that hard."

Following the Georgia Tech victory, Alabama was ranked No. 1 in the Associated Press poll for the first time that season, which it would maintain through a 10–3 victory against Arkansas in the Sugar Bowl for the national championship.

"Regardless of who was coaching them, they still would have been a great team," said Bryant, who was also named national coach of the year for the first time. "I said early in the season that they were the nicest, even the sissiest bunch I'd ever had. I think they read it, because later on they got unfriendly."

Fullback Mike Fracchia was named the most valuable player of Alabama's first victory at the Sugar Bowl in three attempts. Neighbors was a unanimous All-American selection, the Crimson

Tide's first since 1954. Jordan and Trammell were second-team picks and joined Fracchia as All-SEC selections.

"He can't run, he can't pass, and he can't kick," Bryant said about Trammell. "All he can do is beat you."

However, the title did have one lingering negative consequence, due to linebacker Darwin Holt catching Georgia Tech quarterback Chick Granning with an elbow on a late hit, fracturing his jaw. A year later, Alabama fans were dreaming of back-to-back titles until November 17, when the inspired Yellow Jackets pulled out a hard-hitting 7–6 victory after Alabama fell inches short of completing a two-point conversion.

The No. 5 Tide finished 10–1, with Jordan, a unanimous All-American who finished fourth in Heisman Trophy balloting, recording 30 tackles against Oklahoma in the Orange Bowl, a 17–0 victory. Fifteen seniors finished their careers after going 29–2–2 during their last three seasons.

16 Tailgate on the Quad

Tailgating at most places is considered a pleasant and leisurely event.

Usually, it's done in a parking lot, features a cooler or two, maybe a small grill, and, depending where you are, some sort of local cuisine. For example, burning a bratwurst is considered all but a sacred rite in most parts of Wisconsin, just like Cajun food is the main staple in Louisiana. Try something different, like a kabob, and they'll acknowledge your contribution and original thinking, but might look at you a little funny the moment you turn your back.

"Tourist."

At Alabama, they take their tailgating seriously. Very seriously. Anyone without a generator is either an amateur or a student, and one frequently comes across people who have been cooking since the night before, if not longer.

Grills and smokers that look like they could power small cities can be found around town, parked in strategic locations, and smelled from far away. Ribs are generally considered the primary delicacy year-round in Tuscaloosa, but on game days you'll also find a number of other delicious (and unhealthy) staples like brisket, pork shoulder, and, well, just about any kind of pork and beef imaginable—frequently together. For a change of pace, they might cook some chicken.

Brave souls may also take a stab at fish and vegetables, but usually very quietly. The various premade side dishes include everything from casseroles to cookies and are only rarely store-bought.

Alabama's All-Century Team (Selected by Fans)

Offense

E Don Hutson, 1932–34; E Ozzie Newsome, 1974–77; L Fred Sington, 1928–30; L Vaughn Mancha, 1944–47; C Dwight Stephenson, 1977–79; L Billy Neighbors, 1959–61; L John Hannah, 1970–72; QB Joe Namath, 1962–64; QB Ken Stabler, 1965–67; RB Bobby Marlow, 1950–52; RB Johnny Musso, 1969–71; RB Bobby Humphrey, 1985–88; K Van Tiffin, 1983–86.

Defense

L Bob Baumhower, 1973, 1976; L Marty Lyons, 1975–78; L Jon Hand, 1982–85; LB Lee Roy Jordan, 1960–62; LB Barry Krauss, 1976–78; OLB Cornelius Bennett, 1983–86; OLB Derrick Thomas, 1985–88; DB Harry Gilmer, 1944–47; DB Don McNeal, 1977–79; DB Jeremiah Castille, 1979–82; DB Tommy Wilcox, 1979–82; P Johnny Cain, 1930–32.

Coach

Paul W. "Bear" Bryant.

Some consider it heaven on earth, especially if they get the barbeque sauce just right, and many recipes are held on to more intensely than some family secrets, and second only to game tickets.

That's kind of fitting because *the* place to be a couple of hours before kickoff is the campus area known as the Quad, the green in the heart of the campus, which on Saturdays takes on the aura of a giant family reunion.

The bigger the game (and the better the season), the more family members who show up.

Fans clamor for prime predetermined spots long before the teams show up to the stadium. They throw footballs and Frisbees in open areas and walk around as if to inspect the grounds. Satellite dishes and televisions nicer than what many people have in their homes are only outnumbered by lawn chairs and eating utensils, and cheers are heard from all around whenever a Southeastern Conference rival gives up a touchdown, especially Auburn.

Kids can enjoy various carnival-type attractions, the marching band warms up and plays a few songs, a variety of radio stations/networks broadcast pregame shows, and the University of Alabama Supply Store is on-hand to meet any specific need (like replace a forgotten No. 12 jersey or a misplaced shaker). There might even be a famous former player signing autographs along with the author of a book about Alabama football.

However there are other, more subtle, indicators of how seriously Alabama fans take their tailgating. These include some of the items they make sure to have on-hand, such as rain gear, fans, toilet paper, pillows, extra cups, toothpicks, beanbag chairs, blankets, sun block, extra ice, a first-aid kit, ice chests, and extension cords (and jumper cables in the car, just in case).

Just don't ask what's in the sauce or how anyone sneaks anything into the stadium—and under no circumstances wear orange.

17 The Shutout

There's no doubt that when Alabama defeated LSU 21–0 in the BCS Championship Game to win the 2011 national title, the Crimson Tide made history—especially the defense.

Not only did Alabama pull off the first shutout in Bowl Championship Series history, it was the first time since 1946 (the famous 0–0 tie between No. 1 Army and No. 2 Notre Dame at Yankee Stadium) that the No. 1 team was held scoreless in a No. 1 vs. No. 2 matchup.

"You're talking about one of the most competitive groups of guys as a group," Coach Nick Saban said. "Sometimes I get mad at them at practice because they get a little bit hurt and they don't run to the ball like I want them to or like we want them to or whatever. But I always know, *all right, when you throw the ball out, they're going to go get it.* Because they are a hateful bunch and they are as competitive as you can ever imagine, and I think that's probably why they played really well in big games."

Led by defensive game MVP Courtney Upshaw, who had seven tackles and a sack, Alabama finished with a 21–5 edge in first downs, 69–44 in plays, and 384–92 in total yards. LSU's longest possession went just 23 yards and its biggest play was for 19. It went three-and-out six times, with an interception by linebacker C.J. Mosley on the second play of a possession, and converted just two third-down opportunities.

LSU crossed midfield just once and then promptly went backwards and fumbled away the ball. In contrast, Alabama failed to cross the 50-yard line only twice, and with the defense yielding nothing each one of the Crimson Tide's five field goals took a little more out of the previously undefeated Tigers until Trent Richardson closed the scoring with his final collegiate touchdown.

"We knew it was going to be a physical game," senior nose tackle Josh Chapman said. "I love a physical game."

Consequently, the 2011 Crimson Tide forced its way into the discussion about which is the best defense in college football history.

"It was unbelievable," Hall of Fame coach Lou Holtz said. "It was a complete mismatch.

Joe Paterno's Final Loss

Over the years a very respectful rivalry with Penn State developed as the games between Paul W. "Bear" Bryant and Joe Paterno were nothing short of epic. Among them were the 1982 meeting when Bryant notched victory No. 314 to tie Amos Alonzo Stagg's record for career victories and the 1979 Sugar Bowl to determine the national championship.

"I don't talk about wanting to play much, but I would love to have a chance to play against Penn State again," Cornelius Bennett said after Alabama agreed to home-and-home meetings in 2010 and 2011. "We never should have stopped the series.

"You know, Coach Bryant, Joe Paterno. Need I say more?"

Paterno was one of the few coaches with a winning record against Nick Saban, 3–2 from his Michigan State days, when Penn State visited Bryant-Denny Stadium in 2010. Former Florida State coach Bobby Bowden received a special invitation to attend and the three legends shook hands at midfield before the Crimson Tide's 24–3 victory.

No one knew that when Alabama visited Beaver Stadium on September 10, 2011, and won 27–11, that it would be Paterno's final loss as a head coach. After notching 409 wins he was fired in November for his "failure of leadership" regarding a sex scandal surrounding an assistant coach. Similar to Bryant, he died shortly after the conclusion of his coaching career, on January 22, 2012. He was 85.

"I've coached against Coach Saban. I have the utmost respect for him as a person, as a coach. I love being around him, but he's a greedy sucker. Some people get you first-and-ten, second-and-twelve, third-and-nine and they're content at fourth-and-five. Not Nick. He wants it first-and-ten, second-and-twelve, third-and fourteen, fourth-and-nineteen. He wants to move you back, he doesn't want to give you a yard. You can see it the way they practice out there, they just don't want you to make a yard. Some people don't want you to make a first down, not Nick."

Alabama finished the season by leading the nation in pass-efficiency defense (83.7 rating), pass defense (111.5 yards per game), rushing defense (72.2), scoring defense (8.2 points), and total defense (183.6 yards per game)—in addition to third-down defense, red-zone defense, and three-and-outs.

Alabama also topped each category convincingly.

Defensive category	**Second-best team**	**Statistic**	**Difference**
Pass-efficiency defense	South Carolina	94.23	+10.54
Pass defense	South Carolina	131.69	+20.23
Rushing defense	Florida State	82.69	+10.54
Scoring defense	LSU	11.29	+3.14
Total defense	LSU	261.5	+77.88

Additionally, while Alabama gave up just 10.08 first downs, the next-best team was Georgia at 14.36.

Only one other time since the NCAA started keeping track in 1937 has a team finished No. 1 in all four key defensive categories, Oklahoma in 1986. The Sooners yielded 169.6 total yards, 60.7 rushing yards, 102.4 passing yards, and 6.6 points per game.

Granted, there's more passing and offense since then, but Oklahoma also failed to win the national championship, finishing third in the final Associated Press poll.

"Before the game against LSU I was comparing the defense from Alabama to the 1986 Oklahoma defense, which was considered by many to be the best defense in college football history," said ESPN analyst and former coach Lee Corso. "After that game, they went down as the greatest defense in college football history, and I want to congratulate [Saban]."

Here's how Alabama's defensive numbers compared with its previous two national championship teams:

2011: Rushing: 72.2; Passing: 111.5; Pass efficiency: 83.7; Total: 183.6; Scoring: 8.2; Turnovers: 1.5; Third downs: 24.0; TFL: 7.3; 1st downs: 10.1.

2009: Rushing: 78.1; Passing: 166.0; Pass efficiency: 87.6; Total: 244.1; Scoring: 11.7; Turnovers: 2.2; Third downs: 30.0; TFL: 7.0; 1st downs: 13.4.

1992: Rushing: 55.0; Passing: 139.2; Pass efficiency: 83.9; Total: 194.16; Scoring: 9.1; Turnovers: 3.2; Third downs: 22.4; TFL: 5.4; 1st downs: 11.3.

Additionally, the 1961 Crimson Tide gave up just 25 points over 11 games and went into the Sugar Bowl with a streak of five consecutive shutouts, but of the four big categories only led the nation in two: total defense and scoring defense.

"This defense is as good as any I've ever been around," defensive coordinator Kirby Smart said. "Obviously the 2009 group was really special. This group is kind of different because we're really good on the edges, and really stout inside with [Josh Chapman] and got some good backers and got good secondary. It's similar to the other team, the only difference is I think this one has a little more speed on it."

Still, the debate will go on....

"The character, the attitude, the resiliency of this group, the work and the commitment, and the buy-in was what made this team different," Saban said. "I can't tell you what defense was the best. I can just tell you this was one of the most enjoyable teams to coach."

18 1926 Rose Bowl (First Championship)

The first "bowl" game was played in 1902 as part of the Tournament of Roses celebration, held primarily because many of Pasadena's transplanted residents were looking for an excuse to enjoy the fact that it wasn't snowing or cold like it was where they used to live in the East and Midwest.

That first game featured Stanford (3–0–2) against Michigan (10–0), which hadn't yielded a point all season. The Wolverines crushed the local favorites, 49–0.

In part due to wounded pride, organizers turned their attention to other sports/activities to serve as a centerpiece event, including polo and chariot races, which failed to hold the same kind of attention. So in 1916 football was back in, with Washington State playing Brown and pulling off a 14–0 victory.

It wasn't long until the Rose Bowl became the marquee event of the college football season and in some ways the de facto national championship. However, for the next 10 years no Southern team played in the game, although Georgia Tech turned down an invitation in 1917 because players didn't want to wait any longer to enroll in the military during World War I.

That changed during the 1925 season after Alabama, under the direction of Wallace Wade, got off to an 8–0 start while giving up just one touchdown. A pounding 7–0 victory against Georgia Tech set up a showdown with Georgia for the Southern Conference title, which was dominated by Alabama, 27–0.

On hand for that victory were representatives of the Rose Bowl Committee, who left unimpressed and instead extended invitations to Dartmouth, Yale, and Colgate, teams that were all under pressure from the American Association of University Professors to decline. Finally, Alabama received the offer to play heavily favored Washington, which it eagerly accepted, with the entire region rallying behind the Crimson Tide. Even Auburn president Dr. Spright Dowell sent a telegram wishing the team good luck.

After the Tide fell behind 12–0 in the first half, the third quarter saw a complete momentum shift after Alabama knocked Washington's best player, George "Wildcat" Wilson, who finished with 134 rushing yards and completed five passes for 77 yards and two touchdowns, out of the game, and Wade unleashed Pooley Hubert's ground game.

Hubert punched in one touchdown, and Johnny Mack Brown scored on both a 59-yard reception from Grant Gillis and a 30–yard catch from Hubert to give Alabama a 20–12 lead.

"When I reached the 3 I looked around, and sure enough the ball was coming down over my shoulder," Brown said of Hubert's pass after being told to run as fast as he could toward the end zone. "I took it in stride, used my stiff arm on one man, and went over carrying somebody. The place was really in an uproar."

Wilson was able to return and led another scoring drive, but his open-field tackle by Brown ended the final threat for a 20–19 victory.

Although Alabama had to share the national title with Dartmouth, the result shook the very foundation of college football. It was, and still is by some, considered one of the greatest Rose Bowl games ever played, and a rare moment of pride in the post–Civil War South, which was in desperate need of something to celebrate.

19 Ozzie Newsome

Except for coaching, there's not much Ozzie Newsome hasn't done in football.

He had an exceptional collegiate career, an even better pro career, and he has gained entry into four halls of fame: the Pro Football Hall of Fame (inducted 1999), the National Football Foundation's College Hall of Fame (1994), the NCAA Hall of Fame (1994), and Alabama Sports Hall of Fame (1995).

Not too bad for a 6'4", 210-pound player from Muscle Shoals, Alabama.

Newsome was a four-year starter from 1974 to 1977, during which he set many Crimson Tide reception records. He caught 102 passes for 2,070 yards, with an average gain per pass of 20.3 yards, a conference record.

Alabama's season records with Newsome were 11–1, 11–1, 9–3, and 11–1, with three Southeastern Conference championships and a No. 2 finish in 1977 when voters leapfrogged Notre Dame up from No. 5 after it defeated Texas. He was twice named all-conference, and an All-American his senior year. The Touchdown Club of Atlanta and the Birmingham Monday Morning Quarterback Club named Newsome the Southeastern Conference's Lineman of the Year in 1977, when he was also Alabama's co-captain.

Paul W. "Bear" Bryant called him "the greatest end in Alabama history and that includes Don Hutson. A total team player, fine blocker, outstanding leader, great receiver with concentration, speed, hands."

In the 1976 Sugar Bowl, Newsome's slant-and-go for a 55-yard gain set up the only touchdown of the game as Alabama

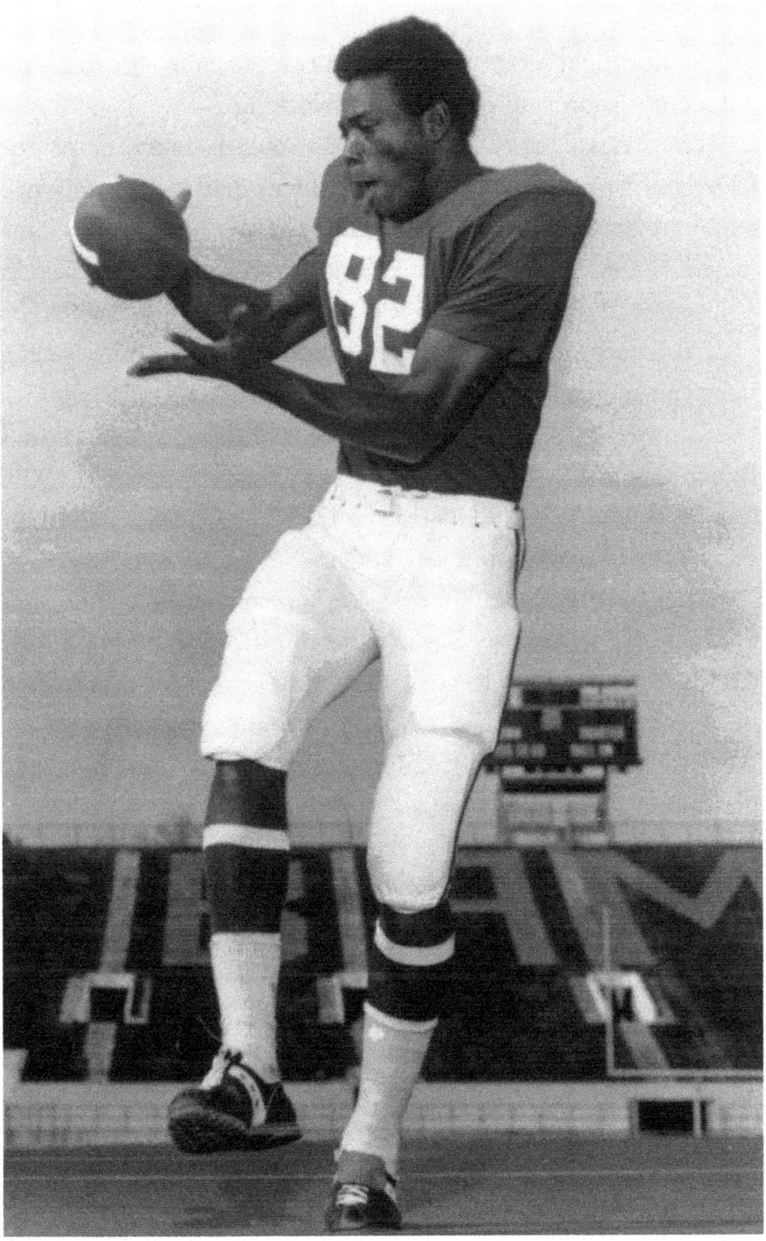

As a four-year starter from 1974–77, Ozzie Newsome set numerous Alabama receiving records, most of which stood until 2007. He caught 102 passes for 2,070 yards with an average gain per pass of 20.3 yards, a conference record.

defeated Penn State 13–6. Against Notre Dame the following season, he caught seven passes, scored two touchdowns and a two-point conversion, and graded 90 on blocking.

The Wizard of Oz was the 23rd-overall selection of the Cleveland Browns in the 1978 NFL Draft and needed only two seasons to earn All-Pro honors (he did so again in 1984). Newsome played in 198 consecutive games as a Brown and caught a pass in 150 consecutive games, which was the second-longest streak in the National Football League when he retired as its all-time leading tight end in receiving with 662 receptions, 7,980 yards, and 47 touchdowns. Additionally, he won the NFL Players Association's Byron "Whizzer" White Award for community service in 1990, four years after being presented the Ed Block Courage Award for continuing to play in spite of injuries.

After his playing days were over, Newsome wasn't done with the NFL. He joined the Cleveland front office and on November 22, 2002, became the league's first black general manager when the franchise (which had since moved and was renamed the Baltimore Ravens) promoted him from vice president of player personnel.

Known for maximizing the Ravens' success in the NFL Draft, Newsome's strategy is, "Select the best available player on the board." Newsome was the architect of the Ravens' Super Bowl XXXV championship team in 2000 and voted the NFL's Executive of the Year that same year.

On the wall of his Baltimore office is a sideline portrait of his mentor, Bryant, wearing his trademark houndstooth hat.

"Coach [Bryant] helped me grow up. He pushed me further than I thought I could go, both on and off the field," Newsome said.

Many believe that Newsome will someday become the director of athletics at Alabama. In the spring of 2007, he told Mobile's *Press-Register*, "People keep talking about me being the AD. If there's the opportunity to come back maybe to be the janitor at the University of Alabama, hey, I'll take that."

20 1992: The Return to Greatness

It was the centennial season of Alabama football, and the Crimson Tide was looking for its first national championship since Paul W. "Bear" Bryant's final title in 1979. Even though it was coming off an 11–1 season and a No. 5 final ranking, few believed this would be the year, as Alabama began the season ninth.

The victories started piling up, though many were not pretty: 25–8 against Vanderbilt, 17–0 vs. Southern Miss, 38–11 at Arkansas, 13–0 vs. Louisiana Tech, 48–7 vs. South Carolina, 37–0 at Tulane. Against Tennessee, running back Derrick Lassic had 142 rushing yards to help lead a 17–10 victory in Knoxville.

"We finally got a little bit of respect," Lassic said.

When the defense limited LSU to just 22 rushing yards in a commanding 31–11 road victory and top-ranked Washington lost to Arizona, Alabama finally had control of its eventual outcome, but only if it could run the table and win its final three games.

The first was the Iron Bowl, with Auburn coach Pat Dye announcing his resignation the day before the game. The defense allowed 20 rushing yards and had five sacks, and Antonio Langham returned an interception 61 yards to key a 17–0 victory.

"Ten to nothing isn't a very big deal unless you've got a defense like Alabama's got, and then it's monumental," Dye said after his only shutout at Auburn. "Alabama may have the best defense I've seen in our conference."

Alabama went into the first-ever SEC Championship Game having outscored opponents 304–88. Again Langham returned an interception for a touchdown as the Tide defeated Florida, 28–21.

The third and final test was at the Sugar Bowl against No. 1 Miami, which was riding a 29-game winning streak and wanted to make sure everyone knew it. Among the numerous boastful things the Hurricanes said before the game was linebacker Michael Barrow's taunting "We seek, we destroy. We fear no one, but everyone fears us."

But Alabama didn't and for the most part kept quiet during its preparations. Although the Crimson Tide was considered a heavy underdog, its mission became simple: make the Hurricanes eat their words.

Did they ever.

Again led by the defense, Alabama began to take control in the second quarter. After shutting down the run, with the Hurricanes accumulating only 48 rushing yards, the Tide went to work on quarterback Gino Torretta, who had just won the Heisman Trophy.

"In the second quarter, I saw Torretta look over at me and he froze for a second," defensive end John Copeland said. "I saw fear."

At times, the Tide put all 11 defenders on the line of scrimmage and dared Torretta to try and beat the man coverage by defensive backs like Langham and safety George Teague, behind swarming ends Copeland and Eric Curry, and linebackers Lemanski Hall and Derrick Oden.

Meanwhile, the Tide offense never got around to establishing the passing game because it never had to. Quarterback Jay Barker threw for just 18 yards, with the ground game pounding out 267 rushing yards for an impressive 34–13 victory.

"There is a quote I've used before from Sir Isaac Newton," Coach Gene Stallings said in a speech during the on-campus "Salute to Champions" weekend. "It says, 'If I can see farther than most, it is because I have stood on the shoulders of giants.' Ladies and gentlemen, I have stood on the shoulders of giants."

Fittingly, Stallings was a unanimous selection for coach of the year and was presented the Paul "Bear" Bryant Award by the Football Writers Association of America.

21 The Bear Returns

Although Paul W. "Bear" Bryant had Texas A&M ranked No. 1 in the country and was on the verge of winning the national championship, he met in secret with Crimson Tide officials prior to his team's key showdown with Rice in 1958. Coming off a three-year stretch that resulted in a dismal 4–24–1 record, Alabama was desperate to reclaim its lost glory and pried him away with a 10-year contract, an annual salary of $17,000, and a house (not to mention other assurances that the coach insisted upon).

"I left Texas A&M because my school called me," Bryant said. "Mama called, and when Mama calls, then you just have to come running."

Although Bryant was already an Alabama fixture from his playing days, he had also developed an imposing reputation from his first training camp at Texas A&M, when he took the Aggies to a barren army base and essentially ran a brutal boot camp in 100-degree heat. More than 100 players made the initial trip, but after 10 days only one-third remained. Those who stuck it out became known as the "Junction Boys."

"I don't want ordinary people," Bryant said. "I want people who are willing to sacrifice and do without a lot of those things ordinary students get to do. That's what it takes to win."

Alabama Head Coaches (Through 2015)

Coach	Year(s)	Record
E.B. Beaumont	1892	2–2
Eli Abbott	1893–95, 1902	7–13
Otto Wagonhurst	1896	2–1
Allen McCants	1897	1–0
W.A. Martin	1899	3–1
M. Griffin	1900	2–3
M.H. Harvey	1901	2–1–2
W.B. Blount	1903–04	10–7
Jack Leavenworth	1905	6–4
J.W.H. Pollard	1906–09	21–4–5
Guy Lowman	1910	4–4–0
D.V. Graves	1911–14	21–12–3
Thomas Kelly	1915–17	17–7–1
Xen C. Scott	1919–22	29–9–3
Wallace Wade	1923–30	61–13–3
Frank Thomas	1931–46	115–24–7
Harold "Red" Drew	1947–54	54–28–7
J.B. Whitworth	1955–57	4–24–2
Paul W. "Bear" Bryant	1958–82	232–46–9
Ray Perkins	1983–86	32–15–1
Bill Curry	1987–89	26–10–0
Gene Stallings	1990–96	62–25–0–x
Mike DuBose	1997–2000	24–23–0
Dennis Franchione	2001–02	17–8
Mike Shula	2003–06	10–23
Joe Kines (interim)	2006	0–1
Nick Saban	2007–15	100–18

x-includes forfeits imposed by NCAA. *-Wins later vacated by an NCAA ruling. Shula's actual record was 26–23, while Saban's actual record was 55–12 through 2011.

The Aggies went 1–9 in 1954, the only losing season of Bryant's career. Two years later, they finished 9–0–1 and won the Southwest Conference championship.

As he did at Texas A&M, Bryant put players through the wringer during his first training camp at Alabama, causing many veterans to quit. But the change was immediate and noticeable in the opener against LSU in Mobile. The Tide had a 3–0 halftime lead but eventually succumbed, 13–3.

The turning point of the game came after Alabama recovered a fumble near the 3-yard line, when LSU coach Paul Dietzel put in his third platoon, which yielded only a field goal.

LSU lineman Emile Fournet described the match as "The game in which the Chinese Bandits were born." He added, "That convinced the coaches, and everyone else, that we could play."

LSU, which had Billy Cannon, who won the Heisman Trophy a year later in 1959, went 11–0 and won the national championship.

Alabama finished 5–4–1, which was the program's best showing since 1953, when it won the Southeastern Conference title despite a 6–3–3 record. The other losses were all close, 14–7 to Tennessee, 13–7 to Tulane, and 14–8 to undefeated Auburn. The 14 points were the most given up in a game the entire season, and Alabama outscored the opposition 106–75, the fewest points allowed since 1935.

The following season, Alabama went 7–2–2 to finish 10th in the polls and started a string of 24 straight postseason appearances. In 1961, Alabama finished 11–0 to win the national title, the first of six for Bryant.

22 Gene Stallings

In 1990 the Alabama football program was at a crossroads. Despite winning a Southeastern Conference championship, Bill Curry, who had lost all three of his games against Auburn, resigned as head coach only to take the same job at Kentucky. He had been the first since Frank Thomas to coach the Crimson Tide without having a previous tie to the program, something school officials weren't about to attempt with his replacement.

Instead, Alabama looked to the same place it found Paul W. "Bear" Bryant, Texas A&M, where one of the former Aggies coaches and Junction Boys members had also been a Bryant assistant with the Tide (1958–64) and was ready to follow in the Bear's footsteps after working in the National Football League.

"The expectation level is high at the University of Alabama and it should be," Gene Stallings said. "What's wrong with people expecting excellence?"

Many believed that Bryant wanted Stallings to replace him at Alabama in 1982, but it took another eight years for that to become reality. Although many fans were still vainly awaiting the second coming of Bryant, they were thrilled with the choice. He was one of them.

"I know that I picked up a great deal of things during my association with Coach Bryant," Stallings said. "I know he influenced me as a coach by teaching me to never give up on your talent. And he told me there was no substitution for work. He convinced his people. And when players and coaches are convinced they can win, they're going to win."

The 1990 season got off to a rocky start with losses to Southern Miss (led by quarterback Brett Favre), Florida, and Georgia, combined with season-ending injuries to running back Siran Stacy and wide receivers Craig Sanderson and Prince Wimbley. But the Crimson Tide turned things around to beat No. 3 Tennessee, 9–6.

"This has to rank right up there with the biggest wins I've ever had in my career," Stallings said.

Alabama finished the season 7–5 and roared back the following year with an 11–1 record and No. 5 final ranking after it beat defending national champion Colorado in the Blockbuster Bowl,

Gene Stallings (right) guided the 1992 Crimson Tide to the national championship, but Alabama fans were equally well acquainted with his son, Johnny (left), who was born with Down syndrome.

30–25. But it was only a stepping stone to the amazing 1992 season, when Alabama ran the table, won the SEC Championship Game in dramatic fashion, and crushed Miami in the Sugar Bowl, 34–13, to win the national title.

For the season, Alabama outscored its opponents 366–122, prompting defensive coordinator Bill Oliver to say, "I wish Coach Bryant were here to see this defense play."

Unfortunately, after a 9–3–1 season in 1993, including an appearance in the SEC Championship Game (a 28–13 loss to Florida), Alabama would later have to forfeit every win except one when the NCAA determined that Antonio Langham should have been ruled ineligible after signing with an agent in the early-morning hours following the national championship game. With NCAA sanctions looming in 1994, Alabama managed to return to the SEC Championship Game (another loss to the Gators, 24–23), and the senior class graduated with a 45–5–1 record (before the forfeited games became official).

When he was hired, Stallings mentioned winning 70 games as a goal, and players had a chance to deliver that goal to him during his final season in 1996. Although it didn't happen in the SEC Championship Game (Florida again, 45–30), they came through at the Outback Bowl against Michigan, 17–14.

John Copeland and Eric Curry

They were bookends on the defensive line and helped key Alabama's amazing 1992 national championship run. Curry, who placed 10th in voting for the Heisman Trophy, was a unanimous All-American, and Copeland was a consensus selection, which is nearly unheard of for linemates during the same year. In 1992 opponents averaged just 1.67 yards per carry, and the two combined for 21 sacks and 105 tackles. Fittingly, they were selected with successive picks in the 1993 NFL Draft, Copeland fifth by the Cincinnati Bengals, and Curry sixth to the Tampa Bay Buccaneers.

"It was real emotional," Stallings said after the coaching staff presented him with the game ball. "I can't think of a more fitting game."

23 See Alabama Win the SEC Championship

The answer that Alabama senior guard Mike Johnson was looking for was 1,628 miles.

"A long way," he said after being asked how far the Crimson Tide had come since Coach Nick Saban arrived in 2007. "I guess you could say it's the distance from Shreveport to Pasadena."

Actually, in many ways it's a lot longer than that.

On December 5, 2009, Alabama looked like it came into the Georgia Dome with a mile-wide chip on its shoulder and promptly smashed it down on the heads of the defending national champion Florida Gators. Not only did the Crimson Tide vanquish any lingering disappointment from the year before in the initial No. 1 vs. No. 2 meeting for the Southeastern Conference title, but also a decade of frustration, scandal, and sanctions.

Even when the Gators were clearly dead, the pounding continued until the fourth quarter, just to be certain. Unlike in 2008, when reigning Heisman Trophy winner Tim Tebow twice led his team into the end zone, this time the game was well in hand before Alabama finished off a 17-play touchdown drive that went 88 yards and ate up eight minutes and 47 seconds of the second half.

It wasn't as close as the 32–13 score indicated, and for every word to describe the complete victory, like dominating and crushing, there was an equally positive corresponding word, usually with a tip to the past.

"This means everything to me, all of our coaches, everybody," director of athletics Mal Moore said two years after the Crimson Tide played in back-to-back Independence Bowls. "I'm very proud."

Overall, Alabama pummeled Florida nearly across the board statistically, including first downs (26 to 13), rushing yards (251 to 88), time of possession (39:27 to 20:23), and third-down conversions (11 of 15 vs. 4 of 11). The Tide never trailed, scored on six of its first seven possessions (minus running out the clock before halftime), and pulled up in the fourth quarter before game MVP Greg McElroy took a knee at the Florida 16 after many of the other starters had been pulled.

"We came with the attitude that we weren't going to be denied," said running back Mark Ingram, who won his Heisman showdown with Tebow, gaining 113 rushing yards on 28 carries and three touchdowns against the nation's No. 1 defense, and also had a key 69-yard screen to finish with 76 receiving yards for a 189 total.

Tebow completed 20 of 35 passes for 247 yards, to go with 10 carries for 63 rushing yards, one touchdown, and a red-zone interception that killed any slim chance of a comeback.

"It was frustrating," said Tebow, who wasn't sacked but relentlessly pursued with Alabama credited with 14 hurries. "To say it wasn't, it would be a lie."

While the victory changed the landscape of the league, if not all of college football as the Crimson Tide went on to win its first national championship since 1992, it also gave Alabama its 22nd SEC title—a number that's so far in front of every other program that it's sometimes overlooked.

Before being one of the charter-founding schools in 1933, the Crimson Tide played in the huge Southern Conference, where it won four titles, the first of which was in 1924. Alabama was 8–1 overall with the lone loss to Centre College from Kentucky, but Georgia had been rated the top team in the region before the

Crimson Tide pounded it 33–0. That initial conference title served as a springboard for Alabama's first appearance in the Rose Bowl and national title one year later.

Alabama didn't win the Southern Conference championship in the final year before the split into the Southeastern Conference and what would essentially evolve into the Atlantic Coast Conference, but it did fittingly win the first SEC title—even after its first league game was a 0–0 tie with Ole Miss. The Tide came back to earn an 18–6 victory against Mississippi State and then avenged the previous year's loss to Tennessee, 12–6, in Knoxville.

The Crimson Tide went undefeated against conference opponents to finish 7–1–1, with the lone loss a 2–0 controversial decision against Fordham in front of 60,000 fans at the Polo Grounds in

SEC Conference Titles (through 2015)

School	SEC Titles	Most Recent	Divisional Titles
Alabama	25	2015	11
Tennessee	13	1998	6
Georgia	12	2005	7
LSU	11	2011	8
Florida	8*	2008	13
Auburn	8	2013	8
Ole Miss	6	1963	1
Georgia Tech	5	1952-x	--
Tulane	3	1949-x	--
Kentucky	2	1976	0
Mississippi State	1	1941	1
Arkansas	0	---	1
Missouri	0	---	2
South Carolina	0	---	1
Sewanee	0	----x	--
Texas A&M	0	---	0
Vanderbilt	0	---	0

*One vacated. x-no longer in conference

New York. But Alabama was 5–0–1 in SEC play, which edged LSU (3–0–2) for bragging rights, even though the league was years from having a balanced schedule or teams playing the same number of conference games.

Alabama had another notable first when it came to SEC titles, winning the first SEC Championship Game in 1992, just down the road from Tuscaloosa in Birmingham at its home away from home, Legion Field.

The game featured Florida, of course, and Steve Spurrier's high-flying offense against Alabama's top-ranked defense. Although the Gators struck first, with quarterback Shane Matthews opening the game by completing his first seven passes, including a 5-yard touchdown to running back Errict Rhett, the Tide's strong defensive play won out in the end.

With 3:16 remaining, Florida had first-and-10 at its own 21, when Alabama cornerback Antonio Langham jumped in front of a receiver and returned the interception 27 yards for the game-winning score. Just one week previous, it was Langham's interception returned 61 yards for a touchdown that broke open the Iron Bowl.

"When we hit [Matthews] and got pressure on him, he threw interceptions," defensive end Jeremy Nunley said. "Antonio Langham just made an awesome play. He's a great guy and I love him to death."

Alabama lost the rematch in the 1993 title game, and again to Florida in 1994. The two teams met again for the title in 1996 and 1999, with the Tide winning the latter, 34–7, and then 2008 and 2009—when it had yet to face a different opponent in the SEC Championship Game.

24 The Goal-Line Stand

In 1978 Alabama lost an early-season meeting with Southern California, 24–14, but clawed its way back into the national title picture despite playing a vicious schedule including Nebraska, Missouri, Washington, and Virginia Tech in addition to the already difficult Southeastern Conference lineup. Led by its defense, the Crimson Tide closed out the regular season with a 34–16 victory against Auburn, sending No. 2 Alabama back to the Sugar Bowl to face No. 1 Penn State.

A 30-yard pass from quarterback Jeff Rutledge to split end Bruce Bolton with eight seconds remaining in the first half gave Alabama a 7–0 lead, and the two teams traded touchdowns in the third quarter with running back Major Ogilvie following a block by tight end Rick Neal. But Alabama's defense was setting the tone for the game, as Penn State's longest gain in the first half was a 10-yard run by fullback Matt Suhey. A 32-yard reception by tailback Mike Guman was negated by an illegal-motion penalty.

However, in the final minutes Penn State recovered a misdirected pitch at the Alabama 19 and soon found itself with third down at the 1-yard line.

"It was gut-check time," linebacker Barry Krauss said. "We looked at each other. We knew this could be it. When they broke the huddle, everything got silent. Boy, talk about gut-checks."

Defensive back Don McNeal made the first stop roughly a foot away from the end zone. When Nittany Lions quarterback Chuck Fusina walked to the line of scrimmage to see how far the ball was from the goal line, defensive tackle Marty Lyons supposedly warned him, "You'd better pass."

Instead, Paterno called Guman's name for a run up the middle.

Immediately after the snap, the pile started to form. Lineman David Hannah had an injured knee drained by doctors the day of the game and wasn't supposed to play, but he went in for the stand. Byron Braggs and Lyons did their part, neutralizing the Penn State blockers. When Guman hit the hole, he and Krauss met in a bone-jarring head-on collision. With the fullback stood straight up short of the end zone, defensive back Murray Legg and linebacker Rich Wingo quickly closed to push Guman backward and finish him off.

The blow broke Krauss's helmet, and he fell to the ground. Due to a pinched nerve, he remained on the field unable to move his left side until Lyons reached down and grabbed him and the two made their way to the sideline.

Alabama held on for the 14–7 victory and topped the final Associated Press poll, but Southern California leapfrogged the Tide to No. 1 in United Press voting, resulting in a split national title. Krauss, an All-American and the Sugar Bowl MVP, was selected in the first round of the NFL Draft. He played 10 years for the Baltimore Colts before finishing his career with the Miami Dolphins.

1975

After a surprising 20–7 loss to Missouri in the season opener, Alabama came back with a vengeance. Despite playing a very difficult schedule, the team allowed only 52 points the rest of the season, with no regular-season opponent able to score more than 10. Along the way, Alabama beat Clemson 56–0, Washington 52–0, Tennessee 30–7, and Auburn 28–0. Against the Volunteers, the Tide defense, led by end Leroy Cook, linebacker Woodrow Lowe, and tackle Bob Baumhower, sacked quarterback Randy Wallace 13 times. With its 11–1 record, Alabama finished third in the final polls while Oklahoma defended its national title.

His No. 77 on the goal-line stand was the image of the 1978 season and graced the cover of numerous magazines, including *Sports Illustrated*.

"That goal-line stand was something I'll never forget," Bryant said.

25 Frank Thomas

When Wallace Wade turned in his resignation at the end of the 1929 season, there were two important developments after the fact. The first was that he promised to fulfill the last year of his contract to the best of his ability, and Alabama went on to win the national championship.

The other was suggesting that former Georgia assistant coach Frank Thomas replace him. As a college quarterback, "Shrewd Tommy" had been George Gipp's roommate at Notre Dame, and sportswriter Naylor Stone, in *Coach Tommy of the Crimson Tide*, credited Knute Rockne with telling his coaches, "It's amazing the amount of football sense that Thomas kid has. He can't miss becoming a great coach some day. I want him on our staff next fall."

Instead, Thomas chose to attend law school.

According to *The Atlanta Journal*, Dr. George Hutcheson Denny said when hiring him, "Now that you have accepted our position, I will give you the benefit of my views, based on many years of observation. It is my conviction that material is 90 percent, coaching 10 percent. I desire to further say that you will be provided with the 90 percent and that you will be held to strict accounting for delivering the remaining 10 percent."

After leaving the meeting in Birmingham, Thomas said to writer Ed Camp, "Those were the hardest and coldest words I ever heard."

But Thomas lived up to them and was in Tuscaloosa well before Wade departed to help ease the transition.

"Keep the players high, and make practice a pleasure but not a lark," he said. "Be a disciplinarian, but not a slave-driver."

Even though 10 of the 11 starters from Wade's final title team were gone and Rockne's non-traditional box-formation offense was installed, the Crimson Tide went on to average 36 points a game and post a 9–1 record that first season. It remains the best coaching debut in Alabama history.

Under the direction of Frank Thomas, who was frequently seen in a letterman's jacket, the Crimson Tide won the first Southeastern Conference championship in 1933 and national titles in 1934 and 1941.

Under Thomas's direction, the Tide won the first Southeastern Conference championship in 1933 and national titles in 1934 and 1941. It was during the undefeated 1934 season, when Alabama outscored the opposition 316–45, that Tennessee coach General Robert Neyland made this famous comment: "You never know what a football player is made of until he plays against Alabama."

With standouts like Millard Fillmore "Dixie" Howell, Don Hutson, Bill Lee, and a young end named Paul W. "Bear" Bryant, the Tide returned to the Rose Bowl, where it dominated Stanford, 29–13.

Alabama went back at the end of the 1937 season to suffer its only loss in the Rose Bowl, 13–0 to California.

Despite having two losses in 1941, the Tide made its first postseason appearance other than at the Rose Bowl, and tallied 12 turnovers to defeat Texas A&M in the Cotton Bowl, 29–21. Although Minnesota was the consensus No. 1, Alabama was able to claim a share of the title thanks to the Houlgate System (a mathematical rating syndicated in newspapers).

After World War II forced him to scrap the 1943 season, Thomas pieced together the famous War Baby Tiders. Alabama went undefeated in 1945, including a dominating 34–14 victory over Southern California in the Rose Bowl, which prompted Trojans coach Jeff Cravath to say, "There goes a great man. I'll never forget what he did today. If he wanted, he could have named the score."

The Tide outscored opponents 430–80. However, this resulted only in a No. 2 ranking behind Army.

Failing health forced Thomas to step aside after the 1946 season with a record of 115–24–7. He resigned as athletic director in 1952 and died two years later, on May 10, 1954.

26 The Perfect Onside Kick

There were a little less than 11 minutes remaining on the clock of the National Championship Game and the University of Alabama had just tied the score when Nick Saban made the call of a lifetime.

With Alabama struggling to stop Clemson quarterback Deshaun Watson and the momentum up for grabs he decided to go for an onside kick in hopes of catching the Tigers by surprise.

It did more than that.

With kicker Adam Griffith striking the ball perfectly and redshirt freshman Marlon Humphrey racing to jump up and catch it before anyone from the other side could sufficiently react, Alabama went on to survive a wild 45–40 victory at University of Phoenix Stadium and claim the national championship trophy for the 2015 season.

"The way we line up on kickoffs with squeeze formation and try to corner kick the ball, when a team squeezes the formation like that, we call it pop kick," Saban described. "I thought we had it in the game any time we wanted to do it. I made the decision to do it because the score was [24–24] and we were tired on defense and weren't doing a great job of getting them stopped, and I felt like if we didn't do something or take a chance to change the momentum of the game that we wouldn't have a chance to win.

"Getting that onside kick, I think, did change the momentum of the game. We scored on a big play two plays later, and then we had a kickoff return for a touchdown, too, which was huge. So special teams was really big for us in this game."

Even with Kenyan Drake's 95-yard kick return for a touchdown and three scoring plays from the 50-yard line and beyond the onside kick was the one most people were talking about afterward.

Many of the Crimson Tide players called it the gutsiest call they'd ever seen.

"That was amazing," senior wide receiver Richard Mullaney said.

Although the play looked completely spontaneous, Alabama had actually been practicing it since Week 3 of the season and was just waiting for the right opportunity. When Saban saw how Clemson lined up after running back Derrick Henry opened the scoring with a 50-yard touchdown run he knew he had that potential ace in the hole to play.

"We have a fake field goal, we have a fake when we punt, we have an onside kick, a surprise onside kick," Saban said during his postgame press conference. "So basically we have someone assigned in the press box who's saying, 'Did they line up like we thought they would? Did they have the play that we want in any of these circumstances?'

"The first time that we kicked off, after Derrick's touchdown, we said okay, we've got that. If we want to try that, we think we have a good chance because of the spacing on the field that's available to us. So it worked."

Jerry Duncan

Jerry Duncan was never an All-American, but he more than made his mark on the Capstone as a player and beyond.

In 1965, when Duncan was a junior, he caught four passes on Coach Paul W. "Bear" Bryant's famous tackle-eligible play to help lead the Crimson Tide to the national championship. He grabbed five more as a senior before the formation was banned.

For 24 years, Duncan was the sideline reporter for the Alabama Radio Network, while also working with the Birmingham Monday Morning Quarterback Club and the Crippled Children Foundation. In 1997 Duncan was awarded the prestigious Paul W. Bryant Alumni-Athlete Award.

But how many coaches would call it in the fourth quarter with everything on the line, including Saban's place in history after winning all four of his previous shots at a national title?

"It was just a matter of Adam Griffth kicking the ball to the right spot, and us not being offside," said special-teams coach Bobby Williams, who estimated that the play's success rate during practices was about "50/50."

"I almost dropped the ball almost every time," Humphrey said about the misses, as catching a bouncing ball like that is tougher than it looks.

What further prompted the decision was Clemson having controlled the clock for 9:45 of the third quarter, resulting in 10 unanswered points. After Watson had accounted for 207 total yards in the first half, he tallied another 101 in the third quarter and was having more success running as the game progressed.

So when Griffith made a 33-yard field goal with 10:34 to go, Saban decided that the upside of giving Watson one fewer opportunity was worth the risk.

Probably the toughest part of the play was not doing anything that might tip Clemson off, and Alabama lined up just like it had every other time in the game, with, to the kicker's right, Michael Nyswander, Dillon Lee, Keith Holcombe, Drake, and Humphrey on the end.

Someone who hadn't done his homework may have simply thought "freshman," and nothing more. But in addition to being the son of Alabama legend Bobby Humphrey, he was a sprinter for the Alabama track team during the football offseason.

Humphrey got off to such a good jump with the kick into open space that combined with the nearest Clemson players caught flat-footed, Swinney could only scream and hope for an offsides penalty that didn't exist and was never called. While everyone else's reaction seemed to be "wow," cameras caught Saban's beaming smile on the sideline while the broadcast crew prepared to show the first of numerous replays that confirmed the Crimson Tide had just pulled off highway robbery.

"I felt pretty good about our chances of getting the onside kick because Griff kicks it well," Saban said. "We did it in practice most of the time. And I didn't think it was—I had confidence in the players. I trusted them, that they would go out and execute it and do it.

"I mean, if we didn't get it, they'd have got the ball on the 45- or 50-yard line, so it's not really like it would have been the end of the world, but it was worth the risk I felt. But it was calculated on the fact that I thought we could execute it and the way they lined up, it was available to us. And it was something that I knew that we would use in this game if we needed to."

Nevertheless, Alabama subsequently never looked back, especially after two plays later when tight end O.J. Howard ran uncovered through the Clemson secondary and caught a 51-yard touchdown pass for a lead the Crimson Tide would never relinquish.

"It got the sideline energized," Howard said. "Everybody was pumped up."

Down 31–24, stunned Clemson finally shook it off and countered with a quick field goal, but Drake's answering touchdown made it a two-score game with 7:31 remaining. The Tigers still didn't give up, yet the outcome was no longer in doubt.

"But let me say this," said Saban to a room full of reporters after getting a Gatorade bath. "You don't look like the type that would do it to me, but if we wouldn't have got that, y'all would be killing me now."

27 Smoke a Cigar on the "Third Saturday of October"

Even though the Tennessee game is known as the "Third Saturday in October," it has often been played on a different weekend due to scheduling fluctuations. Nonetheless, the rivalry continues despite the teams playing in different Southeastern Conference divisions.

The first meeting dates all the way back to 1901. When that game was called due to darkness with the score tied 6–6, spectators rushed the Birmingham field in protest. If anything, it certainly set the tone.

Another notable early game occurred in 1913, which again ran into the problem of darkness, but instead resulted in Alabama's first night game—sort of. Due to a number of injuries, play lasted past sunset and spectators with automobiles were asked to encircle the Tuscaloosa field and turn on their headlights so it could continue. Alabama held on for a 6–0 victory, marking the seventh straight shutout against the Volunteers.

The rivalry really began to take off in 1928, when Alabama and Coach Wallace Wade hosted Tennessee in Tuscaloosa. Alabama was considered a sizable favorite. However, before kickoff, Volunteers coach Robert Neyland introduced himself to Wade, whom he had never met, and supposedly asked that the game be shortened if it got out of hand. Wade was taken aback but agreed. To give you an idea of what these men were like, Wade had been a cavalry captain in World War I, and Neyland left Tennessee twice to serve in the military and eventually retired at the rank of brigadier general.

Tennessee's Gene McEver returned the opening kickoff 98 yards for a touchdown, and the Volunteers managed to pull off the 15–13 upset.

Neyland also may have paid the Crimson Tide its greatest compliment after the 1934 game, which was the only close contest (13–6) Alabama had en route to a 10–0 record and the national championship: "You never know what a football player is made of until he plays against Alabama."

Paul W. "Bear" Bryant had a knack for winning big games as a player and a coach, except when he was an assistant coach for Frank Thomas in 1936, when Alabama had first down at the Tennessee 1 as time ran out in the first half. The scoreless tie cost the Crimson Tide both the SEC championship and a bowl appearance.

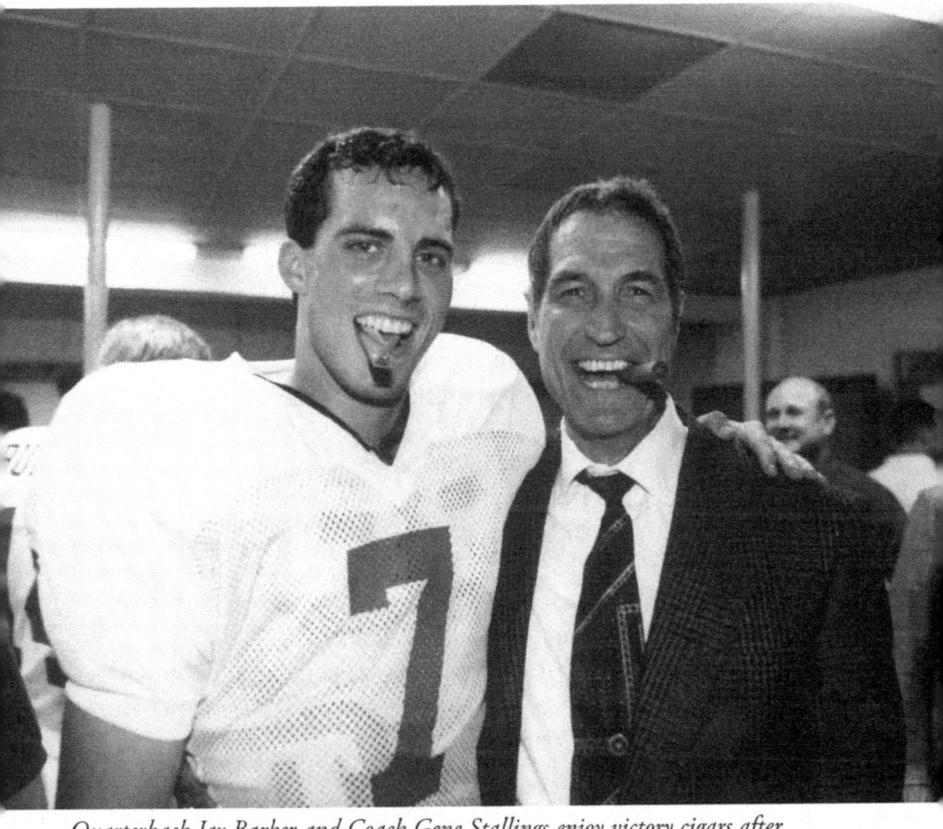

Quarterback Jay Barker and Coach Gene Stallings enjoy victory cigars after a win against Tennessee. Paul W. "Bear" Bryant began the tradition in this famous rivalry, and it continues to this day (although unofficially).

One of the more memorable games for Bryant as a head coach against Tennessee was in 1966, when the Crimson Tide hoped to win its third straight national championship but found itself down 10–0 at halftime in Knoxville. Instead of lashing out at his players, Bryant calmly walked around the locker room and patted them

Visit every SEC stadium

In 2011, the Southeastern Conference's presidents and chancellors unanimously welcomed two new members into the fold, bumping the league up to 14 schools effective the 2012–2013 academic year.

Texas A&M and Missouri were the first additions for the league since September 1991 when South Carolina and Arkansas joined, allowing it to split into divisions and add a conference championship game in 1992.

Although both new members were previously in the Big 12, the football programs were initially separated with Missouri placed in the East Division and Texas A&M in the West. While fans would travel farther, they had two more venues to visit that ranked in the top 25 nationally in attendance.

Here are the schools, stadiums and 2015 capacity:

- Alabama: Bryant-Denny Stadium (101,821)
- Arkansas: Donald W. Reynolds Razorback Stadium (72,000)*
- Auburn: Jordan-Hare Stadium (87,451)
- Florida: Ben Hill Griffin Stadium at Florida Field (89,548)
- Georgia: Sanford Stadium (92,746)
- Kentucky: Commonwealth Stadium (61,000)
- LSU: Tiger Stadium (102,321)
- Ole Miss: Vaught-Hemingway Stadium/Hollingsworth Field (60,580)
- Mississippi State: Davis Wade Stadium at Scott Field (61,337)
- Missouri: Memorial Stadium/Faurot Field (71,168)
- South Carolina: Williams-Brice Stadium (80,250)
- Tennessee: Neyland Stadium/Shields-Watkins Field (102,455)
- Texas A&M: Kyle Field (102,512)
- Vanderbilt: Dudley Field/Vanderbilt Stadium (40,350)

* The Razorbacks also play some games at War Memorial Stadium in Little Rock (53,955).

on their backs. Although initially confusing, it was just what they needed, and Alabama responded by scoring 11 points in the second half to take the lead. Tennessee, in turn, missed a game-winning field goal.

"If he'd kicked it straight, we would have blocked it," Bryant said.

The 1972 meeting saw one of the greatest comebacks in team history. Down 10–3 with a little more than two minutes remaining, quarterback Terry Davis led a rally with Wilbur Jackson punching in a two-yard touchdown. On the subsequent possession, defensive end Mike DuBose swatted the ball away from quarterback Condredge Holloway, with defensive end John Mitchell recovering.

A 22-yard run by Davis secured Alabama's 17–10 victory, and while UT fans left Neyland Stadium in disbelief, the Crimson Tide locker room was full of cigar smoke—a tradition started by Bryant against Tennessee.

Nowadays both teams celebrate wins against the other by enjoying stogies (even though it's technically a National Collegiate Athletic Association violation), as the game remains an important benchmark for each and every season.

28 1930: Wade's Send-Off

Alabama's breakthrough years of 1925 and 1926, which resulted in Rose Bowl appearances and celebrated national championships, were difficult to reproduce over the next three seasons, much to the chagrin of fans who had become accustomed to the program's winning ways.

The 1927 season ended with losses to Florida, Georgia, and Vanderbilt for a disappointing 5–4–1 record. That was followed by 6–3 years in 1928 and 1929, which became best known for the first game played at Legion Field in Birmingham, while Denny Stadium in Tuscaloosa was dedicated on September 28, 1929. Its initial seating capacity was 12,000.

Growing increasingly discontent while simultaneously being targeted by other schools offering a significant raise in salary, Coach Wallace Wade turned in his resignation near the end of the 1929 season, but he agreed to stay on for the final year of his contract before heading to Duke. Clyde Bolton of *The Birmingham News* called the period before Wade's departure the "greatest swan song in the history of football."

Alabama opened the season with a 43–0 victory against Howard and backed it up with two more shutouts, 64–0 against Ole Miss and 25–0 vs. Sewanee. An 18–6 win against Tennessee and a 12–7 victory over Vanderbilt had the Crimson Tide 5–0, and it had already yielded the only points Alabama would give up all season.

A 13–0 victory against Georgia meant both a perfect regular season and another Southern Conference championship, resulting in the third Rose Bowl invitation, this time to play Washington State. Even though the national championship was at stake, Wade started his second stringers, just as he had done previously that season, leaving his best players on the bench until the second quarter when the opposing players began to wear down (it was as much a psychological ploy as physical).

Washington State held its own against the backups, but not against the Tide starters, and Alabama easily won 24–0. Everyone got into the game, and Wade, who was carried off the field by his players, concluded his Alabama career with a 61–13–3 record and third national title.

John "Monk" Campbell was named the most valuable player of the Rose Bowl. Halfback John Henry Suther was named

All-American, while guard John Miller and sophomore fullback Johnny Cain were All–Southern Conference picks.

Wrote Royal Brougham of the *Seattle Post-Intelligencer*:

> Out of the sunny southland came another great Alabama football team and it hit a bewildered Cougar from Washington State like a jug of Dixie gin. By a 24–to-0 score the banjo-plucking, mammy singing troubadours from the land of cotton won the annual Rose Bowl classic, and they were that much the better team. The vaunted defense of the western champions crumpled like the walls of Jericho before an amazing pass attack which caught the northmen flat on their heels.
>
> The Bammers unleashed a passing and cleverly masked running offense which the canny Coach Wade kept stored in the cooler all season long. And before it the touted Cougars were just corn pone and possum pie. That freckled-necked southern gentleman who coaches the Tide won today's game with his noodle, and don't let anybody tell you different. Wade sat out there on the bench and outfigured the lads from the northwest all afternoon long.

29 Harry Gilmer

"He must be too small to play football."

That's what most people said when they first saw Harry Gilmer's trademark leaping passes, which gave the appearance that he couldn't see over his linemen. But he was six feet tall and at times played like a giant.

After not having a team in 1943 due to World War II, Frank Thomas pieced together 20 ragtag players to form a roster that would constitute the Crimson Tide in 1944, with the team centered around a local player from Woodlawn High School in Birmingham who might not have gone to college if not for his high school coach Malcolm Laney being hired as an Alabama assistant coach. Well, that and the Southeastern Conference waiving its rule against freshmen playing with the varsity.

Quarterback Harry Gilmer led the Alabama team appropriately nicknamed the "War Babies" in 1944. Just as unique as the team was Gilmer's leaping throwing style.

Visit the Pro Football, College Football, and Alabama Sports Halls of Fame

Many, if not most, of the players in this book have been enshrined into a football Hall of Fame of some sort, including the Alabama Sports Hall of Fame, the College Football Hall of Fame, or the Pro Football Hall of Fame.

All three halls are open to the public and have regular visiting hours.

Pro Football Hall of Fame: 2121 George Halas Drive NW, Canton, Ohio; (330) 456-8207.
College Football Hall of Fame: 250 Marietta St, Atlanta, GA 30313; (404) 880-4800.
Alabama Sports Hall of Fame: 2150 Richard Arrington Jr. Boulevard N., Birmingham, AL; (205) 323-6665.

Led by Gilmer, the "War Baby Tiders" opened the season against LSU. Gilmer returned a kickoff 95 yards for a touchdown as the teams tied, 27–27. Alabama followed that up with a 63–0 victory against Howard and a 55–0 win over Millsaps. At 5–1–2, the War Baby Tiders secured the school's first invitation to the Sugar Bowl in New Orleans, where Gilmer put on a dazzling performance in front of 72,000 fans. Although a much older Duke team pulled out a 29–26 victory in the final moments, Gilmer completed all eight of his pass attempts and was named the game's most valuable player.

Legendary sportswriter Grantland Rice wrote that Gilmer was "the greatest college passer I've ever seen."

Arguably his best year was his sophomore season, when Alabama (boasting a full roster) finished a perfect 10–0, outscored opponents 430–80, and won the SEC championship. Gilmer, who was named an All-American, led the nation in touchdown passes with 13, ran for nine more, averaged 7.0 yards per carry on 79 attempts, completed roughly 65 percent of his passes on

88 attempts, was second in the nation with 1,457 yards, and also returned punts and kicks.

Against Kentucky, Gilmer became the first player in Alabama history to accumulate 200 rushing yards in a game, on just six carries, and had more than 100 passing yards as well. Alabama won 60–19, and also defeated LSU 26–7, Tennessee 25–7, and Vanderbilt 71–0.

This resulted in Alabama's sixth and final invitation to the Rose Bowl, where the Crimson Tide was considered the underdog but crushed Southern California, 34–14. Gilmer ran for 116 yards and passed for 59, as Thomas made sure every Alabama player got into the game.

Alabama finished 7–4 and 8–3 Gilmer's last two years, with the senior campaign closing with a 27–7 loss to Texas in the Sugar Bowl. His collective record over the four years was 30–9–2.

Gilmer ended his career as Alabama's all-time leader in rushing (1,673), passing (2,894), punt returns (13.5 average), kickoff returns (28.7), and interceptions. He also passed for 26 touchdowns and ran for 24 more. His junior year, Gilmer led the nation in punt returns with a 14.5 average on 37 returns.

After leaving the Capstone, Gilmer was a quarterback in the National Football League with Washington and Detroit from 1948 to 1956. He was also the Lions' head coach from 1965 to 1966.

30 1979: The Bear's Last

Alabama felt it had been robbed by voters in the final polls of the 1977 (when Notre Dame leapfrogged past the Crimson Tide from fifth) and 1978 (when Alabama won a No. 1 versus No. 2 matchup against Penn State in the Sugar Bowl, only to split the national title with Southern California) seasons, but in both cases a loss left the door open for another team to sneak into the top spot.

So there was only one thing to do—remove any doubt by going undefeated in 1979 and cap the most dominating decade in college football.

Led by three first-team All-Americans, guard Jim Bunch, center Dwight Stephenson, and tackle Don McNeal, second-teamers E.J. Junior and Byron Braggs on the defensive line, and five other All-SEC selections, that's exactly what the Crimson Tide did, with Coach Paul W. "Bear" Bryant winning his sixth and final national title.

Thanks to numerous starters returning, the Crimson Tide was the preseason No. 2 team in the national polls and lived up to the high expectations by outscoring its first five opponents 219–9. But like most championship seasons, Alabama did have its share of close calls and scares, including a 3–0 victory at LSU, and, led by backup quarterback Don Jacobs, the team stormed back from a 17–7 halftime deficit to beat Tennessee 27–17.

Against Auburn, turnovers nearly did in the Tide, but quarterback Steadman Shealy led an 82-yard drive on 13 plays for a 25–18 victory. Prior to the game, Bryant made comments that he would have to go back to Arkansas and plow if the Tide lost to its biggest rival, prompting Auburn fans to yell "Plow, Bear, Plow!"

"Our winning drive was one of the finest I've ever seen," Bryant said after the game. "We had to have it. I'm just thrilled to death with the win. We've got some mighty fine plow hands on this team."

Once again, the national championship would be settled at the Sugar Bowl, with Alabama paired against future Southeastern Conference addition Arkansas. After turning an early fumble into a field goal, the Razorbacks didn't know what hit them until it was 17–3 in the third quarter. The game's most valuable player, Major Ogilvie, scored two touchdowns and had a 50-yard punt return, and Shealy led a 98-yard touchdown drive for a dominating 24–9 victory.

At 12–0, there would be no debate over which team should be No. 1, and no split national championship. Alabama was the lone contender with a perfect record (Southern California narrowly missed it with 11–0–1).

The Tide defense yielded only 67 points, compared to 383 scored, with five shutouts, against Baylor, Wichita State, Florida, LSU, and Miami. Except for LSU, the fewest points Alabama scored against an opponent was 24.

For the 1970s, Alabama compiled an incredible 103–16–1 record with eight Southeastern Conference titles and three national championships. It was considered the team of the decade, and when LSU fired Charles McClendon in 1979 for not being able to beat Alabama, Auburn's all-time winningest coach (176–83–6 from 1951 to 1975) Shug Jordan said, "You go by that, and they'll have to fire us all."

31 John Hannah

On July 27, 1991, Herb Hannah had the unique experience of standing at the podium at the Pro Football Hall of Fame to present one of its newest inductions, in a class that included Earl Campbell, Stan Jones, Tex Schramm, and Jan Stenerud.

Herb had played in the National Football League himself. He was an offensive lineman for the New York Giants in 1951, after playing for the University of Alabama. Sons Charles and David followed in his footsteps and had been all-conference linemen for the Crimson Tide. Charles played from 1977 to 1988 in the NFL for

Leroy G. Monsky Sr.

In 1937 this guard was honored with the Jacobs Trophy as the Southeastern Conference's best blocker and named an All-American while helping lead Alabama to the Rose Bowl. The Crimson Tide was 9–0 and outscored opponents 225–33, but during a practice on the way to California, a lineman pulled the wrong way and collided with Monsky, who required 25 stitches above his left eye. He played, but the incident foreshadowed the game, won by California, 13–0. It was the only loss Monsky experienced at Alabama.

"It was a heartbreaker," Monsky said. "I still try and blank it from my mind."

However, Frank Thomas and assistant Hank Crisp called Monsky "the smartest and best guard" they ever coached, and sportswriter Grantland Rice dubbed him the best guard in the country: "Leroy Monsky, amazingly fast for his size and power, was outstanding on both offense and defense and was a key man in the Alabama attack which specializes in the use of the guards.

"His fighting courage was the deciding factor in most of these games."

the Tampa Bay Buccaneers and the Los Angeles Raiders, including the 1983 Super Bowl team.

But on that day, Hannah was there to introduce his other son, the one some believe was the greatest offensive lineman to ever play the game.

"When John was born, God gave him all the attributes of a great offensive guard," he said. "He had the intelligence, physical talents, a winning attitude, a friendly desire for excellence, a competitive nature, and an unusual tolerance for pain. I, like the many fans who enjoyed watching John play, will always remember his exploding into a linebacker or a defensive lineman, leading the back-off tackle around end or dropping back on pass protection. Always giving it 100 percent on each and every play. The intensity of his play was always by the rules of the game and without any fanfare. He just went about doing his job Sunday after Sunday as good as or better than any offensive lineman that I ever saw play the game."

"He didn't tell you about the times he ran me around the house with a switch to improve my sweep," John Hannah replied in his speech. "God, I love football. And to be inducted into the Hall of Fame is probably the one fulfillment of a lifelong dream. You just don't know what it means to me.

"I remember when I was growing up in Albertville, Alabama, and mom and dad would take us to church and as soon as church was over we would fly home to try to see guys like Ray Nitschke, Gale Sayers, Dick Butkus, and all those guys play and, man, I would sit there and froth at the mouth and say, 'Wonder if I would ever be good enough to play with those guys and wonder if I will ever be able to play with them.' And I remember even playing in the NFL and I had a coach, Jim Ringo, that had played the game and I went to him one time and said 'Coach, do you think I could have played with those teams in the '60s, do you think I was good enough?' Well, what today means to me is I made the cut, I'm on the team and right now I have the honor of playing alongside the greatest heroes that ever played football."

Fittingly, Hannah was born in Canton (even if it was Georgia), and in addition to football was an individual national champion in wrestling. He was a football All-American in 1971 and a unanimous selection the following year when he also won the Southeastern Conference's Jacobs Trophy as its best blocker along with Lineman of the Year by the Birmingham Monday Morning Quarterback Club, Touchdown Club of Atlanta, and Miami Touchdown Club.

After being the fourth overall pick in the 1973 draft, Hannah played his entire professional career with the New England Patriots. He was named All-Pro 10 times (1976–85) and selected for nine Pro Bowls. Other honors included being one of the few players named to an NFL All-Decade Team twice, for the 1970s and 1980s. He was also the top guard listed on the NFL 75th Anniversary All-Time Team in 1994.

Bryant once said of Hannah, "In over 30 years with the game, he's the finest offensive lineman I've ever been around."

"Coach Bryant left for me a lesson of setting lofty goals," Hannah said. "And not only that but to run life's race to reach those goals. The greatest lesson that he left with me was that you have to beat your body, you got to make it your slave if you ever want to get where you want to go."

32 Kenny Stabler

Even though it's not one of the University of Alabama's primary colors, they wore black in Tuscaloosa during the 2015 season.

Some did so in remembrance, others in support of the efforts to finally get Kenny Stabler into the Pro Football of Fame, which happened a year later.

Regardless, Bryant-Denny Stadium wasn't the same without Kenny Stabler's gentlemanly disposition and silver hair that had been noticeably absent from the place was that was essentially his second home for 50-plus years. Granted, the trips had become few and far between, but his presence and influence could always be felt. That part, at least, would never change.

With a pregame ceremony before Alabama dismantled LSU, fans finally said goodbye to one of its fallen sons, heroes, and icons, who died on July 9, 2015, at the age of 69.

"He loved the University of Alabama, he truly did," Stabler's oldest daughter, Kendra Stabler Moyes, said. "He was proud to be from Alabama and of the University, and he always said so."

Under the direction of Kenny "Snake" Stabler, Alabama went 28–3–2, including the perfect 11–0 1966 season. Stabler was an early-round baseball selection by the Houston Astros, but he opted instead to play pro football for the Oakland Raiders.

One would be hard-pressed to find a Crimson Tide fan anywhere who doesn't have some sort of Stabler story, but the best seem to be told by his former teammates. They can still hear his voice in their heads, like when he would enter a huddle and say something like: "Alright guys let's take this thing down here, knock it in and get us a touchdown, and go out tonight and have a good time.

"He loved life and he loved to have a good time and he was a tremendous football player," Jerry Duncan said.

Nick Saban called him a "legend," and one retrospective comment that got his attention in particular was from Stabler's former coach with the Oakland Raiders, John Madden. In addition to saying "the hotter the game, the cooler he got," he still maintained that if he had one drive to win a game and could pick any quarterback, past or present, he'd go with Stabler.

Saban called it the ultimate compliment for a quarterback.

After taking over the starting job in 1973 he led the Raiders to a 50–11–1 regular-season record over an amazing five years, including the 32–14 victory over the Minnesota Vikings in Super Bowl XI.

Overall he played 10 seasons in Oakland (1970–79), and also briefly with the Houston Oilers and New Orleans Saints, totaling 194 touchdown passes (222 interceptions) and 27,398 passing yards. Stabler's record as an NFL starter was 94–49–1, and he ended up playing in more "name" games than anyone, including "The Ghost to the Post," "The Holy Roller," and "The Sea of Hands." Named All-Pro three times, he was the league's offensive player of the year in 1974, and both the player of the year and passing champion in 1976.

"Kenny is one of those guys that whatever you throw in front of him it's not going to get him down. Then, when you hear Kenny Stabler died, it's like a kick in the gut," Madden told Raiders reporters. "You think of the good times and the memories, all of the games and all of the practices and all of the meetings. No matter what you throw in front of him, he enjoyed it. He always had a twinkle in his eye and a smile. He was one of the greatest competitors ever."

But Stabler's legacy was arguably even greater at Alabama, where he compiled a starting record of 28–3–2 and helped lead the 11–0 season of 1966 that didn't result in a national championship.

"That '66 team he rarely got his uniform dirty at all because no one ever touched him," Duncan joked about the player known for the "Run in the Mud," a 47-yard touchdown that was the difference in a 7–3 victory against Auburn in the 1967 Iron Bowl.

After his playing career concluded he again became a fixture on campus as a color analyst on the Crimson Tide Sports Network (1998–2007). By then he was more than viewed as being a state treasure.

Stabler was born Christmas Day in 1945 in Foley, Alabama, where he was a highly regarded high school player, and it was after a long, winding touchdown run that Coach Denzel Hollis first

Dennis Homan

Split end Dennis Homan was Kenny Stabler's favorite target in 1967, when he caught 54 passes for 820 yards and nine touchdowns to be a consensus All-American. Also an Academic All-American, Homan caught 87 passes during his three-year career, for 1,495 yards and 18 touchdowns.

Homan went on to be a first-round draft choice of the Dallas Cowboys, and after three years he briefly played with the Kansas City Chiefs. His career NFL numbers were 37 catches for 619 yards and two touchdowns. Homan also played two seasons with Birmingham in the World Football League and was the team's leading receiver both years. In 1974, he had 930 yards and eight touchdowns, and in 1975 he accumulated 18 catches for 277 yards after the offense became more run-oriented.

called him "Snake." Over the years he raised a lot of money for local charities, and spent most of his final years in the Gulf Shores area.

"There is no way to describe the pride an Alabama player feels in himself and the tradition of the school," Stabler once said about the love affair he had with the university and its fans.

As a result, when the man who seemed to collect friends and memories like they were the most valuable commodities died, people reached out in droves any way they could, with the family receiving thousands of cards, emails and messages. They were simply overwhelmed.

"We knew that he was loved, but we had no idea the magnitude," Moyes said. "They were from all over the world, from places like Japan and Germany, and the really cool thing was that 95 percent of the messages had the same theme, about how he made them feel. 'He made me feel so special.'"

Above all else that may have been Stabler's greatest gift. He played the rebel while leading the Raiders, often with a mischievous grin, and maybe made as many headlines off the field as on. But when a game started he was all business, and when it was over he was all charm.

"Traveling the country with him was truly like traveling with a rock star," Stabler's radio broadcast partner Eli Gold said. "He'd walk through the airport and it would take forever because folks would want his autograph, take pictures, and he'd never turn down a request for any of that. He was just one of those people that everybody knew.

"Kenny loved people and people loved Kenny. If you didn't like Kenny Stabler you've got a problem. He was just a great, great guy....The fact that he's gone now is very, very sad."

33 Dixie Howell

Although he's considered one of the greatest players to ever wear crimson for the University of Alabama, Millard Fillmore Howell, who was named for the 13th president of the United States but was known as Dixie, became a national legend when he had one of the greatest final games in college football history.

In addition to being on the throwing end of the famous "Howell-to-Hutson" passing combination that was instrumental in Alabama winning the first Southeastern Conference title in 1933, he also had an 80-yard run the previous year against Vanderbilt and recorded epic punts of 89, 83, and 80 yards.

Led by Howell, the 1934 Crimson Tide had no peers nationally. As part of its 9–0 regular season, Alabama closed the campaign with wins of 40–0 against both Clemson and Georgia Tech, and 34–0 to Vanderbilt, to secure an invitation to play Stanford (9–0–1) in the Rose Bowl.

In scoring the Tide's first touchdown, Howell bolted into the end zone from the 5-yard line, doing a complete somersault and landing on his feet. But he was just getting started that day. He later added a 67-yard touchdown run and threw a touchdown pass to Hutson.

"Open that page once more in the *Book of Football Revelations* and under these names—Dorais to Rockne, Wyman to Baston, Friedman to Oosterbaan—add to those 'HOWELL TO HUTSON,'" Los Angeles sportswriter Mark Kelly wrote. "And let the last stay in capital letters because they should top the list."

Howell completed 9 of 12 passes for 160 yards to go with 111 rushing yards, and he handled kick returns and punts.

Needless to say, Howell left Pasadena with the game's most valuable player honor.

"Dixie Howell, the human howitzer from Hartford, Alabama, blasted the Rose Bowl dreams of Stanford today with one of the greatest all-around exhibitions football has ever known," sportswriter Grantland Rice wrote about the performance.

"No team in the history of football, anywhere, anytime, has passed the ball as Alabama passed it today," said Ralph McGill in *The Atlanta Constitution*. "And no man ever passed as did Dixie Howell, the swift sword of the Crimson attack."

Alabama won its fourth national championship, averaging 31.6 points per game while yielding just 4.5. Howell was named Southeastern Conference Player of the Year in addition to All-American with tackle Bill Lee and Don Hutson.

For an encore, Howell helped the baseball team post a 14–2 Southeastern Conference record to win the conference title. He went on to play one year with the Washington Redskins, 1937, before

James W. "Jim" Whatley

This Tuscaloosa native was a tackle on the 1934 Rose Bowl team and voted All-SEC in 1935, but his career extended well beyond the football field.

Whatley lettered in four different sports at the Capstone and was an All-SEC center in basketball. He played three years of professional football for the Brooklyn Dodgers, from 1936 to 1938, before coaching football, basketball, and baseball at the collegiate level.

From 1939 to 1941 Whatley was the head coach in football, basketball, and baseball at Western Carolina. From there he bounced around, from the U.S. Naval Station to San Diego, California, and Ole Miss before landing at Georgia in 1950. Whatley was an assistant football coach for 11 years, head basketball coach for two years, and the head baseball coach for 25 years. In baseball, he recorded 336 wins, second most in Bulldog history, and was twice named the Southeastern Conference's baseball coach of the year (1953–54).

becoming a coach. From 1938 to 1941, he guided Arizona State to a 23–15–4 record, and at Idaho he went 13–20–1 (1947–50).

34 Amari Cooper

Throughout the 2014 season, Nick Saban was regularly asked about junior wide receiver Amari Cooper and what he brought to the University of Alabama football team.

Actually, the coach got so many questions about him that he ran out of descriptive words to use with reporters. "Outstanding" was the staple for much of the fall and then by November he started using "phenomenal."

But following the 55–44 victory over Auburn, during which Cooper established numerous program records while helping lead the Crimson Tide's dramatic comeback, not even that seemed sufficient.

"Cooper, what do you say about him?" Missouri coach Gary Pinkel said the week of the SEC Championship Game in Atlanta.

Regardless, it was pretty obvious that the wide receiver was without peer, which might be the greatest compliment of all.

"Amari is not worthy of anyone comparing him to anybody else," Saban said. "He is Amari Cooper. He has his own style. He's a very competitive guy who works really, really hard. Has really good speed getting in and out of breaks. Works hard in the game to get open. Does a good job of executing, has made a lot of really big plays for us this year.

"He's certainly been a dynamic player for our team and has made a great contribution to our season."

His final Iron Bowl may have been the perfect example because as he heated up so did the Crimson Tide.

With his first reception, a 5-yard gain to help set up Alabama's initial touchdown, Cooper established a new program record for career catches.

With three touchdown receptions, which tied the Crimson Tide single-game record, he broke his own single-season record of 11 set two years previous as a freshman. Cooper had previously tied his mark and had notched 14.

With 224 receiving yards he tied his own single-game record, set against Tennessee earlier in the season. His 14th career 100-yard game was another career record after being tied with DJ Hall (13, 2004–07).

Cooper also set numerous Iron Bowl records including for receiving yards in a game, and was the only player to have three 100-yard performances in the rivalry. He had 109 yards in 2012 and 178 for an encore, giving him 511 for his career, topping the all-time record held by Julio Jones (318, 2008–10).

Yet at halftime he had just six receptions for 60 yards and a 17-yard touchdown.

"You know we didn't throw the ball downfield that much in the first half," Saban said. "The only time we did was a touchdown and I kept saying to [offensive coordinator] Lane [Kiffin], 'We made a lot of explosive plays throwing the ball downfield, let's take some shots on these guys.'

"They're certainly doing that to us and we're not having much success. I thought a couple of those big plays really changed the momentum of the game."

Saban credited Cooper's 39-yard touchdown reception in particular as being a turning point in the third quarter, and he then topped it with a 75-yard bomb.

Regardless, the Tigers obviously never had an answer, causing Crimson Tide tackle Austin Shepherd to quip: "I'd have the whole defense on him."

"He's a great player," junior center Ryan Kelly said. "I've got a buddy who said they tried to play two on him at some point in time. But if they're going try to put the entire team on him then other guys are going to be open."

Regardless, Cooper put up most of his biggest numbers against some of the best pass defenses in college football.

At the end of the regular season he had faced seven of the top 50, including two in the top 10 and three in the top 20. In those seven games he caught 69 passes (9.9 per game) for 1,041 yards (148.7 yards) with 10 touchdowns. He had three 200-yard performances while his lowest output was eight catches for 83 yards and a touchdown at LSU, which had the nation's No. 2 pass-efficiency defense.

Harold "Red" Drew

Harold D. Drew first arrived on the Capstone in 1931 and was an assistant coach for Frank Thomas for 14 years before leaving to take over Ole Miss. However, when Thomas's health caused him to step aside and be the athletic director, he convinced Drew to return after just one season with the Rebels.

Drew was the coach during Alabama's 61–6 victory against Syracuse in the Orange Bowl at the end of the 1952 season (referring to his players running up the score, Drew said, "I just couldn't stop them."), when he was named the Southeastern Conference Coach of the Year and joined Xen Scott, Thomas, and Wallace Wade as the only Alabama coaches with 10-win seasons. His two other bowl appearances were the 1948 Sugar Bowl, a 27–7 loss to Texas, and the 1954 Cotton Bowl, a 28–6 defeat by Rice highlighted by Tommy Lewis's tackle off the bench. Drew's coaching career at Alabama came to an end in 1954, with a 54–28–7 record.

Against the six opponents ranked in the Associated Press poll he caught 58 passes for 756 yards and seven touchdowns. That's an average of 9.7 catches and 126.0 yards.

"You never know what kind of route he's going to run by the way he moves," junior safety Landon Collins said. "That's just Coop."

Saban expanded on that: "He really pays attention to detail, tries to do things right, doesn't get frustrated when it doesn't go right and sort of just keeps being a relentless competitor out there....He's got really good speed and he's got good size and he's got really good hands, and he plays with really good toughness.

"Because he's smart we can move him around a lot of different places and utilize what he can do in different spots which makes it difficult for the defense to track him."

Saban added that Cooper played through "a lot of injuries," obviously including having one of the greatest performances in Iron Bowl history while wearing a knee brace to protect the deep bruise from a helmet hit the week before against Western Carolina.

"The brace actually helped me," said Cooper, who had 13 receptions against Auburn. "It eased some of the pain."

Naturally, after the SEC Championship Game, the accolades started pouring in for Cooper, including the SEC offensive Player of the Year, and All-American status, which will make him someday eligible for the College Football Hall of Fame.

He became the first player in Alabama history, and just the second from Southeastern Conference, to win the prestigious Biletnikoff Award as receiver of the year. Cooper was also a finalist for the Walter Camp Player of the Year and invited to New York for the Heisman Trophy presentation.

35 The Greatest Play That Sort Of Never Counted

It was the game that the rest of the college football world didn't give Alabama much of a chance to win. The Crimson Tide began the 1992 season ranked near the bottom of the top 10 but after a perfect regular season found itself playing for the national championship at the Sugar Bowl.

What so many people couldn't overlook was that Alabama's opponent was defending champion Miami, ranked No. 1 and riding a 29-game winning streak. The Hurricanes felt the same way, too, and didn't think the Tide posed much of a threat—so much so that they openly admitted it in the days and weeks leading up to the game.

One pregame comment that especially attracted attention came from Hurricanes wide receiver Lamar Thomas: "Alabama's cornerbacks don't impress me one bit. They're overrated. Real men don't play zone defense, and we'll show them a thing or two come January 1."

After taking a 13–6 halftime lead, Alabama went for the kill. On Miami's first offensive play of the third quarter, cornerback Tommy Johnson intercepted a pass and returned it to the Hurricanes' 20. Six plays later, running back Derrick Lassic, who was named game MVP, scored from the 1.

Down 20–6, Miami—including Heisman Trophy quarterback Gino Torretta—was flabbergasted.

"He was so shaken up he couldn't help but throw it to you," Johnson said. "The rush was coming and he looked scared. We'd put 11 men on the line and he'd call timeout. He didn't know what to do."

On the subsequent possession, Torretta again found himself looking at all 11 defenders on the line, only this time the result was an interception George Teague returned for a 31–yard high-stepping touchdown.

That was followed by possibly the greatest play in college football history that never appeared on a statistics page. When Torretta hit Thomas in stride, the wide receiver appeared to be gone for a long touchdown, but Teague had other ideas. Not only did he chase down Thomas before reaching the end zone, he fluidly ripped the ball away and started running in the opposite direction.

Even though it was nullified by a penalty, it's called the "Play of the Century" at Alabama.

George Teague and Friends

During his pro career, George Teague again made a name for himself in ways that didn't show statistically, especially while playing for the Dallas Cowboys.

In a memorable game during the 2000 season, the safety took exception to the San Francisco 49ers' Terrell Owens celebrating on the midfield Dallas logo after scoring a touchdown. Just as he kneeled on the star, Teague drilled him, setting off a confrontation between the teams. Teague was ejected, but Owens was not (only to later be suspended for a game and fined).

"No matter how negative this is, the game and the action that happened, it all comes from having pride and getting our butts kicked over and over," Teague said at the time. "I think it will help us in the long run to be able to not feel that way and not want to feel that way anymore."

On September 23, 2001, just two weeks after the 9/11 tragedy, Teague carried the American flag as the Cowboys took the field for the first time following the terrorist attacks.

Also in 2001, he started the George Teague and Friends Foundation, a charity organization that includes and features many of his former Crimson Tide teammates.

"We had great respect for Alabama, especially its defense," Miami coach Dennis Erickson said after the 34–13 loss. "We knew they were a formidable opponent. But in retrospect, I think they were a lot stronger than a lot of our people thought."

Alabama accumulated 267 rushing yards on 60 carries, led by Lassic's 135 yards and two touchdowns. In contrast, Miami had just 48 yards rushing.

But the buzz of the game was Teague, and how the Tide shut the Hurricanes up, not to mention *down*.

"It's better to be seen and not heard," Lassic said. "They were doing a lot of talking. When you do that, you've got a lot to prove. They didn't do it. They talked about it, but they didn't walk it. There's a new king on the throne.

"My hat goes off to Coach Stallings. You couldn't have written up a better script, winning the national championship during the year we celebrate 100 years of Alabama football."

36 Don Hutson

When most people think of receivers who changed the way football is played, usually Jerry Rice or maybe even Randy Moss come to mind.

Well, more than 50 years before them was Don Hutson, who completely revolutionized receiving during an era when football was still considered almost exclusively a running sport.

Tall, skinny, and having deceptive speed, Hutson was considered the pioneer of modern pass patterns, the first to perfect the techniques of catching a pass "in traffic," and he made the end-around a potent weapon.

Charles Baxter "Foots" Clement

Charles Baxter "Foots" Clement was an All-American tackle in 1930, when as team captain he helped lead the undefeated Crimson Tide to both the Rose Bowl, where it defeated Washington State 24–0, and the national championship. Alabama outscored its opponents 271–13 and shut out eight of 10 teams. In addition to football, Clement was on the track and boxing teams and also served as Cadet Colonel of the University Regiment, business manager of the Corolla yearbook, and senior class president.

"For every pass I caught in a game, I caught a thousand in practice," Hutson once said.

Hutson and Millard Fillmore "Dixie" Howell became football's most celebrated passing combination in the 1930s. In 1934 Hutson was named an All-American. He scored the winning touchdown against Tennessee on a nine-yard end-around and caught two touchdown passes against Clemson. And when he had six receptions for 165 yards against Stanford in the Rose Bowl, West Coast writers hailed him as "the greatest pass-catching speed merchant end."

"Don had the most fluid motion you had ever seen when he was running," said the other end on that team, Paul W. "Bear" Bryant. "It looked like he was going just as fast as possible when all of a sudden he would put on an extra burst of speed and be gone."

Hutson also played center field for the baseball team and ran track, once competing in both on the same day. He was also once timed at 9.8 seconds in the 100-yard dash.

If it wasn't for a unique ruling by NFL President Joe Carr, Hutson might have never made such a splash in the professional ranks. After leaving the Capstone, he signed contracts with both the Green Bay Packers and the football version of the Brooklyn Dodgers, a team that rarely passed (but ironically would be turned down by Bryant). Carr ruled that the deal with the earliest postmark would be honored. The Packers' contract was postmarked 8:30 AM, 17 minutes earlier than the Dodgers' deal. Thus Hutson became a Packer.

He played 11 years with Green Bay, 1935 to 1945, was All-Pro nine times, led the league in pass receptions eight times, led the league in scoring five times, and twice was named Most Valuable Player (1941–42). He finished his pro career with 488 pass receptions, topping the next-best player by more than 200.

His 99 career touchdown receptions stood as a National Football League record for more than four decades, and his 29 points in a quarter has yet to be broken. When he retired, Hutson held 18 NFL records.

He's been enshrined into numerous halls of fame, including Alabama, Arkansas, Rose Bowl, College Football, Pro Football, Green Bay Packers, Helms Foundation, and Wisconsin. When the Packers built their indoor practice facility in 1994, it was named in his honor, the Don Hutson Center.

"I don't know if there is such a thing as royalty in professional football, but this is the closest I've ever come to it," Packers general manager Ron Wolf said at the dedication ceremony.

37 Cornelius Bennett

At Alabama, it's simply known as "the Sack."

It came during the 1986 game against the Notre Dame Fighting Irish, a team the Crimson Tide had never defeated, when Steve Beuerlein dropped back to pass and was hit so hard by linebacker Cornelius Bennett that he was knocked cleanly off his feet. The vicious blow helped pace a 28–10 victory at Legion Field in Birmingham.

The Jacobs Award

True or false: The Jacobs Award for the Southeastern Conference's best blocker has never been won by a tight end.
Answer: False. Alabama's Howard Cross won it in 1988. He had 41 career receptions for 459 yards and four touchdowns before being drafted by the New York Giants. During his 13-year NFL career he won a Super Bowl, had 201 receptions for 2,194 yards and 17 touchdowns, and once held the franchise record with 207 games played.

True or false: He's the only non-lineman to win the award at Alabama.
Answer: False, and it's not even close. Before passing became so popular, the quarterback was frequently the lead blocker out of the backfield.

Alabama's Jacobs Award winners:

1935	Riley Smith (QB)
1937	Leroy Monsky (G)
1946	Hal Self (QB)
1949	Butch Avinger (QB)
1950	Butch Avinger (QB)
1961	Billy Neighbors (T)
1962	Butch Wilson (B)
1966	Cecil Dowdy (T)
1972	John Hannah (G)
1973	Buddy Brown (G)
1974	Sylvester Croom (C)
1977	Bob Cryder (G)
1979	Dwight Stephenson (C)
1986	Wes Neighbors (C)
1988	Howard Cross (TE)
1993	Tobie Sheils (C)
1999	Chris Samuels (OT)
2004	Wesley Britt (OT)
2007	Andre Smith (OT)
2011	Barrett Jones (OT)
2015	Ryan Kelly (C)

"He knocked me woozy," Beuerlein said. "I have never been hit like that before, and hopefully I'll never be hit like that again."

Bennett was a three-time all-conference selection, two-time All-American, and named defensive player of the game at both the 1985 Aloha Bowl and the 1986 Sun Bowl. His senior year, he compiled 61 tackles, 10 sacks, and six forced fumbles en route to unanimous All-America honors. In addition, he finished seventh in

Cornelius Bennett received the Lombardi Award as the nation's best lineman, but he is best remembered by Crimson Tide fans for the vicious hit he put on Notre Dame quarterback Steve Beuerlein in 1986. At Alabama it's known simply as "the Sack."

Heisman Trophy voting and received the Lombardi Award, which is given to the nation's top lineman.

For his collegiate career, Bennett tallied 287 tackles, 15 sacks, and three fumble recoveries.

"Signing my letter of intent to play at the University of Alabama, and then playing against the University of Washington in the Sun Bowl my last game senior year, those two things really stand out more than anything else," Bennett said. "The first part was becoming part of a great tradition and the last was finishing off a career where I tried my best to continue that tradition."

But Bennett was just getting started. After being the second overall selection in the 1987 NFL Draft by the Indianapolis Colts, the two sides were unable to come to an agreement on a contract. Shortly before the trade deadline, Bennett was part of an unusual massive three-way deal that also included Los Angeles Rams running back Eric Dickerson and Buffalo running back Greg Bell, sending his negotiating rights to the Bills.

It's considered the move that made Buffalo a title contender, although some didn't see it that way at the time.

"I don't know how we ever made the trade for Cornelius Bennett," former Bills general manager Marv Levy said. "I was opposed to what we had to give up, it was so much. A first, a second, Greg Bell, and so on. Finally at three in the morning I told Bill Polian, 'Okay, let's go along with it.' The next year, we didn't have a first-round pick and we needed a top-shelf running back. We took one in the second round. A guy named Thurman Thomas."

Because of his holdout, Bennett played in only eight games as a rookie but recorded eight and a half sacks. A year later he helped the Bills win their first AFC Eastern Division title in eight years and made his first of five appearances in the Pro Bowl.

Bennett played in four consecutive Super Bowls with the Bills (1990–93), and a fifth with Atlanta (1998).

During his 14 National Football League seasons, Bennett notched 71½ sacks and seven interceptions, and his 26 defensive fumble recoveries ranked third in league history. He was a six-time All-Pro.

38 Got Crimson?

The University of Alabama's current colors were actually used for the first football season in 1892, when the team that would become known as the Crimson Tide wore large white sweaters, with "U of A" in large crimson letters on the front, or crimson sweaters with a large white *A* and crimson stockings.

At the time, the sweaters cost $6.

Original accounts simply refer to the team as the "varsity," or the occasional "Crimson White," referring to the colors worn. Incidentally, in 1894 *Crimson White* also became the name of the student newspaper on campus, which is still published on a regular basis.

Another early nickname for the team was "the Thin Red Line." Author Winston Groom, in his book *The Crimson Tide: An Illustrated History of Football at the University of Alabama*, speculated that this nickname was borrowed from Rudyard Kipling's poem "Tommy," about a British soldier.

However, that nickname started to fall out of favor by the 1906 game against Auburn, which Alabama won 10–0. The coach that year was J.W.H. "Doc" Pollard, whose team finished 5–1. The lone loss, 78–0 to Vanderbilt, came after Pollard tried to reschedule or cancel the game because seven of his 11 starters were injured or sick and the coach knew his backups couldn't match up. Naturally, Vanderbilt balked.

A year later Alabama was 3–1–1 when it faced 6–1 Auburn but was considered a clear underdog (both teams had lost to Sewanee, Alabama 54–4 and Auburn 12–6). The team was known as "Pollard's Pets," but sportswriter Hugh Roberts of the *Birmingham Age-Herald* had a better idea after Alabama managed a 6–6 tie. In part due to the thick, red mud the team regularly kicked up during games in Birmingham, and surrounding the field that day, he coined the name "Crimson Tide."

Incidentally, due to a dispute between the schools, Alabama and Auburn didn't play again until 1948.

With a 5–0 victory against Tennessee on Thanksgiving Day, in which the only touchdown was off a blocked punt returned for a touchdown by Derrill Pratt (scoring was different then), Alabama finished the season 5–1–2.

Alabama was also briefly called the "Red Elephants" in 1930, but otherwise the nickname has never changed.

However, it's made other appearances in pop culture, including the 1995 submarine movie *Crimson Tide*, starring Denzel

Got White?

Although Alabama traditionally wears crimson-colored helmets, it has at times worn white. While some players still didn't wear leather helmets in the mid-1920s, it's believed the first time the team sported white helmets (with crimson markings) was 1930. However, it switched to a dark helmet the following year.

Other notable years the Crimson Tide wore white helmets include 1949 (with a crimson stripe), 1955 (all white), 1956 (the stripe returned), 1971 (in the opener against Southern California and again against Houston), and 1983–84 (Alabama used both white and crimson helmets). During the 1960s, Alabama used white helmets on eligible receivers during night games or when the opposing team's color was close to the Tide's.

Washington and Gene Hackman and directed by Tony Scott. Incidentally, there actually is a nuclear-powered submarine named the USS *Alabama*.

Crimson Tide is also referenced in the Steely Dan song "Deacon Blues," though somewhat sarcastically. In a *Rolling Stone* interview, Donald Fagen said, "Walter [Becker] and I had been working on that song at a house in Malibu. I played him that line, and he said, 'You mean it's like, "They call these cracker [jerks] this grandiose name like the Crimson Tide, and I'm this loser, so they call me this other grandiose name, Deacon Blues?"'

"And I said, 'Yeah!'

"He said, 'Cool! Let's finish it!'"

39 Visit the Paul W. Bryant Museum

It was a little surreal for Mark Ingram Jr. to be standing in the Paul W. Bryant Museum on a warm summer Friday night before his first training camp with the New Orleans Saints in 2011. There in various display cases were the national championship trophy, the gloves he held up after scoring a touchdown in the Rose Bowl, and all sorts of photos and awards from his Crimson Tide career.

He even got to see the permanently stained shirt that Nick Saban wore when Alabama players gave him the Gatorade treatment and accidentally hit him in the head with the bucket. "It wasn't long ago at all," Ingram said while reflecting. "I think it was three-and-a-half years ago I was reporting here and then started summer workouts. It went by really quick. I remember all the older guys telling me that it flies by and they didn't lie. Those are guys who played five years and I only played three, so it went by really fast.

"I definitely miss it, but I'm looking forward to the next chapter as well."

Although his Crimson Tide years were already in the rear-view mirror, Ingram was back in Tuscaloosa with his family to participate in the unveiling of a painting, which was completed by Birmingham sports artist Steve Skipper, donated by George Landegger, and sponsored by Ingram's foundation to help kids of incarcerated parents.

The painting shows Ingram scoring a touchdown against Texas in the BCS National Championship Game, overlooked by a shadowy image of the Heisman Trophy.

"Take it by force, you have to get it however you can," Ingram said of the artistic representation of one of his signature moments at Alabama. "There are [defenders] laying down there everywhere. It's a perfectly executed play. All I had to do was jump over one guy.

"Why not? It was a touchdown in the national championship game."

Not to minimize the painting, which took roughly 1,300 hours of work to complete, but such ceremonies and dignitaries can be almost commonplace at the museum, which was founded at 1985 and opened its doors down the street from Bryant-Denny Stadium in 1988.

With exhibits, video presentations, and more hardware than a Home Depot, many fans make a point to visit annually, whether as a pilgrimage or part of their pre-game ritual. Coach Paul W. "Bear" Bryant himself suggested its creation to honor the former players and assistant coaches who contributed to all the championship teams and his record-setting career, but also preserve, educate, and inspire.

"Winning helps, obviously," museum director Ken Gaddy said. "We're the repository for all the old game films, the media guides, game programs, all that. We're kind of the gatekeeper for all that information. If anybody wants to write a story or write a book, even do a painting, a lot of people start here. We have newspaper clippings and those kinds of things."

Gaddy was being modest, because even more impressive than what people see on display every day is what's in the back rooms and in storage. In addition to having scores of trophies, paintings, photographs, press clippings, books, and so forth, which help make the museum one of the country's best college football research facilities, there are things like personal items and a scrapbook of William G. Little, the founder of Alabama football.

After introducing the sport to the Capstone in 1892, Little gathered a group of students to form a team that included a future Speaker of the U.S. House of Representatives, a state governor, a state senator, a judge, a doctor, and prominent businessmen and lawyers.

There are a lot of other things going on behind the scenes as well, including the massive conversion of everything into a digital format—photos, video, and audio are all being enhanced, which can be a several-step process. Given the condition of, say, old coaching tapes, trying to turn these items into something that's usable today is more than a tall order.

Yet the advantages of doing so are great. From the photo galleries to the video series "Crimson Classics," having a complete digital library will allow for more flexibility and the opportunity to do so much more.

"I'm sure it's not exciting to the folks who might read this, but it's exciting to us, and they'll like what will come out of it," Gaddy said. "A lot of new videos can come out of that project."

Additionally, the museum self-published the book *When Winning Was Everything*, by Delbert Reed, which tells the story and honors the more than 300 former Crimson Tide players and coaches who saw military duty during World War II.

Fans never quite know who might be there promoting a book, speaking to a group, or signing autographs. Nowhere else can they

Attend a Neutral-Site Game

Although Alabama no longer plays Auburn at Legion Field every year, neutral-site games are back in vogue again in college football and with the Crimson Tide.

In 2007, Alabama met Florida State and Bobby Bowden in Jacksonville, even though it was the Seminoles' second home. Dubbed the "River City Showdown," the two schools split more than $4.5 million, which was financially comparable to a home game, and were each given 30,000 tickets to sell.

The 85,412 fans attending the 21–14 Florida State victory were the most to ever see a game in Jacksonville, exceeding attendance at the 2005 Super Bowl game or any of the annual Florida-Georgia rivalry games at Alltel Stadium (home of the Gator Bowl and the NFL's Jacksonville Jaguars).

Alabama also played in the first Chick-fil-A Kickoff game in Atlanta, beating Clemson 34–10 in 2008, and used the same venue to springboard the 2009 national championship season by defeating Virginia Tech, 34–24. Eager to reap the rewards of traveling Tide fans, Jerry Jones signed Michigan as an opponent to open the 2012 season, and Wisconsin in 2015 at Cowboys Stadium. The Crimson Tide went on to win both national titles.

see the Hall of Honor, which has a photo of each team Bryant coached surrounding a bust of the legend. Or the Waterford Crystal houndstooth hat, the original LeRoy Neiman, or the replica of Bryant's office including his low-seated couch.

Some of the new things that patrons have enjoyed recently include the clay model (called a *maquette*) created by student Jeremy Davis that was essentially transformed into the Nick Saban statue standing along the Walk of Champions. There are more items and paraphernalia from the 2009, 2011, 2012 and 2015 national championship teams. A Big Al display has been added. The coaching exhibits, from Ray Perkins to Mike Shula, have been revamped, and the museum has started producing its own live shows on the website.

It's even tackled the emotional topic of the 2011 tornados and how football and the Crimson Tide have helped with the recovery. Consequently, the museum added an unscheduled display depicting the devastation and the storm's aftermath, including a gut-wrenching video.

"It's kind of hard for me to look at, still," Gaddy said.

40 Pooley Hubert

The January 11, 1926, issue of *Time* magazine said this about the first Rose Bowl to feature a Southern team:

> Pasadena was flooded with sunshine. Businessmen swelled with pride, policemen with importance. Through the streets it was raining roses—white ones, red ones, pink ones, yellow ones, in bunches and basketfuls, automobiles full, motor trucks full. To the gay Rose Bowl went Pasadena, 300 gorgeous floats and a hilarious walking multitude, for the 37th annual Tournament of Roses on New Year's Day.
>
> Out upon the chalk-lined sward trotted the eleven purple-banded "Huskies" of the University of Washington. They slapped their padded thighs, they pranced their cleated feet. Came the slighter, nimbler Dixie boys of the University of Alabama, flitting through signal practice, twitching their pigskin this way, that way.
>
> It was the old, old contrast, the thunder and the lightning.

Hoyt "Wu" Winslett

During Winslett's three years playing with the varsity (1924–26), Alabama won three Southern Conference championships, two national titles, and lost a grand total of one game. When the Crimson Tide returned from the 1926 Rose Bowl, the first victory for the region at the prestigious game, he was credited with saying, "We were the South's baby."

Winslett was primarily known as a defensive end, a position in which he earned All-America honors in 1926. According to Tide lore, no opponent recorded a first down when running to his side of the field.

A little more believable, and substantiated by statistics, is that "Wu" was a triple threat offensively. He could pass and run, and didn't have a single fumble during his career.

Led by Allison "Pooley" Hubert, Alabama was the lightning, which helps explain why Coach Wallace Wade supposedly told him before kickoff, "Run the game any way you want to, Pooley, but don't run the football yourself or they'll kill you."

With nothing to lose, Wade finally unleashed Hubert in the third quarter. He punched in one touchdown, and Johnny Mack Brown caught two touchdown passes, one from Hubert, as Alabama won 20–19. With the victory, Hubert capped a prolific career as Alabama's field general with 38 touchdowns, including six games in which he scored at least three.

"Pooley was the greatest team leader and playmaker that I ever coached in my long career," Wade said.

Hubert was a proficient defensive back and defensive leader as well, which prompted Southern sportswriters to refer to him as "the greatest defensive back ever to appear on Grant Field in Atlanta."

Pooley also helped lead Alabama to a couple of the program's other great victories, including one for Coach Xen Scott during the 1922 season. Southern football was still considered inferior to what was being played in the Northeast, where the game originated, and the November 4 face-off between the Crimson Tide and Penn was expected to be a blowout.

With a field goal by Bull Wesley and center Shorty Propst's recovery of Hubert's fumble in the end zone, Alabama pulled off a jaw-dropping 9–7 victory in Philadelphia that led to the team parading in the streets before heading home. With thousands greeting them at the Tuscaloosa train depot, it served as a precursor to the Rose Bowl game that would change college football in the South and the nation.

During Hubert's career, Alabama teams went a combined 31–6–2, and he was an All-Southern selection in both 1924 and 1925, when the Crimson Tide also won its first conference titles. In 1924, Georgia was rated the No. 1 team in the region before getting pounded by Alabama. Hubert threw touchdown passes in the 33–0 victory.

"Undoubtedly one of the greatest football players of all time," Wade said.

41 The 1966 Undefeated Team

Alabama was the two-time defending national champion (though both the 1964 and 1965 titles were somewhat controversial) and ranked No. 1 in the preseason polls. Led by players like quarterback Kenny "Snake" Stabler, end Ray Perkins, and tackle Cecil Dowdy—not to mention All-American defensive tackle Richard Cole, guard John Calvert, and back Dicky Thompson—the Crimson Tide destroyed every team it faced minus one, Tennessee, which it still came back to defeat in the Knoxville rain, 11–10.

Tommy Wilcox

If there were 101 things every Crimson Tide fan should know or do, number 101 would probably be Tommy Wilcox, a two-time All-American safety who was SEC Freshman of the Year in 1979, when Alabama won the national championship, and went on to finish his career with 243 tackles. Among his 10 interceptions were two game-saving pickoffs in the end zone, against Mississippi State in 1981 and against Auburn in Paul W. "Bear" Bryant's 315th career victory. His pro career ended after just two years because of a neck injury, but Wilcox kept hunting and fishing on the side and became the host of the regional television program "Tommy Wilcox Outdoors."

The defense allowed just 37 points all regular season with six shutouts, including 21–0 against LSU and 31–0 over Auburn.

Even the Orange Bowl was a complete Crimson affair, as Alabama played Nebraska in a rematch of the previous year's decisive title game. With Stabler throwing a 45-yard pass to Perkins on the first play from scrimmage to set up the first score, and defensive back Bobby Johns making three interceptions, Alabama crushed Nebraska in a 34–7 rout.

However, it didn't lead to the coveted three-peat.

Despite the perfect season, the Crimson Tide was ranked third behind Notre Dame and Michigan State heading into the postseason—with both the Associated Press and United Press International polls holding their final voting before the bowl games were played. (The AP held its final voting after the bowls in 1965 but switched back in 1966 before making the switch permanent in 1969. The coaches' poll followed suit in 1973.)

On top of that, the Spartans and Fighting Irish had played to a 10–10 tie earlier in the season in what was hyped as the "Game of the Century," with Notre Dame, No. 1 at the time, running out the clock instead of going for the road win.

Coach Paul W. "Bear" Bryant was quoted as saying, "At Alabama, we teach our men to win," and the Crimson Tide felt it was robbed of its place in history as the first program to win three consecutive national titles.

Numerous ranking services, including the National Championship Foundation and Clyde Berryman's Quality Point Rating System had the 11–0 Tide No. 1, but Alabama didn't count it. Author Keith Dunnavant later referred to the season as *The Missing Ring*, in his book with the same title.

Many believe that the state's racial issues, which were the focal point of national debate, including Governor George Wallace's "Stand in the Schoolhouse Door," the Rosa Parks bus protest in Montgomery, and the Selma civil rights march, were a crucial factor in the snubbing. Additionally, the Crimson Tide had yet to integrate the football team, with Bryant publicly saying the time wasn't right while helping some standout black athletes land at other top programs, including Michigan State with Bryant's friend Duffy Daugherty.

Daugherty is believed to have coined the phrase, "A tie is like kissing your sister," a line Bryant himself used.

42 Johnny Musso

They called him the "Italian Stallion," but Johnny Musso was the kind of football player who evoked words like *gritty*, *drive*, *determination*, and *chutzpah*.

He also embodied the word *class*.

The running back, who grew up in the Birmingham area, was one of those rare players who had exceptional brains *and* brawn.

Robert Marlow

Robert Ross Marlow was an All-American halfback in 1952 and gained 2,560 yards from 1950 to 1952. His 233 rushing yards against Auburn in 1951 set a school record that stood for 35 years, and he's still Alabama's career leader in net-per-carry at 6.3 yards.

Marlow was one of the few bright spots of the 1951 season, Alabama's first losing campaign since 1903. Consequently, he was the only Crimson Tide player named All-SEC that year.

In 1952, Marlow had a little more help with Bobby Luna joining him in the backfield, and he tallied 950 rushing yards on 176 carries as Alabama finished 10–2.

Marlow was a first-round draft pick by the New York Giants in 1953, but he opted to play in the Canadian Football League, where he was later named to the All-Time All-Star CFL team.

Not only was he a two-time All-American but a two-time Academic All-American as well. He truly was Crimson through and through.

"I grew up sneaking into Legion Field to see Alabama play," Musso once told *Alabama Illustrated*. "I vividly remember Joe Namath's first varsity game. I remember Kenny Stabler running down the sideline in the rain and mud against Auburn. I remember Lee Roy Jordan chasing down a running back and intimidating without even hitting.

"I really appreciate the people who have contributed to this legacy and the tradition that has been passed down, and the people who have continued it, the goal-line stand and Van Tiffin's kick and all those memories of people who have carried on the tradition of Alabama football. I really feel blessed to have had the opportunity to be part of the tradition of Alabama football."

Although Musso led the Southeastern Conference in rushing in 1970 (when he also accumulated 221 rushing yards against Auburn), he's better known for the 1971 season (when he scored four touchdowns against Florida), when he did it again.

His senior numbers of 191 carries for 1,088 yards told only part of the story because Musso was also a devastating blocker, led the conference in scoring (100 points), and helped the Crimson Tide to an 11–1 finish and SEC championship.

That season was also well remembered by Alabama fans for the first meeting against Auburn when both teams were undefeated. The Tide won easily, 31–7, and even though Tigers quarterback Pat Sullivan would go on to win the Heisman Trophy, he had to share Southeastern Conference Player of the Year honors with his friend from the rival school.

Musso placed fourth in Heisman voting but was named Player of the Year by *Football News*, the Miami Touchdown Club, and the Touchdown Club of Atlanta. He received the National Football Foundation scholarship, and the American Football Coaches Association gave him the Ernie Davis Award, presented annually to a football player, past or present, who exemplifies Davis's qualities of "excellence of character and integrity, and service to mankind."

When he left the Capstone, Musso held the school records for career rushing yards (2,741) and rushing touchdowns (34), which stood for nearly three decades.

After a short professional career in the Canadian Football League (1972 to 1974) and with the Chicago Bears in the National Football League (1975 to 1977), Musso settled in the Chicago area and began a business career. He became president of a commodities firm and a deacon in the Baptist Church of Hinsdale, Illinois, serving in youth ministry and working with inner-city citizens.

43 1934: Thomas' Turn

In 1934 Alabama was coming off a 7–1–1 season and won the inaugural championship of the new Southeastern Conference, which included Sewanee, Georgia Tech, and Tulane. But the team also had an amazing collection of young talent, including fullback Joe Demyanovich, halfback Dixie Howell, end Don Hutson, tackle Bill Lee, quarterback Riley Smith, and a rugged end named Paul W. "Bear" Bryant.

It was easily the best team Coach Frank Thomas had ever had. After opening with a 24–0 victory over Howard, a team that was coached by former Alabama All-American center Clyde "Shorty" Propst, the Crimson Tide blew through its Southeastern Conference schedule, with the lone close game a 13–6 victory against Tennessee.

The wins kept piling up, with an impressive season-ending stretch of 40–0 against Clemson, 40–0 at Georgia Tech, and 34–0 vs. Vanderbilt in Birmingham. Consequently, Alabama was headed back to Pasadena to play in the Rose Bowl, but for the first time without Wallace Wade. Thomas pushed all the right buttons to motivate his players, including making sure they knew that many sportswriters had declared Minnesota would have been a better choice to face Stanford, and again the West Coast team was expected to win.

"I'll never forget going to the Rose Bowl," Bryant said. "I remember everything about it. We were on the train and Coach Thomas was talking to three coaches and Red Heard, the athletic trainer at LSU. Coach Thomas said, 'Red, this is my football player. This is the best player on my team.' Well shoot, I could have gone right out the top. He was getting me ready, and I was, too. I would have gone out there and killed myself for Alabama that day."

Duly inspired, and aided by scouting reports from former standout Johnny Mack Brown, Alabama dominated, 29–13, before a sellout crowd of 84,474.

Rose Bowl archives describe the game this way: "Frank Thomas's Alabama (9–0) brings the first great aerial circus in Rose Bowl history to Pasadena to hand Stanford's 'Vow Boys' (9–0–1) another Rose Bowl defeat, 29–13. The 85,000 spectators are amazed by the soaring footballs propelled by Dixie Howell to Don Hutson. Howell completes nine of 12 passes and averages 44.8 yards with six punts."

Howell scored two touchdowns, one on a 67-yard run, and threw 59 yards to Hutson for another. He passed for 160 yards and ran for 111 more to be named the game's most valuable player.

Thomas called Howell's performance the "greatest I've ever seen."

"That boy has ice water in his veins, if ever a competitive athlete had. I've never seen him nervous before, but that morning he couldn't look at his breakfast, let alone eat it. And he couldn't eat lunch."

Alabama had won its fourth national championship by averaging 31.6 points per game while yielding just 4.5. Howell was named Southeastern Conference Player of the Year in addition to All-American along with Lee and Hutson, who would go on to revolutionize the National Football League with the Green Bay Packers.

Noted Will Rogers, "Stanford made a mistake in scoring first. It just made those Alabama boys mad."

44 Take Lots of Photos at the Walk of Champions

When construction began to expand beyond the north end zone following the 2004 season, director of athletics Mal Moore didn't want changes to just Bryant-Denny Stadium.

In addition to the upper-deck stands, three levels of skyboxes collectively known as "the Zone," and large video screens, Moore wanted to really embrace the program's history and have it reflected both inside and outside the stadium. He wanted it to have more of a presence along the school's main thoroughfare, University Boulevard.

To accomplish this goal, a seven-story glass curtain gave the northernmost wall a formal face, creating a permanent front entrance that, when lit up, could easily be seen from the street and beyond (well, it could after a fraternity was razed and rebuilt across the street).

In addition, the university landscaped the area for a new brick plaza, which included both the Walk of Champions and Coaches Walk to celebrate the program's success. It instantly became a must-visit for Crimson Tide fans.

The Walk of Champions serves as a pathway to the entrance, running perpendicular from the street, inlaid with granite tablets commemorating the school's title seasons. The national championship plaques include the year, coach, record, and team members. The Southeastern Conference title markers include just the year, coach, and record.

Overlooking the walkway are two bronze statues of Crimson Tide football players at the north entrance, with one holding an Alabama flag and the other pointing ahead into the distance. The player on the left is wearing the number 18, and the one on the right is wearing the number 92, which is not a coincidence as the

A Student Literally Made History

For months it wasn't the biggest question on the Alabama campus, but probably the largest secret.

Although Crimson Tide fans had been aware since January 7, 2010, after Alabama defeated Texas in the BCS Championship Game at the Rose Bowl 37–21, that a statue of Nick Saban would eventually be unveiled along the Walk of Champions plaza, what nearly no one knew was who was working on it...or that he was a student.

"It's kind of crazy, something of this magnitude that will affect, not necessarily the art world, but the public in general because a lot of people will see that," Jeremy Davis said. "I come from a very small town. We don't even have a red light."

Davis was selected for the project after MTM Recognition, which did the other statues outside of Bryant-Denny Stadium, submitted designs that were lacking a number of fine details.

A consensus decision was made to get someone locally involved who could have access to the coach and devote the necessary time and energy. The list of candidates had only one name on it. Davis was asked to draw a couple of preliminary sketches, which he did at his mother's house in West Blocton the night before presenting them.

"[Terry] Saban came into the meeting room, looked at it, and just went, 'Oh, this is what we're looking for,'" said Alabama art professor Craig Wedderspoon, who oversaw Davis along with instructor Daniel Livingston. "Jeremy was freaking out of course."

That's when the real work began. After studying Saban's physical idiosyncrasies and nuances, he made a 3-foot maquette, which is essentially a model that would be enlarged into the 9-foot final version—a process that would normally take two or three years to complete. Instead, it was unveiled just 15 months after the title game.

Meanwhile, everything was done behind closed doors and on a need-to-know basis, with only Terry Saban getting regular updates.

"It was small things that she wanted fixed," Davis said. "I remember on one of the better drawings I didn't have the shadow on his ear just right, it was off just a little bit. She said that he had very distinct earlobes. His nose didn't round off enough. It's amazing how much she knew about this man's face. I guess if you've been married for 40 years you know."

football program was founded in 1892. Although the statues were meant to honor the entire football program, they were modeled by two real Alabama players on the roster at the time—center Antoine Caldwell and linebacker Matt Collins.

Prior to each home game, Alabama's team buses drop the players and coaches off at the walkway, where after surveying the path through cheering fans (roughly 100 yards), they enter the stadium's inner sanctum to their locker room approximately two hours prior to kickoff.

The Coaches Walk is off to the side of the Walk of Champions, and features 9-foot-tall bronze statues, weighing 2,000 pounds, celebrating the coaches who led Alabama to a national title: Wallace Wade, Frank Thomas, Paul W. "Bear" Bryant, Gene Stallings, and Nick Saban. All display the coaches in their game-day garb, so naturally Bryant's statue includes his houndstooth hat, and instead of a suit Thomas has on the letterman's jacket in which he was frequently photographed.

At the end of the walkway was initially an open spot, apparently reserved for the next coach to win a national title at Alabama. It didn't take long to fill as Saban joined the school's version of a bronze garden after winning the 2009 national title. His statue was unveiled before the 2011 A-Day Game.

45 2011 National Championship

If the disappointment of not returning to a BCS bowl in 2010 wasn't enough motivation for the Alabama football team, it got an overdose of tragedy during the months building up to the 2011 season.

Mere days after the annual A-Day scrimmage and unveiling of Nick Saban's statue for winning the 2009 national title, a series of horrific tornados struck the state on April 27, killing 53 people in Tuscaloosa alone—including long-snapper Carson Tinker's girlfriend Ashley Harrison. He barely survived with a concussion, a broken wrist, and an ankle injury.

In May, reserve offensive lineman Aaron Douglas was found dead on a balcony the morning after attending a party in Jacksonville.

Despite all that, and a 9–6 overtime loss to LSU at Bryant-Denny Stadium on November 5, Alabama managed to reach the BCS National Championship Game in New Orleans, where it dominated the rematch against the Southeastern Conference–rival Tigers with a 21–0 victory.

"I've never coached a team that was more determined, more dedicated to overcoming adversity than this group of guys," Saban said. "I've never seen a more dominant performance than what they did in the national championship game against LSU."

Although running back Trent Richardson was a Heisman Trophy finalist who set the Alabama single-season rushing record, and after moving from right guard to left tackle Barrett Jones became the third Crimson Tide player to win the Outland Trophy (best interior lineman), the defense put itself on the short list for best-ever consideration.

Alabama finished the season by leading the nation in pass-efficiency defense (83.69 rating), pass defense (111.46 yards per game), rushing defense (72.15), scoring defense (8.15 points), and total defense (183.62 yards per game)—in addition to third-down defense, red-zone defense, first downs allowed, and three-and-outs—all by wide margins.

It pulled off the first shutout in BCS history, never mind the title game, and the Tigers crossed the 50-yard line only once.

Trent Richardson holds up the crystal trophy after Alabama defeated SEC rival LSU 21–0 on January 9, 2012, to win the BCS National Championship. (AP Images)

Meanwhile, with AJ McCarron often passing on first down he became the first sophomore quarterback to lead his team to victory in the BCS title game and was named the offensive MVP.

"We knew coming into the game somebody else had to step up, and coach just gave me an opportunity," said McCarron, who completed 23 of 34 attempts for 234 yards and had no turnovers. "I don't think I did anything special."

If so, he was the only one.

"Tonight, he was on a whole other level, he actually blew me away," center William Vlachos said. "He talked to us at halftime, he talked to us pregame, he's on the stage getting offensive MVP. The guy is unbelievable."

With 4:36 remaining, Alabama scored the one and only touchdown between the two teams in eight quarters and one overtime of play on the season. Richardson recorded his 21st rushing touchdown of the season by bouncing outside on a 34-yard run.

"That was probably the most fun touchdown I've ever scored," Jones said. "Two games of frustration of not finding the end zone, just to seal the deal, that was a great feeling."

In addition to winning its second crystal football in three years, Richardson won the program's first Doak Walker Award (best running back), Jones collected the ACA Sportsmanship Award and Wuerffel Trophy, and Alabama was also presented with the Disney Spirit Award that annually goes to college football's most inspirational player, team, or figure. Tinker accepted on behalf of the Crimson Tide roughly a month before the championship.

"It's awesome," Tinker said between hugs and falling pieces of crimson and white confetti at Mercedes-Benz Superdome. "There are no words that can describe this. Just a lot of work paid off. Everyone here faced some kind of adversity, and just to see how they all came out of that is a great thing."

But that didn't keep the Crimson Tide from relishing the finality of the moment and all it had accomplished. For example, after playing in his final game for the Crimson Tide, Vlachos refused to let go of the game ball, even in the locker room, while offensive coordinator Jim McElwain walked arm-in-arm with his family off the field and subsequently stepped into his new job as the head coach at Colorado State.

Everyone else headed back to Tuscaloosa where the rebuilding continued but another crown jewel would be prominently displayed, and a championship like none other celebrated.

"It means a lot, we went through a lot this season, last year," Richardson said. "The tornado, we lost a teammate, it was big for our team. We needed this here and we're glad to bring it back to Tuscaloosa, and try and bring hope and faith back to our town.

"That accomplishment is big. You dream of stuff like that, some dreams don't even be that big, but when stuff like that happens it's incredible. That tells you about the program we have here and the kind of program we built here, and we're still building. We're not done yet."

46 The Block

An undefeated season being on the line was nothing new for Alabama fans, especially against a rival like Tennessee. Factor in that it was a tired No. 1-ranked Crimson Tide team playing its fifth straight week against a Southeastern Conference opponent, and it shouldn't have surprised anyone that the game was a lot closer than expected with numerous uncharacteristic mistakes giving the Volunteers a chance to steal away an epic win for new coach Lane Kiffin at Bryant-Denny Stadium.

But, oh, *how* the Crimson Tide won was what made the cigars blaze brightly into the Tuscaloosa night in 2009. Massive senior nose tackle Terrence Cody stole the moment with not one, but two

Javier Arenas

At 5'9", they said he was too small to play Division I college football. Numerous schools bet that Alabama made a mistake in offering him a scholarship—his next best offer was from Florida Atlantic.

Javier Arenas not only proved them wrong but was on the field more than any of his teammates, both as a return specialist and as a starting defensive back—something else he supposedly couldn't do.

"He is an outstanding competitor," Coach Nick Saban said. "You talk about a guy who's a perfectionist, works really hard every day to be the best he can be."

From 2006 to 2009, he played in 52 games and scored eight touchdowns—seven punt returns, one interception—to finish one shy of the NCAA record set by Notre Dame's Allen Rossum (1994–97). One of the most dynamic players in Alabama history, he returned 125 punts for 1,752 yards, second in NCAA history behind Texas Tech's Wes Welker (2000–03), and combined with his 90 career kick returns for 2,166 yards (24.1 avg.) is the only college football player to ever amass over 1,500 punt return yards and 2,000 kickoff return yards in his career.

He also notched 154 tackles, including 17.5 for a loss and seven sacks, and six interceptions. Eventually, opponents started giving Arenas the ultimate compliment when they deliberately started going away from him and challenging other defenders.

Arenas silenced his critics once again when the Kansas City Chiefs took him in the second round of the 2010 draft.

"Just consistency and being mentally tough," Arenas said. "Being physically tough has never been a problem for me. Just never taking a play off. In each and every thing that I do, I'm trying to max out at 100 percent.

"If a guy catches a ball and I knock it, that's not even good enough. I want to have it bounce off his foot and I grab it for a pick. Punt return, not drop any balls. My job is to catch the ball, look it in, and make a play."

blocked field goals, including Tennessee's 44-yard attempt with four seconds remaining to preserve the dramatic 12–10 victory.

"For the whole team, this was a big win," said Cody, who didn't face Tennessee the previous year due to a sprained knee. "We knew they were a tough team. They have real good players over there and a good coaching staff. We knew we had to come in strong and it was going to be tough. We had to grind all day."

That's because the Crimson Tide didn't quite play like its top ranking for much of the game, squandering numerous chances throughout, but most notably the final six minutes and 31 seconds following senior Leigh Tiffin's 49-yard field goal to go up 12–3.

Tennessee went three-and-out, but when trying to kill the clock sophomore running back Mark Ingram Jr. lost the first fumble of his career, with the ball stripped and recovered by All-American safety Eric Berry with 3:39 remaining.

"I made a mistake that could have cost us dearly," Ingram said.

Alabama's pass defense then buckled, allowing Tennessee to go 43 yards on eight plays to score the only touchdown of the day. To make matters worse, the Volunteers (3–4, 1–3) perfectly executed the subsequent onside kick with Denarius Moore recovering for first-and-10 at the UT 41 with 1:19 left.

Yeah, it was that close, with Kiffin calling it "A difficult loss to deal with," and Nick Saban saying, "It shows you, you talk about how fragile a season is."

"I'm really proud of our players," Saban said. "I didn't want to say this, but I felt like our team was really tired this week psychologically, probably more mentally than really physically. We had a lot of guys beat up, a lot of guys missed practice, and a lot of guys struggling to do what we need to do, but there are a lot of positives in this game today."

Still, it was more than just another memorable chapter in the "Third Saturday in October," rivalry, with the teams going toe-to-toe from the start. Julio Jones had seven receptions for 54 yards while Ingram quietly pounded out 99 yards on 18 carries (5.5 average), many out of the wildcat formation.

It set the Crimson Tide up for a big second half, yet Tennessee managed to turn the tables and played Alabama-type football against it. Thanks to a 13-play drive that went forward 50 yards and then backward 20, the Vols ate up 7 minutes and 49 seconds of the third quarter, followed by a 12-play possession.

Cody blocked that attempt from 43 yards.

"He'll be remembered for that, and many other things," senior linebacker Cory Reamer said.

Tennessee ended up outgaining Alabama 341 to 256, and had an edge in time of possession of 32:18 to 27:42, but still it came down to that one last memorable play—sort of.

"I just dove and me and Kareem [Jackson] collided and I blacked out," said senior cornerback Javier Arenas, who made 13 tackles despite playing with sore ribs. "I was sitting on the ground and I didn't know if they made it or not. All I saw was crimson jumping. Before the snap was probably the worst feeling I've ever had in my whole entire life because of what we did to put ourselves in our position."

Jones had an easier summation of the block.

"Ball game," he said.

47 Billy Neighbors

Lineman Billy Neighbors was a freshman at the Capstone when he and all of the other football players were suddenly called to a meeting with the new coach of the Crimson Tide, Paul W. "Bear" Bryant.

Paul Crane

Although Paul Crane was a center and linebacker, he was named Southeastern Conference Lineman of the Year in 1964 and a unanimous All-America selection at center in 1965 when Alabama defended its national championship. Crane was a captain of the 1965 team, and Alabama went 28–4–1 during his career. He spent seven years with the New York Jets and was on the Super Bowl champion team of 1968 along with Joe Namath. He was voted Most Popular Jet in 1970. He returned to the Capstone in 1974 to serve as an assistant coach and was an assistant at Ole Miss from 1978 to 1981.

"Coach [J.B. 'Ears'] Whitworth was the coach when I was being recruited, although Pat James was the coach who actually recruited me," Neighbors told sportswriter Tommy Hicks for the Alabama edition of the *Game of My Life* book series. "In that meeting, he told us that if we all stayed there and did what he told us to do, we would win a national championship.

"We thought he was crazy."

Actually, they had good reason to think that. Alabama had won just 14 games the previous five seasons combined, which prompted school officials to lure Bryant away from Texas A&M.

Neighbors had grown up in Tuscaloosa and, in addition to idolizing the Crimson Tide, his older brother, Sidney, was on the team as well, so his recruitment from Tuscaloosa County High School had been extremely easy for the previous coaching staff. But even he needed a wake-up call.

"I wasn't doing too well in school my freshman year, and my second semester, matter of fact, I wasn't doing anything," Neighbors said. "I was cutting classes. So Coach Bryant asked me to eat lunch with him, and man, I was scared to death because I knew I had a problem, but I didn't know why he was mad. To tell you the truth I didn't think he knew what kind of grades I was making. He had the dean of the school with him, and I went and sat down with them. He introduced me to the dean, and we started talking. He pulled out my IQ and pulled out how many classes I'd cut, and boy, I didn't look up, I just kept my head down. Coach Bryant said, 'Look up at me, boy, I'm talking to you.' So I looked up, and he said to the dean, 'Now this boy right here can help us win, but if he doesn't start getting better grades, he isn't going to be here.' The dean started talking about the classes I'd taken, what I should take, and all this stuff, and Coach Bryant said, 'Well, I'm going to give him one more semester. I'm going to move him into my house with me, and I'm going to do him like I do Paul Jr. when he comes home with a C; I'll beat him with a damn dictionary.' So, I got straightened out real fast."

Although Sidney Neighbors didn't last, Billy did and was one of just nine freshmen out of the 108 players who did "stick it out." Not only did he become Alabama's first All-American since 1954, but Bryant proved to be correct when Alabama won the national title in 1961.

Neighbors was a key cog in the championship season, when the defense yielded a total of just 25 points, never gave up more than seven points in a game, and shut out six opponents. His career concluded with the Crimson Tide having finished in the top 10 nationally all three years, and he was named both the top lineman in the Southeastern Conference and the most valuable in the Senior Bowl.

As an offensive lineman in the National Football League, Neighbors played eight seasons with the Patriots and Dolphins, and in the 1963 AFL All-Star Game.

48 1964: Namath Stopped Short

The 1963 season had been turbulent for the Crimson Tide. Quarterback Joe Namath was suspended for the final two games for violating the team's no-drinking policy, and, after accepting an invitation to play in the Sugar Bowl, Coach Paul W. "Bear" Bryant compared his team's chances against Ole Miss as being the same as it snowing in New Orleans.

The next day, Alabama awoke to find the city covered in the white stuff, which obviously drastically changed the dynamics of the game. Although the Tide didn't reach the end zone, it didn't need to. The defense made six fumble recoveries and three interceptions to more than offset the Rebels' statistical advantage of 248 yards to 194. Tim Davis' four field goals, of 31, 46, 22, and 48 yards, led to a 12–7 victory, and for the first time in Sugar Bowl history a kicker was named game MVP.

Namath had earned a fresh start in 1964, when Alabama was ranked sixth in the preseason Associated Press poll, but four games into the schedule he sustained a knee injury against North Carolina State that would limit him for the rest of the year. Steve Sloan replaced him and led victories against Florida, Tennessee, Mississippi State, and LSU. But against Georgia Tech in Atlanta, Namath entered the scoreless game late in the second quarter. By halftime, it was 14–0, en route to a 24–7 victory.

When Namath had a similar performance against Auburn on Thanksgiving Day, with a touchdown pass to end Ray Perkins along with Ray Ogden's 108-yard kickoff return sparking a 21–14 victory, his legendary status really began to take hold. Of course, the undefeated (10–0) record didn't hurt, either.

1964: 10–1, National Champions, SEC Champions

Date	Opponent	Location	W/L	Score
September 19	Georgia	Tuscaloosa	W	31–3
September 26	Tulane	Mobile, Ala.	W	36–6
October 3	Vanderbilt	Birmingham, Ala.	W	24–0
October 10	North Carolina State	Tuscaloosa	W	21–0
October 17	Tennessee	Knoxville, Tenn.	W	19–8
October 24	Florida	Tuscaloosa	W	17–14
October 31	Mississippi State	Jackson, Miss.	W	23–6
November 7	LSU	Birmingham, Ala.	W	17–9
November 14	Georgia Tech	Atlanta, Ga.	W	24–7
November 26	Auburn	Birmingham, Ala.	W	21–14
January 1, 1965	Texas	Orange Bowl	L	21–17
				250–88

Coach: Paul W. "Bear" Bryant
Captains: Joe Namath, Ray Ogden
Ranking (AP): Preseason—No. 6; Postseason—No. 1.
All-American: First team—Wayne Freeman, guard; Dan Kearley, defensive tackle; Joe Namath, quarterback; David Ray, halfback. Second team—Mickey Andrews, back. Academic—Gaylon McCollough, center.
All-SEC (first team): Steve Bowman, back; Wayne Freeman, guard; Dan Kearley, defensive tackle; Joe Namath, quarterback; David Ray, end.
Leaders: Rushing—Steve Bowman (536 yards, 106 carries); Passing—Joe Namath (64 of 100, 757 yards); Receiving—David Ray (19 catches, 271 yards).

Combined with Notre Dame's loss to Southern California, Alabama vaulted to No. 1 in the final Associated Press poll (voted before the postseason) and received an invitation to face Texas in the first Orange Bowl played at night.

Namath again was the spark plug off the bench, completing 18 of 37 passes for 255 yards and two touchdowns. However, in the closing seconds, Alabama was down 21–17 and had the ball inches away from the goal line. The call was a quarterback sneak behind center Gaylon McCollough, who, with the snap, plowed into the end zone. One official signaled touchdown, but another overruled. Namath said afterward, "I'll go to my grave knowing I scored."

Guard Wayne Freeman, tackle Dan Kearley, and halfback/kicker David Ray were named to various All-America teams (back Mickey Andrews was second-team) along with Namath, who for the season completed 64 of 100 passes for 757 yards but was not a consensus selection. Of course, he went on to have a prolific career in the National Football League and is enshrined in the Pro Football Hall of Fame.

49 Go Bowling

One of the best things about being a Crimson Tide fan is that Alabama's season almost always concludes with a bowl appearance, ranging geographically from California to Florida. It isn't by coincidence. Not only does the Tide have one of the most successful programs in college football, but its fans travel as well as, if not better than, everyone else. Consequently, bowl officials all but foam at the mouth when Alabama is mentioned for a potential invitation because of the lucrative ticket sales.

Through the 2015 season, when the Crimson Tide became the first repeat playoff team, Alabama led the NCAA with 64 bowl/playoff game appearances, including a record 37 victories (but not a vacated win in the Cotton Bowl).

Not surprisingly, there have been numerous memorable moments, such as in 2006 when massive freshman left tackle Andre Smith took a lateral and scored a two–yard touchdown run (really, would you want to try and stop him?), and the 1954 Cotton Bowl when no one remembers that Rice's Dickie Moegle set an all-time bowl record with 24.1 yards per rush, but everyone knows that

Tommy Lewis jumped off the bench in the middle of a play to tackle him.

Incidentally, Alabama lost both of those games. Some of the more positive bowl milestones (that can't be found elsewhere in this book) include:

- Alabama set the NCAA record, which will never be broken but has been tied numerous times, by allowing no passing first downs against Texas A&M in the 1942 Cotton Bowl. However, the Tide also set the record for fewest first downs recorded, one, which was tied by Arkansas against LSU in the scoreless 1947 Cotton Bowl. Alabama won by the remarkable final score of 29–21.
- The Tide's 55-point victory against Syracuse in the 1953 Orange Bowl (61–6) was the largest margin of victory in NCAA bowl history.
- Paul W. "Bear" Bryant took the Tide to a school-record 24 consecutive bowl games, from 1959 to 1982, of which 17 were on New Year's Day. Bryant also played in the 1935 Rose Bowl.
- Ray Perkins played in and coached six bowl games. He caught at least one touchdown pass in all three bowl games as a player, and from three different quarterbacks—Joe Namath, Steve Sloan, and Kenny Stabler. He was 3–0 in bowl games as a coach.
- Tailback Sherman Williams set the NCAA bowl record with 359 all-purpose yards in the 24–17 victory against Ohio State in the 1995 Florida Citrus Bowl. He accumulated 166 rushing yards, 155 receiving yards, and 38 yards on kickoff returns. He scored the game-winning touchdown with less than a minute to play on a pass from Jay Barker.
- Three coaches were undefeated in bowl games, Wallace Wade (2–0–1), Perkins, and Dennis Franchione (1–0). Mike DuBose participated in five games as a coach and a player, and was winless in all five, three as a coach.

- Alabama didn't beat its most common bowl opponent, Texas, until the BCS title game at the end of the 2009 season (1–4–1), and didn't defeat Notre Dame (1–2) in the postseason until the 2012 BCS National Championship.

Tommy Brooker

When it came time to piece together his display case as part of the Alabama Sports Hall of Fame's Class of 2009, Tommy Brooker didn't have much he could contribute. There was no old jersey in a frame or helmet in storage, so he wrote "Bama, No. 1 team in the nation" on the one item he could donate, a cheek cushion from his Riddell helmet.

Still, it was the most personal item placed next to a photo of Brooker shaking hands with Joe Namath after playing the New York Jets; a pictorial collage of the 1960 game against Auburn when he scored the only points in the 3–0 victory; a letterman's jacket; and "Coach Bryant's Football Family," a team photo of the 1961 national champions.

"This is probably the ultimate," he said. "It's a dream come true."

The Demopolis, Alabama, native was an honorable mention All-American, but an Academic All-American, and always thought of himself as more than a kicker. For example, during his AFL rookie season he caught four passes for the Dallas Texans (before the franchise became the Kansas City Chiefs), three for touchdowns—including a 92-yard hookup with quarterback Len Dawson at Denver.

Brooker, who founded the Alabama A Club Educational & Charitable Foundation in 1968, also broke George Blanda's record for consecutive extra points. He never missed one during his five years as a pro, making all 149. His most famous kick came in the famous 1962 AFL championship when he made a 25-yard field goal in double overtime, then the longest game in pro football history at 77 minutes and 54 seconds, to beat the Houston Oilers 20–17.

"The conditions were awful and nobody in the huddle was saying a word," he said. "They were just looking at me and standing there, and I looked up to them and said, 'Don't worry baby, it's all over.' I was a brash young rookie. I looked at it this way, kicking was just another play for me."

Under Nick Saban the Crimson Tide became the first program to pull off a "grand slam," winning a national championship in each of the four major title-game venues during the BCS era, the homes of the Rose (2009 season), Sugar (2011), Orange (2012) and Fiesta (2015) bowls.

50 Dr. George Hutcheson Denny

At no other school does football transcend the boundaries of a field or stadium like Alabama. According to the *ESPN College Football Encyclopedia*, "Perhaps no program has meant as much to the identity, even the self-esteem, of its home state as Alabama."

That was, in part, by design.

Dr. George Hutcheson Denny was born in the Hanover, Virginia, courthouse in 1870, the son of a Presbyterian minister. He earned his bachelor's and master's degrees at Hampden-Sydney College, received his PhD from Virginia, and was president at both Hampden-Sydney and Washington and Lee before arriving at the Capstone. His published works include *The Subjunctive Sequence after Adjective and Substantive Predicates and Phrases* and a collegiate edition of *Cicero's Letters.*

Football at Washington and Lee, a liberal arts school in Lexington, Virginia, dated back to 1873, when the Generals faced Virginia Military Institute in the first game ever played in the South. The program had some of its greatest success when Denny was president, and it peaked shortly after his departure. From 1912 to 1915, Washington and Lee went 31–3–1, and the 1914 team coached by Jogger Elcock went undefeated (9–0) while outscoring opponents 324–12.

It would be another 20 years before the Generals won another Southern Conference title, and Washington and Lee currently plays in Division III.

When Denny was hired as Alabama's president in 1912, he was a visionary in that he saw football as a tool to build enrollment and gain notoriety. At the time, the campus had just 652 students and nine principal buildings.

Denny, a massive football fan, was personally involved in the hiring of coaches, including Thomas Kelly, Xen Scott, Wallace Wade, and Frank Thomas. During his reign, the roots of the program's success were firmly entrenched, including the building of a 12,000-seat football stadium on campus. George Hutcheson Denny Stadium (now known as Bryant-Denny Stadium) opened in 1929.

During Denny's reign, Alabama won four national championships, made four trips to the Rose Bowl (without a loss), captured four Southern Conference championships, and was a founding member of the Southeastern Conference, winning its first title in 1933.

Today, one can't go anywhere on campus without seeing Denny's influence, or at least something named in his honor. In the

1936

Although it wasn't ranked in the first-ever Associated Press poll, released October 19, 1936, Alabama did make a title run that year and finished unbeaten. Led by guard Arthur "Tarzan" White, fullback James "Bubber" Nesbit, and quarterback Riley Smith, the Crimson Tide outscored its first three opponents, 73–0, and then sputtered. A 0–0 tie with Tennessee in Birmingham, in which it had first down at the Volunteers' 1-yard line when time ran out in the first half, cost it both the Southeastern Conference championship and a bowl appearance. In the final AP poll, Alabama (8–0–1) finished fourth. Incidentally, former Alabama player Paul W. "Bear" Bryant joined the staff that year as an assistant coach for Frank Thomas.

heart of the Capstone is Denny Chimes, which serves as Alabama's key landmark and was dedicated in 1929. Starting in 1948, team captains would have the honor of their names, handprints, and footprints set in concrete around the bell tower on the Walk of Fame.

However, Denny's success also helped bring about his departure from his post. Disputes with both the state legislature and student faculty contributed to his resignation after a quarter century of growth.

When he left in 1936, Alabama boasted more than 5,000 students and 23 major buildings, which still form the central core of the modern campus. Considered one of the most distinguished educators of the South, Denny died in 1955.

51 1926: Back to the Rose Bowl

In 1925 Alabama was not the first choice of the selection committee to play in the Rose Bowl, but it proved worthy by pulling off a 20–19 upset of Washington to win its first national championship.

A year later, many wondered if it could possibly do so again, especially after being thrust into the national spotlight by being the first Southern team to play in the high-profile game.

Although standouts Pooley Hubert and Johnny Mack Brown had moved on, Alabama continued to discredit its naysayers and critics with another undefeated regular season that included six shutouts. The only close game was a 2–0 victory against Sewanee decided by a blocked punt that went out of the end zone.

Led by All-Americans Fred Pickhard and Hoyt "Wu" Winslett, along with All–Southern Conference backs Herschel Caldwell and

1926: 9–0–1, National Champions, Southern Conference Champions

Date	Opponent	Location	W/L	Score
September 24	Millsaps	Tuscaloosa	W	54–0
October 2	Vanderbilt	Nashville, Tenn.	W	19–7
October 9	Mississippi State	Meridian, Miss.	W	26–7
October 16	Georgia Tech	Atlanta, Ga.	W	21–0
October 23	Sewanee	Birmingham, Ala.	W	2–0
October 30	LSU	Tuscaloosa	W	24–0
November 6	Kentucky	Birmingham, Ala.	W	14–0
November 13	Florida	Montgomery, Ala.	W	49–0
November 25	Georgia	Birmingham, Ala.	W	33–6
January 1, 1927	Stanford	Rose Bowl	T	7–7
				249–27

Coach: Wallace Wade
Captain: Emile "Red" Barnes
All-American: First team—Hoyt "Wu" Winslett, end; Fred Pickhard, tackle.
All–Southern Conference: Emile Barnes, back; Herschel Caldwell, back; Gordon Holmes, center; Fred Pickhard, tackle; Hoyt Winslett, end.

Emile Barnes, and center Gordon "Sherlock" Holmes, the Crimson Tide outscored its regular-season opponents 242–20. Similar to the previous year, the Southern Conference championship came down to a season-ending showdown with Georgia, and for the third straight year Alabama left with the title in tow—thanks to a convincing 33–6 Thanksgiving victory.

This time, Alabama didn't have to wait for Rose Bowl officials to first ask a host of East Coast powers to make the trip to play on January 1, 1927. Alabama was the clear and obvious choice, and eager for an opportunity to both defend its accomplishments and prove that the previous year was not a fluke. Again, the hopes of the South rested on the men from Tuscaloosa, who were, not surprisingly, considered underdogs.

On the opposing side was Stanford, coached by the legendary Glenn "Pop" Warner, who had already made quite a name for himself and boasted the West Coast's finest team that season. Jack James of the International News Service wrote the following in reference to Stanford's 13–12 victory against Southern California: "Football followers of this vicinity cannot forget the bewildering deception, the concentrated power, the grim determination of the afternoon. And because they remember, they figure that Alabama, or any other ball club, would have to be just short of super-human to deny a repetition of that attack."

Alabama was outplayed, but Stanford could never put the game away. In the closing minutes, the Crimson Tide scored a touchdown for a 7–7 standoff and 9–0–1 record. Pickhard was selected MVP of the Rose Bowl, and the game was the first transcontinental radio broadcast of a sporting event on NBC.

Because most services at the time held their final rankings at the conclusion of the regular season, both teams, along with Lafayette College and Navy, had already been declared national champions by at least one organization prior to the game—Alabama's second title.

52 No Wardrobe Is Complete without Houndstooth

In 1975, when the Crimson Tide celebrated the 50-year anniversary of the original Rose Bowl victory, Alabama opened with a 20–7 loss to Missouri but allowed only 52 points the rest of the season to win the Southeastern Conference title.

With the conference having reached an agreement for its top team to annually play in the Sugar Bowl, which had been relocated

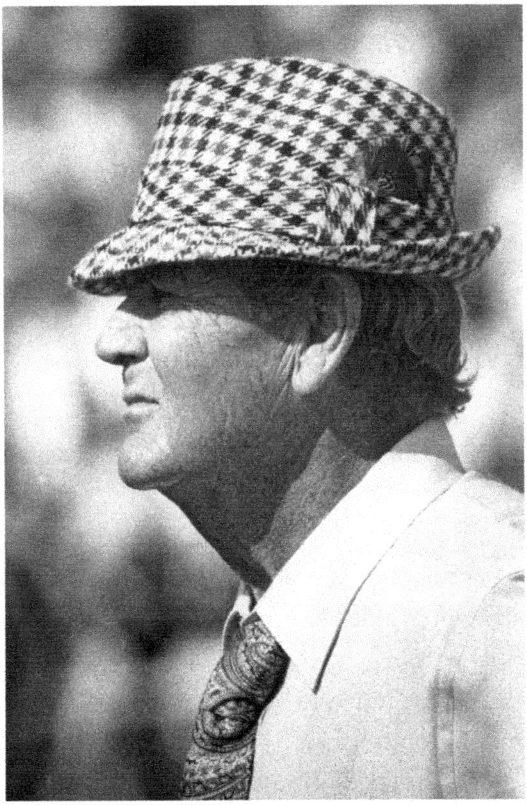

In terms of college football icons, one would be hard-pressed to find anything more popular or well known than Paul W. "Bear" Bryant's houndstooth hat. Now the design is a fashion staple on the Tuscaloosa campus.

to the Louisiana Superdome, Alabama would try to snap its eight-game winless streak in the postseason against Penn State and Joe Paterno.

The key play came in the fourth quarter, after Tide quarterback Richard Todd called a timeout.

"We had a sweep called to the left side, but I didn't like the defense they were in. I didn't want to take the chance of running a play," Todd said. "So I called time. I went over to the sidelines and Coach Bryant sort of winked at me. He called a pass."

Sophomore wide receiver Ozzie Newsome, who was already well on his way to a Hall of Fame career, ran a slant-and-go route and beat the single coverage for a 55-yard gain to set up the only touchdown of the game, an 11-yard sweep by halfback Mike Stock.

The Origin of the Houndstooth Tradition

Paul W. "Bear" Bryant was known for wearing hats on the sideline long before first being seen in his trademark houndstooth and there are numerous photos of him sporting a fedora. According to Ken Gaddy, director of the Paul W. Bryant Museum, Bryant started wearing the houndstooth hat after winning the 1966 Orange Bowl, when New York Jets owner Sonny Werblin tried to hire him away. Instead, they developed a friendship, and after being turned down Werblin sent a houndstooth hat. When Bryant started wearing it to games, Werblin kept sending new hats.

Alabama won 13–6, and Todd, who completed 10 of 12 passes for 205 yards, was named the game's most valuable player. But afterward, the most pressing question reporters had for Bryant wasn't about the timeout, Newsome's reception, or the fact that the No. 3 Tide would not move up and would remain third in the final polls.

They wanted to know why the coach didn't wear his trademark houndstooth hat.

"My mother always taught me not to wear a hat indoors," he replied, much to the delight of Crimson Tide fans everywhere.

Although Georgia has its bulldog mascot, Uga, and the conference has an overall abundance of iconic images ranging from Colonel Reb (now retired) to Arkansas's Tusk, a 380-pound Russian boar, none may be as prevalent as Bryant's houndstooth hat, which is as much of a staple on the Tuscaloosa campus today as when the coach was dominating college football in the 1960s and 1970s.

In terms of coaching headgear, perhaps only Tom Landry's fedora comes close, and Steve Spurrier's trademark visor would have to be considered a very distant third. But overall, there's never been a stronger fashion statement in sports, including Tiger Woods's baseball-style cap and red shirts on Sundays, Bum Phillips's cowboy hat, and Jim Brown's skullcap.

In addition to wearing a replica houndstooth hat to games, many fans have made the black-and-white checkerboard design a part of their year-round wardrobe, including shirts, jackets, scarves, skirts, coats, purses, gloves, shoes, belts, and even pants.

In 2006 Alabama wore special commemorative crimson jerseys with a houndstooth trim on the collars against Ole Miss to honor the 25th anniversary of Bryant's 315th win (the Tide won in overtime).

Also, the Bryant Museum has a specially made Waterford crystal replica of Bryant's houndstooth hat on display along with the real thing.

53 Johnny Mack Brown

If one title best exemplified Johnny Mack Brown both on and off the playing field, it would have to be "leading man."

As a back, he helped propel Alabama to its first conference title in 1924 and to the Rose Bowl a year later for one of the most important football games in region history.

Down 12–0 at halftime, Coach Wallace Wade changed his offensive strategy, which worked and led to three touchdowns in the third quarter, including two touchdown receptions by Brown. The first was a 59-yard catch from Grant Gillis (although how far the pass actually traveled remains unknown because statistics weren't precise), with the other a 30-yard pass.

With Brown making a clutch open-field tackle of Washington standout George "Wildcat" Wilson in the waning moments, Alabama held on for a dramatic 20–19 victory.

"Johnny Mack Brown has the sweetest feet I have ever seen," the head linesman was quoted as saying. "The way he managed to elude Washington tacklers in his long runs was marvelous. He has a weaving elusive style that is beautiful to watch."

Not only did the victory put Southern football on the map, but Alabama finished off a 10–0 season that included eight shutouts and claimed its first national championship.

For Brown, who was named the Rose Bowl's Most Valuable Player, the trip to Pasadena also gave him a glimpse into his future as one of the first collegiate standouts to seriously pursue a career as an actor in motion pictures. He went on to become one of Hollywood's most popular western stars.

Brown had numerous minor roles until 1930, when he was cast as the lead in director King Vidor's *Billy the Kid*, one of the earliest widescreen films. That same year, he played Joan Crawford's love interest in *Montana Moon*, and he later was paired with Greta Garbo and Norma Shearer. He was being groomed by MGM to be one of its feature headliners, but some studio executives didn't think his Southern accent was becoming of a Hollywood marquee

Joseph Flinn "Joe" Kilgrow

Joe Kilgrow could pretty much do everything in football, and he proved it against Mississippi State in 1936 when he faked a punt and ran 83 yards for a touchdown and made the extra point to score the only points in the game. Kilgrow was best known as a halfback, but he did most of the passing and punting as well and played safety on defense—rarely coming off the field.

During his three years, Alabama compiled a 23–3–2 record, during which he was named an All-American as a senior in 1937 and finished fifth in Heisman Trophy voting.

Kilgrow was also a standout baseball player. He played two seasons for the Crimson Tide and coached at both Mercer and Alabama.

attraction. He was replaced on a film in 1931, with all of his scenes reshot with Clark Gable.

However, Brown's love for football seemingly never diminished, and in 1934 when the Crimson Tide returned to Pasadena to play Stanford, he served as an advance scout for the team and provided information on players, formations, and game plans. Alabama dominated, 29–13, to win its fourth national title.

Brown's acting career spanned four decades, and he appeared in more than 160 movies in addition to a few television shows. Consequently, he was given a star on the Hollywood Walk of Fame at 6101 Hollywood Boulevard.

54 Family Traditions

There are legends of Alabama football, and there are *legends.*

Bully Van de Graaff definitely fits into the latter, and in many ways into a category all of his own. Not only was he the Crimson Tide's first All-American, but also the first Southerner to be named an All-American by both Parke Davis and Walter Camp, whose annual lists of honorees had been dominated by players from the Northeast.

There were three reasons why it sometimes seemed like Van de Graaff was everywhere on the field.

1) He was a terrific player.

2) Not only was he a tackle on both the offensive and defensive sides, Van de Graaff was also Alabama's kicker and punter.

3) He wasn't alone.

In 1912, Alabama had the unusual distinction of having three Van de Graaff brothers playing at same time: Bully, back Adrian, and end Hargrove, who hailed from Tuscaloosa. Their love for the game came from their father, Adrian Van de Graaff Sr., who was a sub on Yale's first 11-man football team in 1880.

In their collegiate debut together, Adrian and Hargrove both scored touchdowns against Marion Institute, while Bully saw playing time.

Hargrove was the team captain in 1913 when the game against Tennessee turned into the program's first unofficial night event.

Robert Van de Graaff

Although Robert Van de Graaff's name isn't nearly as recognized in Tuscaloosa as his brother Bully's, he had a profound effect on how we all live our lives today.

In 2004 there was a dinner at the Jemison–Van de Graaff Mansion in honor of the 75th anniversary of Robert's atomic generator. The keynote speaker was 87-year-old L. Worth Seagondollar, who worked on the famous Manhattan Project.

"He's the guy who physically built the bomb that was dropped on Hiroshima," mansion manager Jim Young told *The Tuscaloosa News.* "What he talked about was the importance of the Van de Graaff accelerator in determining what the nucleus of plutonium was in regard to how they would cause the explosion. They were only able to do that using the Van de Graaff accelerator.

"And he said if we hadn't had the Van de Graaff accelerator or generator, the war would have lasted a whole lot longer. It would have taken hundreds of thousands of additional lives, not only United States soldiers but Japanese as well. The bomb killed 185,000 Japanese, but many times more would have been killed if the troops on Okinawa and in the east would have made the invasion into Japan."

Robert's influence as a scientist and inventor didn't end with the war or at Princeton University. In 1946, he started his own company, the High Voltage Engineering Corporation. The beam-control techniques it developed made possible the manufacture of microchips by shooting atoms into silicon, laying the foundation for the Computer Age.

Due to a number of injuries, play lasted past sunset and spectators with automobiles were asked to encircle the Tuscaloosa field and turn on their headlights so it could continue. Alabama held on for a 6–0 victory, marking the seventh straight shutout against the Volunteers, who remembered Bully more than the lighting problems, and not because he made Alabama's two field goals that day.

"His ear had a real nasty cut and it was dangling from his head, bleeding badly," Tennessee lineman Bull Bayer said. "He grabbed his own ear and tried to yank it from his head. His teammates stopped him and the managers bandaged him. Man, was that guy a tough one. He wanted to tear off his own ear so he could keep playing."

Bully was an all-conference selection in 1914, and played through 1915, when he received the All-American honors. The 23–10 victory over Sewanee was the Crimson Tide's first against the Southern power since 1894, and not only did Van de Graaff score 17 of Alabama's 23 points, but he also had a 78-yard punt.

Alabama wouldn't have three brothers playing on the same team together again until 2004 with the Britts: linemen Wesley, Taylor, and Justin. During that season the program's family tree read like a depth chart, with three sets of brothers, one set of cousins, one third-generation player, and nine second-generation players.

On some college football teams, they all would be splintered into factions like Scottish clans, fighting amongst themselves for influence. That's not the way things work in Tuscaloosa.

"You kind of look at your teammates as kind of like your brother," junior quarterback Brodie Croyle said. "I'm sure there's something different with the Britt clan and the Castilles, but everyone on this team is tight. After everything that we've been through, we're going to be a close-knit team."

Croyle's legacy at the Capstone includes his father, John (defensive end, 1971–73), sister Reagan (basketball, 1994–98), and brother-in-law John David Phillips (quarterback, 1995–98).

That's a lot of people to answer to—on top of teammates, coaches, students, and fans—but Croyle didn't even lead the team in family predecessors that year. Wide receiver Matt Miller's grandfather Floyd lettered as a tackle (1948–49), his father Noah was a linebacker (1973), and oldest brother Marc was a linebacker and strong safety (2001–02).

"Growing up with the family, [we] loved Alabama football and its tradition," Matt Miller said. "Everyone hears about the tradition, but I lived it."

So did fullback Tim and cornerback Simeon Castille. Their father Jeremiah was an All-American defensive back and the most valuable player of Coach Paul W. "Bear" Bryant's last game at the Liberty Bowl. He's still involved with the program as UA's Fellowship of Christian Athletes director.

Younger bother Caleb was a walk-on player who ended up trying his hand at acting. In 2015 he starred in the independent movie "Woodlawn," the inspirational true story of former Alabama and NFL star Tony Nathan, who became the first black football superstar at Woodlawn High School in Birmingham in 1973–74 in the midst of racial turmoil as the school integrated.

On the 2004 team, brothers Freddie and Will Roach were the half-brothers of assistant director of football operations, Tim Bowens. Todd Bates and Tyrone Prothro were cousins. The second-generation players included David Cavan, Clint Johnston, Evan Mathis, Spencer Pennington, Mark Saunders, and Jake Wingo. Mathis' uncle is Bob Baumhower.

For many, the decision to play at Alabama was an easy one, even if family members didn't push them during recruiting.

"There was never any doubt," said Cavan, a tight end whose father Pete was a Crimson Tide running back (1975 to 1977). "You want to try and leave your options open, but I could never see myself going anywhere else."

55 The First Game

In the beginning, there was football.

Okay, there wasn't. But for such a rabid fan base, the question "What came first, the school or the football team?" might cause some of the Crimson Tide faithful to pause.

Obviously, the answer is the University of Alabama, which existed for decades without football, with dedication ceremonies held in 1831 (well before the first college football game was played between Rutgers and Princeton in 1869). At the time, the university consisted of seven buildings and 52 students.

It wasn't until 1892, the year before the first two women enrolled (no cheerleader jokes, please), that football arrived at the Capstone. Student William G. Little had been introduced to the game as a high school student at Phillips Exeter Academy in New England. The death of his brother brought him back to his home state of Alabama to help his family. Once enrolled at the University of Alabama, he collected a group of students to form a team to play the new sport.

At the time, the game was actually a hybrid of soccer and rugby and better resembled an organized riot compared to what football is today. Uniforms were basically a heavy sweater (which would have been nearly impossible—or at least extremely uncomfortable—to wear in the summer months due to the heat and humidity), padded pants, and no helmets.

Little was named the first team captain, and E.B. Beaumont the coach. Because the sport was still virtually unknown in the South, opponents were scarce, but the Birmingham Athletic Club boasted a team made up of former college players from the Northeast.

E.B. Beaumont

E.B. Beaumont was Alabama's first coach and thus the first person to get fired from the job. When William G. Little organized the first football team on the Capstone in 1892, he was named the first captain, with Beaumont, who had become somewhat familiar with the sport at the University of Pennsylvania (although that may essentially mean that he had seen the game played) named coach. This was a little unusual because many of the first coaches were also players.

Beaumont lasted one season and was replaced by Eli Abbott.

Said the Corolla in its first year as Alabama's official yearbook: "We were unfortunate in securing a coach. After keeping him for a short time, we found that his knowledge of the game was very limited. We therefore got rid of him."

However, because Alabama wanted a trial run, or preseason if you will, it first scheduled a practice game against a collection of high school athletes from the Birmingham area. On November 11, 1892, Alabama won its first game, 56–0, against the self-proclaimed Birmingham High School team. It then lost the next day 5–4 to the Birmingham Athletic Club.

A local newspaper described the winning play, a drop-kick by J.P. Ross, who had played rugby in Ireland, as follows: "Just as the Birmingham enthusiasts were beginning to despair of a victory, Ross made a clean kick of sixty-five yards which was the most brilliant feat ever witnessed in a match game. The crowd set up cheer after cheer and his admirers gathered him on their shoulders and paraded him around the grounds."

A month later, much-improved Alabama—which, unlike the much-burlier club team, could practice daily—came back and won the rematch, 14–0. It was described as a "battle royal" and "Waterloo for Birmingham," with Beaumont called "one of the best football coaches in America."

Alabama played one final game that inaugural season, in February of that same school year, against state-rival Auburn. Even back then it was not just another opponent. Fans covered the Caldwell Hotel with red and white banners in support of Alabama.

It didn't help. Auburn won at Lakeview Park in Birmingham, 32–22.

56 The First Player Drafted to Play in the NFL

Riley Smith was a fullback on the 7–1–1 team in 1933, but switched to quarterback the following year when Frank Thomas's team went 10–0, handily defeated Stanford in the Rose Bowl, 29–13, and won the national championship.

Even though the 6'1", 195-pound All-American led impressive victories against Georgia and Tennessee his senior year, and handled kicking duties, Smith also won the Jacobs Trophy as the Southeastern Conference's best blocker.

On February 8, 1936, the National Football League held its first draft at the Ritz-Carlton in Philadelphia, where Jay Berwanger, the first Heisman Trophy winner, from the University of Chicago, was the first-overall pick by the hometown Eagles. Only Berwanger reportedly wanted $1,000 a game, an unheard-of sum then, and didn't sign with either the Eagles or the Chicago Bears after they traded for his rights.

Smith was selected second by the Boston Redskins.

"I signed because I wasn't ready to quit playing ball," Smith told the Professional Football Researchers Association in 1983. "I just wanted to keep playing. I signed for $250 a game and a little bonus. We won the Eastern Division championship twice and the NFL championship once in the three years I played and the most I ever got was $350 a game. I made more money in the offseason.

"I quit in 1938 and took a coaching job at Washington and Lee for a lot more money. But we had it good because some of those fellas down in Philadelphia were playing for $60 and $70 a ball game."

Incidentally, only 24 of the 81 players selected in that initial draft were on National Football League rosters that season. Four more signed the following year, and three opted for the American Football League. Because the substitution rules were different, and players had to play both offense and defense, rosters were limited to 25 players. But still, almost a third of the players were rookies, the majority of whom signed as free agents.

"That's about right for that time," Smith said. "There wasn't any money in [the NFL] so people didn't go in and if they did they didn't stay long."

Smith himself had a short career in the NFL before being sidelined by an injury. In his first year, he helped turn the Redskins from the second-to-last team in the league to Eastern Division champions in 1936. Despite the team's success, lackluster fan support prompted owner George Preston Marshall to host the title game at the Polo Grounds in New York (where the Redskins lost to the Green Bay Packers) and then move the franchise to Washington, D.C.

With the sixth-overall selection in the 1937 draft, the Redskins selected TCU quarterback Sammy Baugh, who would revolutionize the passing game through 1952. In the first home game at Griffith Stadium in Washington, D.C., Smith scored on a 58-yard interception return, two field goals, and an extra point to lead a 13–3 victory. The Redskins went on to win their first championship, defeating the Chicago Bears 28–21 in the title game.

During the 1936–37 seasons, Smith missed only three minutes in 26 Redskins games. In 1939, he served as an assistant coach at Washington and Lee and was promoted to head coach

Alabama's Draft History

It was pretty much assumed when Nick Saban landed at Alabama that the Crimson Tide would essentially become the premier program for potential NFL players, but no one quite expected what happened in the 2011 draft.

While defensive lineman Marcell Dareus and wide receiver Julio Jones were early picks as expected, running back Mark Ingram Jr. was a late selection, and tackle James Carpenter was taken before most expected at No. 25 by the Seattle Seahawks, giving Alabama a program-record four first-round selections.

Previously, Alabama had three first-round selections in both 1993 (John Copeland, Eric Curry, and George Teague) and 1948 (Harry Gilmer, Lowell Tew, and Vaughn Mancha). It also came just three years after the Crimson Tide didn't have a player selected in the draft for the first time in three decades.

"Every time my phone rang and rang and rang it was me, this is my turn," Dareus said after being the third-overall selection by the Buffalo Bills. "I can't explain the way I felt."

Jones went just a few minutes later at No. 6, when after a day of rampant rumors the Atlanta Falcons moved up from No. 26 and in exchange gave the Cleveland Browns their first-, second-, and fourth-round picks in 2011, plus their first and fourth in 2012.

Ingram had a much longer wait, and was flirting with falling out of the first round, but wound up in the same division as Jones, the NFC South. After New Orleans passed on him at No. 24, when it addressed its biggest defensive need, it traded up to snare Ingram at No. 28—the same pick the New York Giants used to take his father in 1987.

When ESPN read an emailed statement from Mark Ingram Sr., who was serving time for bank fraud and money laundering, the emotional 2009 Heisman Trophy winner choked up and said, "I want to tell my dad I love him. I miss you, dog."

A year later, Alabama had four first-round selections again, running back Trent Richardson (No. 3, Cleveland), safety Mark Barron (No. 7, Tampa Bay), cornerback Dre Kirkpatrick (No. 17, Cincinnati), and linebacker Dont'a Hightower (No. 25, New England).

in 1940–42, before serving as a lieutenant commander during World War II.

Incidentally, Alabama had another high pick in that initial draft, Paul W. "Bear" Bryant by the Brooklyn Dodgers in the fourth round. He never played in the league and instead went into coaching.

57 1978: Split Title with USC

Alabama's near-miss for the 1977 national title, when the Crimson Tide finished second in both the final Associated Press and coaches' polls, served as prime motivation the following season. However, if Alabama wasn't enough of a target for opponents after being ranked first in the preseason, the schedule was arguably the toughest to date in program history, with the Tide set to play Nebraska, Missouri, Southern California, Washington, Florida, Tennessee, Virginia Tech, LSU, and Auburn, followed by the presumably difficult bowl opponent.

The chances of finishing undefeated appeared slim, and sure enough Alabama did stumble after cruising through both the Cornhuskers, 20–3, (thanks in part to a 99-yard touchdown drive) and Missouri, 38–20.

When Southern California pulled out a 24–14 victory in Birmingham, it not only knocked Alabama from the top ranking but would come back to haunt the Tide some more.

Led by the defense, Alabama didn't suffer another setback, closing the regular season with a 34–16 victory against Auburn in the Iron Bowl. It set up what appeared to be a natural national championship game between No. 1 Penn State and No. 2 Alabama in the Sugar Bowl—a game they still regularly discuss in Tuscaloosa.

As the scoreless game approached halftime, Alabama was content to run out the clock when Penn State coach Joe Paterno called two timeouts in hopes of getting the ball back and taking a shot at some points. However, the strategy backfired when Tony Nathan broke a 30-yard run and quarterback Jeff Rutledge found

1978: 11–1, co-national champions, SEC champions

Date	Opponent	Location	W/L	Score
September 2	Nebraska	Birmingham, Ala.	W	20–3
September 16	Missouri	Columbia, Mo.	W	38–20
September 23	Southern Cal	Birmingham, Ala.	L	24–14
September 30	Vanderbilt	Tuscaloosa	W	51–28
October 7	Washington	Seattle, Wash.	W	20–17
October 14	Florida	Tuscaloosa	W	23–12
October 21	Tennessee	Knoxville, Tenn.	W	30–17
October 28	Virginia Tech	Tuscaloosa	W	35–0
November 4	Mississippi State	Birmingham	W	35–14
November 11	LSU	Birmingham	W	31–10
December 2	Auburn	Birmingham	W	34–16
January 1, 1979	Penn State	Sugar Bowl	W	14–7
				345–168

Coach: Paul W. "Bear" Bryant
Captains: Marty Lyons, Jeff Rutledge, Tony Nathan
Ranking (AP): Preseason—No. 1; Postseason—No. 1.
All-American: First team—Barry Krauss, linebacker; Marty Lyons, defensive tackle. Second team—Dwight Stephenson, center.
All-SEC (first team): Mike Brock, tackle; Jim Bunch, tackle; Wayne Hamilton, defensive end; E.J. Junior, defensive end; Barry Krauss, linebacker; Murray Legg, safety; Marty Lyons, defensive tackle; Dwight Stephenson, center.
Leaders: Rushing—Tony Nathan (770 yards, 111 carries); Passing—Jeff Rutledge (73 of 140, 1,078 yards); Receiving—Keith Pugh (20 catches, 446 yards).

split end Bruce Bolton for a 30-yard touchdown with eight seconds remaining.

An interception helped the Nittany Lions tie the game in the third quarter, but Alabama again took the lead on an eight-yard touchdown run by running back Major Ogilvie.

Penn State appeared to get a huge break with 7:57 remaining when Joe Lally landed on a misdirected pitch at the Alabama 19, and it wasn't long before the Nittany Lions were on the verge of tying the game, with third-and-goal at the 1.

Paterno decided he wanted to run it in, but the Tide defense refused to buckle. After the third-down play came up short, the call was a run up the gut by Mike Guman, who instead of barging into the end zone was stopped cold by first-team All-American linebacker Barry Krauss and the rest of the defense. Alabama held, but Krauss took the brunt of the collision and, after a few scary seconds from not being able to move, ran off the field under his own power.

Although Alabama went three-and-out on its subsequent possession, with the series-ending punt shanked, giving Penn State first down at the 30, the Nittany Lions were flagged for having too many men on the field. With a second chance, the Tide effectively drove down the field and ran out the clock. Meanwhile, the defense held Penn State to just 19 rushing yards.

With the impressive, and hard-hitting, victory, Alabama began celebrating Bryant's fifth national championship, only to be surprised by the final polls. As expected, the Tide was voted No. 1 by the Associated Press, but United Press International voters promoted Southern California up from No. 3—claiming the Trojans deserved to be ahead of the Tide after their regular-season victory, even though both teams had one loss. The result was a split national title.

58 Johnny Cain

The nickname went back to the 1930 season, when as a sophomore he was the only non-senior in the Crimson Tide's starting lineup. Whenever Coach Wallace Wade wanted Johnny in a game, all he had to do was yell out, "Hurry, Cain!"

"Hurri-Cain" was actually listed on the roster as the quarterback of Wade's swan-song season, when Alabama was a perfect 10–0, outscored the opposition 273–13, and won the national championship. The Crimson Tide was so deep that season that Wade occasionally started his backup players and then, just as the opposition began to wear down a bit, would bring in the fresh starters. The Rose Bowl against Washington State was one of those games, and Alabama crushed the Cougars, 24–0.

After Frank Thomas took over and installed his Notre Dame box formation, it took only one game for the new coach to move his only returning starter to fullback "because he is too modest to call his own signal," Thomas said.

Alabama's offense scored an average of 36 points per game and destroyed most of its opponents, including Clemson 74–7, Ole Miss 55–6, and Mississippi State 53–0. Following the 14–6 victory at Vanderbilt, Claude "Blinky" Horn wrote in *The Tennessean*: "Twas a savage struggle. Vanderbilt has encountered no rival which hit as hard as Alabama. Nor an enemy which tackled so surely. And so viciously."

At 9–1, which was the best coaching debut in Alabama history, the Tide's lone loss that season was 25–0 at Tennessee, which set up a punting showdown the following year between Cain and Volunteers standout Beattie Feathers (punts were considered more of a weapon during that time, and it wasn't uncommon for a coach

Hal Self

When most Alabama fans think of the War Baby Tiders, the first person who comes to mind is usually Harry Gilmer, but Hal Self was also a major force for Alabama during the years surrounding World War II. He helped pass, run, and throw the 1945 team to an undefeated season, and he scored two touchdowns against Southern California in the Rose Bowl.

Self is one of the few people in college football history to play in the Cotton, Orange, Rose, and Sugar bowls, and in 1946 he won the Southeastern Conference's Jacobs Trophy as the league's best blocker.

In 1949, Self began restoring the football program at Florence State, now known as the University of North Alabama, and coached there for 21 years. His teams went 109–81–8, including 13 winning seasons, despite usually playing bigger schools and with a one-person coaching staff of assistant George Weeks.

Self retired from coaching in 1969 to become the school's athletic director.

to call for a quick-kick on third down instead of risking a pass). Cain punted 19 times with an average of 48 yards, and Feathers punted 21 times, but Alabama lost, 7–3.

"John Cain is the best football player I have ever seen on a football field," Alabama line coach and 1924 All-American center Clyde "Shorty" Propst told Owen Merrick of the *San Francisco News.*

Cain and guard Tom Hupke were the last Crimson Tide players to earn All–Southern Conference honors. The following year Alabama would join the offshoot Southeastern Conference, known simply as the SEC. Cain and Feathers also finished tied for the conference lead in scoring at 72 points, even though Cain played one fewer game. At 8–2, the Tide didn't win the final Southern Conference championship but came close.

In his final game for Alabama, Cain's 71-yard touchdown run against St. Mary's in San Francisco—the Tide's first regular-season game on the West Coast—resulted in a 6–0 victory and served as a perfect way to top his career. He would later serve as Southwestern Louisiana's head football coach from 1937 to 1941, and he was athletic director at the same school from 1946 to 1947 before moving on to Ole Miss.

Zipp Newman, who covered Alabama football from 1913 to 1948, wrote, "He could run, block, punt, and play defense, the best all-around back I ever saw."

59 2012: Domination Secures Dynasty

There were roughly two minutes remaining in the game, and University of Alabama senior center Barrett Jones knew that the time was finally at hand. So he grabbed co-captain Damion Square and went for a Gatorade jug, while teammates formed a wall behind Coach Nick Saban.

They subsequently executed the dousing to perfection, which was fitting considering what the Crimson Tide had just done to Notre Dame—dominating from the start and crushing the previously unbeaten Fighting Irish in the BCS Championship Game 42–14.

"I'm not a really emotional guy, but I really enjoyed the moment," Jones said after Alabama won its 15th national title and second straight.

"It's been amazing. I just can't really put it into words right now."

That was a strong sentiment among teammates as well as they tried to put it into perspective what had been accomplished.

With the victory, Alabama become college football's first back-to-back consensus national champion since Nebraska in 1994–95, as well as the first school to win three national titles in the BCS era—nevermind in four years. Outside of the Cornhuskers, one had to go all the way back to Notre Dame in the late 1940s to find a comparison, and those Irish teams didn't play postseason games.

Saban also went from being the first coach to lift the crystal trophy a third time, to now enjoying the fourth (three at Alabama).

2012: 13–1 National Champions, SEC Champions

Date	Opponent	Location	W/L	Score
September 1	Michigan	Arlington, Texas	W	41–14
September 8	Western Kentucky	Tuscaloosa	W	35–0
September 15	Arkansas	Fayetteville	W	52–0
September 22	Florida Atlantic	Tuscaloosa	W	40–7
September 29	Ole Miss	Tuscaloosa	W	33–14
October 13	Missouri	Columbia, Mo.	W	42–10
October 20	Tennessee	Knoxville, Tenn.	W	44–13
October 27	Mississippi State	Tuscaloosa	W	38–7
November 3	LSU	Baton Rouge, La.	W	21–17
November 10	Texas A&M	Tuscaloosa	L	29–24
November 17	Western Carolina	Tuscaloosa	W	49–0
November 24	Auburn	Tuscaloosa	W	49–0
December 1	Georgia	SEC Championship	W	32–28
January 7	Notre Dame	BCS National Championship	W	42–14

Coach: Nick Saban
Captains: Barrett Jones, Damion Square, and Chance Warmack.
Ranking (AP): Preseason—No. 2; Postseason—No. 1
All-American: First team—Barrett Jones, center; Dee Milliner, cornerback; C.J. Mosley, linebacker; Chance Warmack, guard
Second team—D.J. Fluker, tackle
All-SEC (first team): Chance Warmack, guard; D.J. Fluker, tackle; Barrett Jones, center; Eddie Lacy, running back; C.J. Mosley, linebacker; Dee Milliner, cornerback
Leaders: Rushing—Eddie Lacy (1,322 yards, 204 carries); Passing—AJ McCarron (211 of 314, 2,933 yards); Receiving—Amari Cooper (59 catches, 1,000 yards)

In the modern era of the game, only Paul W. "Bear" Bryant (six) and Knute Rockne (five) had more national titles, and many of theirs weren't considered consensus.

It was also the Southeastern Conference's seventh straight championship while Alabama finally vanquished one of its demons, beating the nemesis that cost it the 1973 title among others indirectly.

"It's unbelievable; I really can't say anything," senior long-snapper Carson Tinker tried to explain.

"We wanted to do something no one else has done. I think we did we it tonight. Unprecedented. That's the word that's been in my head the last month or so."

Midway through the second quarter Notre Dame's bench was silent and stunned at the Crimson Tide's proficiency on both sides of the ball.

Notre Dame's defense had given up just nine points in the first quarter that season, and two rushing touchdowns; Alabama posted 14 on its first two possessions and reached the end zone a third time on its first play of the second quarter.

The Fighting Irish was thought to have the nation's best red-zone defense; the Crimson Tide scored touchdowns on all five possessions inside the 20.

Only one opposing running back had reached 100-rushing yards; junior Eddie Lacy had 96 in the first half including a show-stopping spin move into the end zone for an 11-yard touchdown reception.

Lacy finished with 140 rushing yards on 20 carries, and similar to Mark Ingram Jr. and Trent Richardson in the 2009 title game against Texas, the Crimson Tide had two 100-yard backs with freshman T.J. Yeldon finishing with 108 yards on 21 carries.

Destiny? Luck of the Irish? Alabama thumbed its zone at all that and then un-mercilessly squashed the previously unbeaten leprechauns. Notre Dame won the coin toss and nothing else.

"We said we're coming to take it, and we're not leaving here until we get it," junior tackle D.J. Fluker said.

When Alabama scored off the opening kickoff, the 82-yard possession was the longest the Irish had given up all season. The Tide followed with touchdown drives of 61 and 80 yards on its next two possessions, which made everything after that a formality.

"We want to be physical," senior guard Chance Warmack said. "That's our M.O. We want to be a physical team."

With Lacy, the offensive MVP, grinding away, it was almost unfair that the passing game was equally effective. Quarterback AJ McCarron completed 8 of his first 9 passes en route to a 20-of-28 and four-touchdowns performance, with and no interceptions or sacks. Consequently, Alabama finished with 264 passing yards and 265 rushing.

Up 28–0, McCarron found Amari Cooper for a 34-yard touchdown on Alabama's first possession of the second half and later on a 19-yard scoring pass to complete the scoring. The freshman wide receiver finished with six catches for 105 yards.

Meanwhile, led by defensive MVP C.J. Mosley, Alabama keyed stopping the run and ended up giving up just 32 yards, 20 on a single carry by Theo Riddick.

"I told (the defensive backs) they won't run the ball," Square said. "The only way they can win is to throw the football."

Redshirt freshman quarterback Everett Golson did lead Notre Dame on two second-half scoring drives, and completed 21 of 36 passes for 270 yards and one touchdown, but couldn't change the telling words being used to describe the game and Crimson Tide.

Like overwhelming, historic, and "dynasty," junior cornerback Dee Milliner offered.

60 The Kick

If you ask a University of Alabama football fan which game against Auburn is his or her favorite, there's a very good chance the answer will be the 1985 meeting, which was known simply for "the Kick."

"It was kind of a dream come true," Van Tiffin told WHNT in Huntsville in 2005.

"I've kidded with Van a lot about what would have happened if he didn't make it," center Wes Neighbors said.

Alabama was 7–2–1 that season, and Auburn had briefly reached No. 1 in the polls. Both teams had some big-time names on their rosters, including Cornelius Bennett, Jon Hand, Neighbors, and Mike Shula for the Crimson Tide, with the Tigers able to boast Tracy Rocker and Bo Jackson, who soon after won the Heisman Trophy.

Although Jackson was playing with two cracked ribs and wore a protective flak jacket, he had 142 rushing yards and two touchdowns. But the game went back and forth, with the lead changing hands four times in the fourth quarter alone.

Down 23–22, Alabama had one final chance with just 57 seconds remaining on the clock, and its initial efforts nearly resulted in a sack and interception. But on fourth-and-4, a sideline pass to running back Gene Jelks, who had 192 rushing yards, led to a first down and sparked the rally. That was followed by a reverse to junior college transfer Al Bell, who had scored the touchdown to complete a last-minute 20–16 comeback in the season opener against Georgia, for another 20 yards.

The key play, though, was to receiver Greg Richardson, who was barely able to get out of bounds at the Auburn 35 with just six seconds left.

"We had beaten Georgia in the last second and we were talking about it," Neighbors said. "Some offensive linemen, I think it was David Gilmore said, 'Hey, we've done this before. You know, let's win this game.'"

"I thought there was absolutely no way we'd get into field-goal range," Tiffin said. "But a couple big plays later, an end-around to Al Bell and that pass across the middle to Greg Richardson, a couple of great executed plays. The next thing you know we're in field-goal range."

Although Tiffin's career best was 57 yards earlier in the season against Texas A&M, a school record, this was the Iron Bowl, with everything on the line—and never before had the showdown come down to something like a 52-yard field goal, which he promptly drilled with room to spare.

"I didn't have a lot of time to get nervous about it," recalled Tiffin. "Auburn didn't call a timeout. We had just enough time to get the play off. It couldn't have worked out any better."

See a Game-Winning Field Goal

So how many times has Alabama scored a field goal in the final five minutes of the fourth quarter, or in overtime, to win a game? Just 13. Although the second game in school history was decided by a drop kick, the first player credited with doing so was Sandy Sanford in 1937, when his 41-yard field goal in the closing moments provided a 9–6 victory at Tulane. The most famous kick was by Van Tiffin, 52 yards to beat Auburn as time expired in 1985.

However, the only kicker to do it three times was Jamie Christensen, all during the 2005 season. His 31-yard field goal as time expired resulted in a 13–10 victory at Ole Miss, his 34-yard field goal with 13 seconds remaining beat Tennessee 6–3, and his 45-yard knuckler through the uprights was the difference at the Cotton Bowl, 13–10 against Texas Tech.

"A game like this, Alabama players will remember it for the rest of their lives," Tigers coach Pat Dye said afterward. "Auburn players, it'll eat their guts out the rest of their lives."

Actually, Tiffin did eventually finally find something to rattle his nerves at Alabama, when in 2006 his son Leigh walked on to the Crimson Tide as—you guessed it—a kicker. Leigh ended up setting career Crimson Tide records in scoring (385 points), field goals (83), and extra points (136).

61 Tyrone Prothro's Catch

It was September 10, 2005, and Alabama was struggling against Southern Miss, a team it frequently dominated even though the Golden Eagles were playing their first game of the season after the opener against Tulane had to be rescheduled due to Hurricane Katrina. Down 21–10 late in the second quarter at Bryant-Denny Stadium, and with the running game all but non-existent, the Crimson Tide was facing fourth down and 12 yards to go when it decided to go for broke and throw deep, figuring an interception would probably be no worse than a punt. Instead, wide receiver Tyrone Prothro made arguably the greatest catch in program history.

Words cannot accurately describe the play, but here's a valiant effort:

After quarterback Brodie Croyle uncorked the long ball down the middle of the field, Prothro was racing toward it and the end zone along with junior defensive back Jasper Faulk, who had near-perfect coverage. Even though Jasper was literally in Prothro's face, the receiver somehow reached around both sides of the defensive back with his arms and managed to catch the ball.

As the two tumbled head-over-heels into the end zone, Prothro still kept his grip with both hands, even though his right arm was also wrapped around Faulk's head and his left arm was reaching around the defender's right arm and shoulder.

It was initially ruled a touchdown, but the play was reviewed by the instant replay official, who correctly confirmed that it was a catch and that Prothro was down short of the end zone. Croyle quickly swung a pass to fullback Le'Ron McClain for the touchdown, and from then on it was all Alabama, which pulled out a 30–21 victory.

"That's the first time I've ever caught a ball like that," said Prothro, who had seven receptions in the game for 134 yards and 279 all-purpose yards, the sixth-best single-game performance in school history. "It was real big for us. Going on a drive, on their side, it's fourth down, we had to make a play."

What became know as "the Catch" was named the Pontiac Game Changing Performance of the Year, which snagged Alabama $100,000 for its scholarship fund. It also received an ESPY Award for Play of the Year. Prothro edged out Philadelphia Phillies

Paintings and Prints

It pretty much goes without saying that Alabama is always near the top of the list when it comes to collegiate merchandise sales, but an area mostly unique to Crimson Tide fans is that many of them have something team-related on their walls at home.

Alabama prints, paintings, and posters are a huge business and commemorate everything from a favorite player or coach to a spectacular play that was probably mentioned somewhere in this book ("the Sack," "the Kick," "the Goal-Line Stand," etc.). The number of Tuscaloosa restaurants and bars that don't have some sort of paraphernalia prominently displayed are few, and many decorate exclusively with Crimson Tide items.

outfielder Aaron Rowand's dramatic catch while slamming into the wall (FYI, the previous month he told team officials, "I want some padding on that fence because I'm going to run into it," but it had yet to be installed. Rowand broke his nose), Nathan Vasher of the Chicago Bears returning a missed field goal for a touchdown against San Francisco, New York Mets infielder David Wright's over-the-shoulder bare-handed catch, and Reggie Bush's touchdown for Southern California against Washington.

However, many Crimson Tide fans became even more emotional when they saw Prothro, one of the most beloved and exciting players in Alabama history, limp up to the stage to accept his ESPY after sustaining a horrific career-ending leg injury against Florida. After spending weeks in the hospital due to complications, including his leg becoming infected following surgery, it was the first time most people had seen Prothro since he had been carted off the field October 1.

Prothro kept his acceptance speech short: "This says a lot. I just want to thank God, my family, my coaches and my teammates, my pastor, and, last but not least, the fans. Thank you."

62 The 41-Year Feud

When people mention the word *feud* in the state of Alabama, there's no doubt about the reference, and it has nothing to do with a game show.

Alabama vs. Auburn dates all the way back to 1893 and is so intense that among the many legendary anecdotes is that a local television station refused to interrupt the 2000 game for the results of the presidential election recount announcement.

But the "Iron Bowl" had a 41-year gap, from 1908 to 1947, when the schools refused to play each other. Although there are numerous misconceptions about the causes, both sides agree that it had nothing to do with a rumored fight that broke out after the 6–6 tie in 1907. Instead, the spark was something that occurred on the field and spilled over into other areas.

In winning the 1906 game 10–0, Alabama used an offensive formation that Auburn coach Mike Donahue thought was illegal. Specifically, Tide coach Doc Pollard unveiled the Military Shift, which was described as every player except the center lining up on the line of scrimmage and joining hands, but then turning right or left to form an unbalanced line.

Donahue was so upset with the formation, which had never been seen before in the South (Pollard learned it at Dartmouth), that he threatened to cancel the series.

A year later, Pollard used a similar formation, the "Varsity Two-Step," which infuriated Auburn so much that it demanded that the next game be officiated by a referee from outside of the South. Alabama thought the idea ridiculous.

Additionally, a debate over the per diem for players and referees was heating up and proved to be the impetus for the split. Auburn wanted to have 22 players on the roster, and the money per player increased from $2 to $3.50. Alabama wanted just 20 players for $3 each.

The sides argued for months, but by the time a compromise had been reached both schedules were already in place for 1908. Alabama suggested playing after Thanksgiving, which was rejected by Auburn's Board of Trustees. Attempts to revive the series in 1911, 1919, 1932, and 1944 all failed. In fact, the schools stopped playing each other in all sports.

In 1948 the debate on whether to renew the series finally came to an end after state legislators threatened to get involved despite objections from Alabama athletic director Frank Thomas and other

The Hatchet Site

Prior to the first Alabama vs. Auburn game in 40 years, the 1948 student body presidents, Willie Johns and Gillis Cammack, participated in a symbolic "burying of the hatchet" ceremony at Woodrow Wilson Park in Birmingham.

"There were a lot of hard feelings between the students," Auburn's Cammack told *Sports Illustrated* years later. "We were trying to get everyone to settle down and not be so vicious."

Woodrow Wilson Park has undergone several renovations and is now called Linn Park, but the burial site is not marked.

Said Cammack, "I doubt if that hatchet stayed buried very long."

school officials, who believed nothing could be gained by playing a team that had never finished better than third in the Southeastern Conference.

Citing problems, including brawls and other incidents, at rivalry games in Texas, Minnesota, Louisiana, Georgia, South Carolina, Maryland, Kansas, and Tennessee, the school's Committee on Physical Education and Athletics report argued, "We hazard nothing in saying that the game would not make a single constructive contribution to education in the state." It concluded, "The fundamental question is: Do the people of Alabama need a tranquil, sane kind of athletics in their two major institutions, or an irrational rabid kind?"

Although Auburn claims to the contrary, Alabama athletic department notes and documents clearly show that the school was concerned about state representatives threatening to hold back funding to force the football game. Among the final decisions was the neutral-site location, with Birmingham selected over Montgomery and Mobile.

With 46,000 in attendance, and another 2,000 at the Birmingham Armory enjoying a pay-per-view broadcast, Alabama won 55–0.

63 Visit Legion Field

When construction began in 1926, plans were for west-side stands, a press box, and a small seating area on the east side, for a capacity of 21,000 at a cost of $439,000. Legion Field, named in honor of the American Legion, a U.S. organization of military veterans, hosted its dedication game on November 19, 1927, with Howard College (now Samford University) defeating Birmingham-Southern College, 9–0. Alabama's first game there was a week later, a 20–6 loss to Georgia.

Although the stadium, dubbed by Paul W. "Bear" Bryant as the "Old Grand Lady," became the home for UAB games—in addition to the Southwestern Athletic Conference championship, the annual Alabama A&M–Alabama State showdown, and high school games—its most memorable moments were from Alabama games, as the Crimson Tide used to hold most of its marquee contests there instead of Tuscaloosa. Not only was it a larger venue, it was in the state's biggest city—which also happened to be home to many of the program's biggest boosters (not to mention recruits).

In addition to hosting the Iron Bowl from 1948 to 1998, with Alabama and Auburn splitting tickets each year, it was the site of Bryant's 315th career victory, when he became the winningest coach in college football.

The first two Southeastern Conference championship games were held in Birmingham, which is also the home of the conference headquarters, and both games featured the Tide.

On December 5, 1992, the SEC became the first Division 1-A league to stage a title game between its division winners, when Alabama defeated Florida 28–21. Cornerback Antonio Langham's 27-yard interception return for a touchdown earned him MVP

Andrew Zow and Tyler Watts

Although the two had a quarterback controversy, they guided the Crimson Tide offense from 1998 to 2002 and combined to pass for more than 8,000 yards.

Andrew Zow took over the starting job as a freshman in 1998, and his 1,969 passing yards were the seventh most in Alabama history. However, his signature game was one of his last, against rival Auburn. With Santonio Beard (199 yards) and Ahmaad Galloway (127) both exceeding 100 rushing yards, Zow replaced injured Tyler Watts and completed 22 of 29 passes for 221 yards and two touchdowns, to help lead a 31–7 victory.

Zow passed for 5,983 yards during his college career.

As a senior, Watts and Brodie Croyle became the first quarterback combo to each pass for more than 1,000 yards in a season. Watts completed 112 of 181 passes for 1,414 yards, and helped lead the Tide to a 10–3 record.

honors, and the Tide went on to defeat Miami in the Sugar Bowl to win the national championship.

A year later, the teams rematched, with Florida pulling out a 28–13 victory. The title game subsequently moved to the Georgia Dome in Atlanta.

Alabama's last football game at Legion Field was also Mike Shula's debut as the Tide's coach. Alabama won 40–17 and left the stadium with an all-time record of 160–52–12, including a 32–15 mark against Auburn.

Legion Field was the home of the Hall of Fame Bowl from 1977 to 1985, before it relocated to Tampa, Florida, and was renamed the Outback Bowl. It also hosted the Dixie Bowl (1947–1948) and the All-American Bowl (1986–1990).

In 2006 the inaugural PapaJohns.com Bowl, formerly known as the Birmingham Bowl, was played on December 23 and featured South Florida vs. East Carolina, with the Bulls winning 24–7.

The "Football Capital of the South" has also been the home to numerous other football ventures, including the Birmingham Americans and Vulcans of the World Football League (1974–1975), the Alabama Vulcans of the American Football Association (1979), the Birmingham Stallions of the United States Football League (1983–1985), the Birmingham Fire of the World League of American Football (which became NFL Europe) in 1991–92, the expansion Birmingham Barracudas of the Canadian Football League, and the Birmingham Thunderbolts of the XFL (2001).

Finally, Legion Field was a prominent soccer venue, and a host site for the 1996 Olympic Games, with the opening match between Argentina and the United States drawing 83,810 fans to set the stadium attendance record. However, when the field switched from natural grass to an artificial surface, U.S. Soccer no longer considered it a viable location, and when the upper deck was removed due to structural damage, capacity dropped to 71,594.

64 Attend A-Day (If You Can Get In)

When the team buses were pulling up to Bryant-Denny Stadium on April 21, 2007, players already had a good idea that they were in for something special.

Not only was the traffic worse than anything they had ever seen before in Tuscaloosa, but scores of fans were already waiting for them—and to get their first glimpse of Nick Saban at the helm of the Crimson Tide.

"I made a comment to Rashad [Johnson] that maybe Florida or Tennessee was in town," senior defensive end Wallace Gilberry quipped at the time. "It was definitely a sight for sore eyes, but it was a good sight. My hat goes off to the fans who made the trip. I hope they liked what they saw."

Although the atmosphere was similar to a high-profile regular-season game, it was simply to watch A-Day, the final of 15 practices to conclude spring workouts, which has become a major event all of its own. Coming in, school officials expected maybe 50,000 fans to show, and planned for a record-breaking 60,000, but like the players were pleasantly blown away by the volume.

Before long, people were being turned away at the gate by the hundreds, if not thousands, because Bryant-Denny Stadium had exceeded its capacity of 92,138. Inside, the lower bowl filled up first, followed by the western upper deck, the contingency northern upper deck, and finally the eastern deck, which was supposed to remain empty. Fans didn't care if they could find an empty seat or not. They kept pouring in, and the lone single-file line went from section to section until finally all the stands were full, not to mention the ramps while taking advantage of the shade.

"I thought it was awesome," quarterback John Parker Wilson said.

"It's ridiculous," cornerback Simeon Castille added. "I never could have imagined that there would be that many people, but it made it more fun for both teams. We just wanted to go out there and show how hard we've been working."

Even Saban called it a "Special Day."

"It shows what kind of passion and support we have at the University of Alabama," Saban said. "It certainly makes me feel great about being here as the coach. I just hope we can continue to channel all that energy in a positive way so we can get to where we want to go and continue to build this program into something special."

Only it was really just the beginning. The A-Days following Saban's arrival were the most attended in Alabama history, and it's not even close. Whereas the previous record was 51,117 in 1988,

92,310 fans came out in 2011 after another stadium expansion was unveiled.

The amazing thing was that in 1998 it attracted just 8,968 fans. When Paul W. "Bear" Bryant was coaching the biggest attendance recorded was 20,000 in 1972.

"Even in Coach [Gene] Stallings' day players and coaches may have thought it was just another practice," said Ken Gaddy, director of the Paul W. Bryant Museum. "It wasn't the event it is now."

Instead, A-Day has become the museum's busiest day of the year, with more than 5,000 people paying to walk through and see the exhibits, and the economic impact to the community similar to that of a home game in the fall. According to university's 2009-2010 Economic Impacts report that was published in October 2011, that's roughly $23.2 million.

Such are the benefits of being a national football powerhouse.

"They were supportive from the start and when we weren't so good," Saban said about the fans. "I think that was something that really contributed to recruiting. The first A-Day, it was really heartfelt by the Sabans. It really made us feel welcome here. We had gone through some tough times in getting here, leaving Miami and all that. So we really appreciated that.

"I think it sent a message to a lot of people and a lot of people that we're interested in recruiting, too, that there was a lot of positive energy and attitude for what can be accomplished at the University of Alabama, with the program that we were trying to establish. That positive energy that the crowd shows and has shown for years here and the support that they have shown for our players and our team, has contributed tremendously to our success in recruiting as well as the success that we've had on the field."

Barrett Jones, the 2011 Outland Trophy winner as college football's best interior lineman, was there in 2007, and the large crowd made a huge impression. He ended up signing on for the recruiting Class of 2008, which was one of the best in college football history. Each successive big crowd brought similar rewards and added to the program's impressive momentum.

"It was exciting," linebacker Nico Johnson said about attending A-Day as a prospect. "Witness something like that, it was amazing.

"Going through that, I was speechless, having that many people here, just for a spring game. That was unreal."

65 Don Whitmire

When Don Whitmire played tackle at Alabama in 1941–42, he was a mere 5'11" and 215 pounds—yet he played one of the most brutal positions on the football field.

That first season, the Crimson Tide visited Miami for the first time and defeated the Hurricanes 21–7 in the season finale to earn an invitation for the Cotton Bowl, where Alabama beat Texas A&M, 29–21. Despite a 9–2 record, the Tide was able to claim at least a share of the national championship—its fifth title.

In 1942 one of the Crimson Tide's losses was to Georgia Pre-Flight, a military institution featuring players from around the country—an important foreshadow for Whitmire's career. At the end of the season, Alabama returned to Miami to face Boston College in the Orange Bowl.

Facing a 14–0 deficit, Whitmire was one of the players leading the comeback as the Crimson Tide won 37–21. Fittingly, he shared the game's most valuable player honors with his ball-carrying teammates.

Whitmire made only one All-America list that season, but he was a consensus All-American in 1943 and 1944 for another team, Navy, which was able to recruit players from other college football programs due to a wartime exemption (incidentally, Alabama couldn't field a team in 1943 due to World War II). Rip Miller, Navy's line coach, recruited Whitmire after seeing his photo in *Street & Smith's* football annual.

The Clemson Connection

When Frank Howard left his hometown of Barlow Bend, Alabama, for the Capstone, where he had an academic scholarship, he said he was "walking barefoot on a barbed-wire fence with a wildcat under each arm." After lettering three years as a guard in football and also in baseball, he headed to Clemson in 1931.

"My first title was line coach, but I also coached track, managed ticket sales, recruited players, and had charge of equipment," Howard said. "In my spare time I cut grass, lined tennis courts, and operated the canteen while the regular man was out to lunch."

Over the space of 30 years he compiled a record of 165–118–12 before taking over as athletic director.

Danny Ford, an All-SEC tackle for the Crimson Tide, eventually followed. After nine years as an assistant at Alabama and Virginia Tech, he made his debut as a head coach facing Ohio State in the 1978 Gator Bowl, the final game for Woody Hayes. The 30-year-old Ford's team won 17–15.

"When Coach Ford was named coach at Clemson, there were mixed emotions," Clemson player Jeff Davis said. "It was obvious that he had so many things to offer, and what he lacked he made up for in working harder than anyone else and communicating his expectations to the players. He blossomed as well as any coach could."

In 1981 Clemson began the season unranked but won the national championship after defeating Nebraska in the Orange Bowl, 22–15. At the age of 33, Ford became the youngest coach to win a national title.

Dabo Swinney, a walk-on player on the Crimson Tide's 1992 national championship team, nearly brought Clemson its second title in 2015, but ran into his alma mater in the National Championship Game, a dramatic 45-40 victory for the Crimson Tide.

Under the direction of Coach Billick Whelchel, the Midshipmen went 8–1 in 1943, with the lone loss to national champion Notre Dame, 33–6. With Oscar Hagberg taking over the program the following year, Navy went 6–3, including a season-ending 23–7 defeat to national champion Army, but the Washington Touchdown Club awarded Whitmire the Rockne Trophy as the nation's best lineman.

In the four years he played college football, Whitmire's teams compiled a 31–9 record.

Whitmire made an even bigger mark in the military after rising to the rank of brigade commander, the highest rank a midshipman can attain at the Naval Academy.

He eventually became a rear admiral in the U.S. Navy and directed the evacuation of Saigon at the end of the Vietnam War in 1975, which was the largest evacuation in world history, with 82,000 men, women, and children escaping.

"Football taught me the virtue of team play and enhanced my leadership qualities," Whitmire said when he was elected into the College Football of Fame. "These traits have been most valuable in my Navy career. Football taught me to take hard knocks and come up fighting."

66 The 1965 National Title

In 1965 Alabama was coming off a controversial national championship in which the Crimson Tide had finished the regular season undefeated and had already been voted No. 1 in the final polls before narrowly losing to Texas in the Orange Bowl, 21–17.

Consequently, the Associated Press decided that for the first time in its history it would hold the final vote after all the bowl games had been played instead of at the conclusion of the regular season (though this change did not become permanent until 1969).

Amazingly, this worked to Coach Paul W. "Bear" Bryant's advantage again, but it sure didn't seem that way on September 18, when Alabama opened the season with an 18–17 loss at Georgia thanks to a disputed call in which the Bulldogs scored the

1965: 9–1–1, National Champions, SEC Champions

Date	Opponent	Location	W/L	Score
September 18	Georgia	Athens, Ga.	L	18–17
September 25	Tulane	Mobile, Ala.	W	27–0
October 2	Ole Miss	Birmingham, Ala.	W	17–16
October 9	Vanderbilt	Nashville, Tenn.	W	22–7
October 16	Tennessee	Birmingham, Ala.	T	7–7
October 23	Florida State	Tuscaloosa	W	21–0
October 30	Mississippi State	Jackson, Miss.	W	10–7
November 6	LSU	Baton Rouge, La.	W	31–7
November 13	South Carolina	Tuscaloosa	W	35–14
November 27	Auburn	Birmingham, Ala.	W	30–3
January 1, 1966	Nebraska	Orange Bowl	W	39–28
				256–107

Coach: Paul W. "Bear" Bryant
Captains: Steve Sloan, Paul Crane
Ranking (AP): Preseason—No. 5; Postseason—No. 1.
All-American: First team—Paul Crane, center; Steve Sloan, quarterback. Second team—Steve Bowman, fullback. Academic—Dennis Homan, end; Steve Sloan, quarterback.
All-SEC (first team): Steve Bowman, fullback; Paul Crane, center; Creed Gilmer, defensive end; Bobby Johns, defensive back; Tommy Tolleson, split end.
Leaders: Rushing—Steve Bowman (770 yards, 153 carries); Passing—Steve Sloan (97 of 160, 1,453 yards); Tommy Tolleson (32 catches, 374 yards).

game-winning touchdown on a play the receiver should have been ruled down.

The Tide stumbled again on October 16 after young quarterback Kenny Stabler moved Alabama into scoring range late in the game only to throw the ball away on fourth down when he mistakenly thought it was third down (which is what the Legion Field scoreboard indicated), resulting in a 7–7 tie with Tennessee.

But those would be the only blemishes in an otherwise remarkable season. For example, against Mississippi State in Jackson, Mississippi, Bryant surprised the Bulldogs by calling the tackle-eligible play, having Jerry Duncan move off the line of scrimmage to make him able to receive a legal reception.

After defeating LSU 31–7 and Auburn 30–3, Alabama (8–1–1) was ranked No. 4 behind Michigan State (No. 1), Arkansas (No. 2), and Nebraska (No. 3), with seemingly no way to leapfrog all three and defend its title.

Or so it seemed to everyone but Bryant.

Instead of accepting an invitation to play in the Cotton Bowl, Bryant agreed to face Nebraska in the Orange Bowl. His thinking was that if Michigan State lost to UCLA in the Rose Bowl and Arkansas was defeated by LSU in the Cotton Bowl, the Orange Bowl would determine the national champion.

That's exactly what happened.

Despite being outsized, Alabama outgained Nebraska 518 to 377 yards, and Bryant's squads successfully executed both the tackle-eligible play and more than one onside kick in completing a masterful 39–28 victory.

Although Ray Perkins had nine catches for 159 yards, quarterback Steve Sloan was named the game's MVP and, along with center/linebacker Paul Crane, an All-American. All-SEC selections were fullback Steve Bowman, Crane, defensive end Creed Gilmer, defensive back Bobby Johns, and split end Tommy Tolleson.

As Bryant foresaw, when the final Associated Press poll was released, the top five were:

1. Alabama
2. Michigan State
3. Arkansas
4. UCLA
5. Nebraska

In contrast, the final coaches' poll, conducted before the bowls, read:

1. Michigan State
2. Arkansas
3. Nebraska
4. Alabama
5. UCLA

Incidentally, Bryant joined Minnesota's Bernie Bierman (1940–41), Army's Earl "Red" Blaik (1944–45), Notre Dame's Frank Leahy (1946–47), and Oklahoma's Bud Wilkinson (1955–56) as the first coaches to win back-to-back national titles.

67 Marty Lyons

It's pretty much assumed that whenever an athlete or a coach is selected to be enshrined into a particular hall of fame, he or she gets to make an acceptance speech.

That's not true for the College Football Hall of Fame. On the night when a new class is celebrated only one person is chosen to speak on behalf of everyone, because when there are 15 or more individuals being honored it would otherwise go on for several hours.

So when former Alabama defensive tackle Marty Lyons was asked to participate in the announcement of the Class of 2011, and ring the NASDAQ opening bell in Times Square, he didn't hold back and choked up when talking about Crimson Tide fans shortly after the April 27 tornado struck Tuscaloosa.

"Right now they're going through a difficult time in their life with the devastating tornado," he said during the press conference in New York on May 17, 2011. "But come December 6, I'm going to put them all on my back and we're going to get inducted into the College Football Hall of Fame."

He was just as emotional on September 3, 2011, when the Crimson Tide hosted Kent State at Bryant-Denny Stadium in its first game since the storm. Because it was the only weekend Lyons could attend a home game that season, it was coincidentally when the school in conjunction with the National Football Foundation (NFF) and College Football Hall of Fame held the traditional on-campus salute.

"It's truly an honor that you cherish for the rest of your life," Lyons said. "You work so hard in college with your teammates and the coaching staff to accomplish what we did for four years at the University of Alabama, it's truly an honor. I accept on behalf of the university, on behalf of my teammates, on behalf of the coaching staff down there. If it wasn't for them and the fans, this probably wouldn't have happened.

"In 1975 I was an outsider, I was a stranger to Alabama. Now I call Alabama my home. I live in New York, but Alabama is where I started. The fans embraced me."

Lyons grew up in Pinellas Park, Florida, and attended St. Petersburg Catholic High School before heading to Tuscaloosa. He was named All-SEC as a junior in 1977 and led the Crimson

John and Brodie Croyle

John Croyle was a standout defensive end for Coach Paul W. "Bear" Bryant who helped lead the 1973 Crimson Tide to the national championship and was a second-team All-American. However, instead of pursuing a career in the National Football League, Croyle opted to open Big Oak Ranch, a home for abused and neglected children just outside of Gadsden, Alabama.

His son, Brodie, became a quarterback who had the honor of wearing No. 12 and broke most of the school passing records despite a couple of scary moments along the way, like against Western Carolina in 2004 when he blew out a knee on a play—where he didn't take a hit—by planting his foot.

"I was just going to the sideline," he said. "I went to plant and my knee just went out. This isn't how I imagined it happening, but I've been through it before and I'll start over again."

Croyle completed 488 of 869 passes for 6,382 yards with 41 touchdowns and 22 interceptions, good for a 128.4 rating—the yards, completions, attempts, and touchdowns all career Tide records. His 2,499 passing yards in 2005 set the single-season mark but was broken the following year by John Parker Wilson's 2,707.

Unlike his father, Brodie didn't pass on the NFL, and he was selected in the third round of the 2006 NFL Draft by the Kansas City Chiefs. A year later, he made his first pro start and was still wearing No. 12.

Tide in tackles in 1978, when he earned first-team All-American honors and was a co-captain of the national championship team.

He was also part of the goal-line stand in the Sugar Bowl against Penn State, and when Nittany Lions quarterback Chuck Fusina walked up to the line of scrimmage to see how far the ball was from the goal line Lyons supposedly warned him: "You'd better pass."

However, Lyons arguably had his best game in the 1978 Iron Bowl when he had 16 tackles and three sacks to help lead a 34–16 victory against Auburn. For his career he was credited with 202 tackles, six forced fumbles, and four recoveries, while Alabama went 31–5 with two SEC championships to go along with the 1978 national title.

Lyons was subsequently selected in the first round (14th overall) of the 1979 NFL Draft and spent his full 12-year career with the New York Jets, appearing in 147 games over 11 seasons. Along with Mark Gastineau and Joe Klecko he helped form the "New York Sack Exchange," which led the league in sacks in 1981. He was credited with 45 career sacks and for giving Buffalo quarterback Jim Kelly "the business," which was how referee Ben Dreith famously described the personal-foul penalty.

In 1982 he established the Marty Lyons Foundation to improve the quality of life and grant wishes for terminally ill children in nine different states. Two years later, he was named the NFL's Man of the Year, an honor that has since been renamed the Walter Payton Man of the Year Award.

The Senior Vice President of Operations at the LandTek Group, Inc. in Amityville, New York, was initially told of his selection over the phone by NFF President & CEO Steve Hatchell, and said the two of them spent 20 minutes thanking one another.

"You're overwhelmed with emotions, first," Lyons said was his initial reaction. "You thank the Good Lord for surrounding you with good people your entire life. You start to look back at and think about everyone who was instrumental your football career and in your life, starting with your parents, your siblings and your high school coach, and all your teammates that you had in high school. Maybe they weren't good enough to play in college, but they enabled you to become a better athlete and a better person.

"Of course, going to the University of Alabama and playing for Coach [Paul W.] Bryant, you never realize just what kind of influence he would have on your entire life. He wasn't just a great coach he was a great teacher, and a person that I truly loved. Coach Bryant meant the world to me."

It wasn't lost on Lyons that he was about to share college football's highest honor with his former coach. It also didn't seem that long ago when Bryant said while recruiting him, "I can't promise anything if you come to the University of Alabama, all I can promise you is an opportunity. If you're good enough to play the opportunity will be here."

It certainly was.

"You're proud to stand alongside Coach Bryant, but everyone who has gone in underneath that family of Crimson Tide, it's truly a great fraternity to be a part of," Lyons said.

68 Tommy Lewis' Tackle

The 1953 season was one of the most unusual in Alabama history, even though the Crimson Tide won the SEC championship.

Despite three ties, against LSU, Tennessee—which was the first televised home game, with Alabama alum Mel Allen announcing along with Volunteers alum Lindsey Nelson—and Mississippi State, it was Alabama's first conference title in eight years, thanks to a narrow 10–7 victory over Auburn in the Iron Bowl.

Consequently, an invitation was extended to play Rice in the Cotton Bowl, which featured a play remembered much longer than the 28–6 final score. With Alabama already down 7–6, Owls halfback Dickie Moegle broke through the line at the Rice 5, and by the time he was racing past the Crimson Tide sideline it was apparent a touchdown was imminent.

Kennedy's Reverse

On December 6, 1961, President John F. Kennedy attended the Hall of Fame dinner in New York City to honor Alabama's national championship team, as the Crimson Tide had already been voted No. 1 in the final Associated Press poll before it would beat No. 9 Arkansas in the Sugar Bowl, 10–3. Kennedy was made an honorary Crimson Tide letterman, and he's still on the school's all-time list.

However, a year later, after Alabama defeated Oklahoma in the Sugar Bowl, 17–0, Kennedy visited Oklahoma coach Bud Wilkinson, who was on his physical fitness council, but not the Crimson Tide locker room. Many saw it as a snub due to the increasingly hot issue of racial integration.

Alabama was a state Kennedy won against Richard Nixon in the 1960 presidential election. It may be a coincidence, but since then the only Democrat to carry the state was Jimmy Carter in 1976.

Only fullback Tommy Lewis, who had been sitting on the sideline with the other offensive players, stepped on to the field and drilled the startled Moegle.

As if coming out of a daze, Lewis returned to the bench, where he stayed for the remainder of the second quarter, and covered his head with a towel behind stunned Coach Red Drew (who would resign a year later with a career 54–28–7 record after an unimpressive 4–5–2 season) while fans booed.

Referee Cliff Shaw ruled that Moegle should be credited with a touchdown, and at halftime Lewis went to Rice's locker room to apologize.

"I saw him coming a long way off," Lewis said after the game. "The nearer he got to me, the nearer I moved to the field. I don't know what happened. I couldn't realize that I had done it when I returned to the bench. It seemed like a dream.

"I'm too emotional. I kept telling myself, 'I didn't do it. I didn't do it.' But I knew I had. I'm just too full of 'Bama. He just ran too close. I know I'll be hearing about this the rest of my life."

Alabama's fortunes dipped in the second half as Moegle continued to dismantle the defense. He eventually finished with 265 rushing yards—which was more than the entire Alabama offense—averaging a whopping 21.4 yards per carry, and three touchdowns to be voted outstanding back of the game.

Even though Lewis wound up on the losing end, he became a national celebrity, with "I'm just too full of 'Bama" energetically celebrated by the Crimson Tide fan base. *TIME* magazine dubbed him "Alabama's Twelfth Man," and both players traveled to New York to appear on *The Ed Sullivan Show* and talk about one of the most memorable plays in college football history.

However, Moegle didn't quite appreciate the hero treatment Lewis received, which effectively put him in the shadows despite his amazing performance in the game.

"Heck, I was the one who scored the touchdown," said Moegle, who later changed the spelling of his name to Maegle, to match its pronunciation.

69 Be Buddies with Big Al

In 1930 Alabama was off to a 1–0 start when Ole Miss rolled into town on October 4 for both teams' Southern Conference opener. Even though it would be his final season with the Crimson Tide, Wallace Wade knew that he had good team, maybe his best yet—and that included the 1925 and 1926 Rose Bowl squads.

The Tide had opened the season with a 43–0 victory against Howard and would crush the Rebels that day, 64–0.

Big Al has been Alabama's official mascot since the 1979 Sugar Bowl and is a regular fixture at most Crimson Tide sporting events. Here, Al is dragging a tiger by a noose during a 2004 women's basketball game.

Apparently inspired by comments yelled between fans, Everett Strupper of *The Atlanta Journal* wrote:

> That Alabama team of 1930 is a typical Wade machine, powerful, big, tough, fast, aggressive, well-schooled in fundamentals, and the best blocking team for this early in the season that I have ever seen. When those big brutes hit you I mean you go down and stay down, often for an additional two minutes.
>
> "Coach Wade started his second team that was plenty big and they went right to their knitting scoring a touchdown in the first quarter against one of the best fighting small lines that I have seen. For Ole Miss was truly battling the big boys for every inch of ground.
>
> "At the end of the quarter, the earth started to tremble, there was a distant rumble that continued to grow. Some excited fan in the stands bellowed, 'Hold your horses, the elephants are coming,' and out stamped this Alabama varsity.
>
> "It was the first time that I had seen it and the size of the entire eleven nearly knocked me cold, men that I had seen play last year looking like they had nearly doubled in size.

The 1930 team went on to finish its regular season 10–0, with eight shutouts and 13 total points allowed compared to 271 scored. Consequently, Alabama received another invitation to the Rose Bowl, where the "red elephants" crushed Washington State 24–0 to claim their third national championship.

Did You Know?

One of the most unusual and unique places Big Al's likeness has shown up was on the cover of Aerosmith's rock album *Toys in the Attic*, which was released in 1975. No, the rock band doesn't hail from Alabama but from Boston.

For years, Strupper and other sportswriters commonly referred to the football team as the red elephants due to the trademark crimson-colored jerseys the players wore. Before long, seeing a real elephant on campus wasn't unusual, a practice that continued into the 1950s when school officials decided the massive mascots were too expensive.

Big Al's debut as Alabama's official mascot came at the 1979 Sugar Bowl, where the Crimson Tide turned back Penn State at the goal line to earn a 14–7 victory and a national championship. Although the Tide is one of the few teams that does not have a logo on the helmet or uniforms, Big Al's likeness has become a staple on Alabama merchandise, the costumed mascot makes regular appearances around the state, and he's even the subject of some children's books.

70 Alabama's Version of the Trojan Horse

Even though the integration of the football program was already well under way by 1971, Coach Paul W. "Bear" Bryant knew that more dramatic changes were needed, especially if the Crimson Tide was going to keep up with its competition.

After Alabama's amazing attempt to become the first program in college football to win three consecutive national championships from 1964 to 1966, the following years weren't as kind and didn't bring anywhere near the same level of success. As the Tide's record went from 11–0 in 1966 to 8–2–1, 8–3, 6–5, and 6–5–1, some thought the game might be passing the coach by. Instead, one of the greatest reinventions of a program's identity was at hand.

During the summer, Bryant quietly slipped out of Tuscaloosa to go visit his friend Darrell Royal at Texas, who taught him the wishbone offense. In a complete contrast in style and philosophy, the confusing system was designed to give the quarterback the option of handing off, throwing, running the ball himself, or pitching out to a running back.

Without a pure passer on the roster, it would be the Tide's new offensive scheme. Players and coaches were sworn to absolute secrecy because Alabama's first game would be a rematch with Southern California, which had crushed Alabama 42–21 the year before in the infamous game when Sam Cunningham ran all over the Tide.

Major Ogilvie

He never led the Crimson Tide in rushing and never became an All-American, but Major Ogilvie was the kind of player fans say typified what it meant to play for Coach Paul W. "Bear" Bryant, even though the wishbone offense might not have been tailor-made for him.

"Be courteous to everyone, write home to your parents, and keep your rooms neat," Ogilvie was quoted in *Time* magazine about what Bryant told his freshman class. "He's so involved in your future. He teaches us as people, not as football players. He relates football to life rather than life to football."

The running back, an Academic All-American in 1979, has the unique distinction of being the first, and still only, player to score a touchdown in four successive New Year's Day bowls.

He had a key touchdown against Penn State in the 1979 Sugar Bowl to help win the national championship, and a year later he returned to become the game MVP even though Billy Jackson had 120 rushing yards on 13 carries. Ogilvie scored two touchdowns and had a 50-yard punt return against Arkansas as the Tide defended its title.

He capped his career by being named co-MVP (along with Warren Lyles) of the 1981 Cotton Bowl, a 30–2 victory against Baylor.

Bryant even went to the extreme of having campus security and Tuscaloosa police check on the apartments across the street from practice, had any students watching from the rooftops chased off, and told any local reporters who knew of the switch that there would be consequences if they wrote about the wishbone. Somehow, word didn't leak out.

When Alabama arrived in Los Angeles, Southern California was caught completely off guard. Combined with a renewed emphasis on hard-hitting defense and bigger offensive linemen, the Crimson Tide surprised and shocked the heavily favored Trojans to score two early touchdowns and held on for a 17–10 victory.

It also served notice to the rest of college football: 'Bama and Bryant weren't going anywhere for a while.

From there, the Tide rolled through the regular season with impressive victories over nationally ranked Ole Miss (40–6), Houston (34–20), Tennessee (32–15), and LSU (14–7). For the first time, both Alabama and Auburn entered the Iron Bowl undefeated, and the Tigers were led by quarterback Pat Sullivan, who would go on to win the Heisman Trophy. But behind running back Johnny Musso, the Tide pounded out a 31–7 victory on national television.

"I know one thing, I'd rather die now than to have died this morning and missed this game," Bryant said afterward.

Alabama didn't win the national championship, thanks to a 38–6 loss to Nebraska in the Sugar Bowl, but it captured the first of eight Southeastern Conference titles in the decade, a stretch during which it would claim three more national titles.

Bryant, who enjoyed career win number 200 against USC on the day before his 58th birthday, was fittingly named national Coach of the Year.

71 Fred Sington/Barrett Jones

When Barrett Jones was becoming the most decorated player in Alabama football history (at least until Derrick Henry came along), Ken Gaddy, the director of the Paul W. Bryant Museum, thought that he reminded him of another player in Crimson Tide history.

"The name that comes to mind for comparison is Fred Sington," he said. "All-American and a star in the class room who went on to be a true civic leader. It's hard for offensive linemen to stand out in historical terms. They only get their name called when they are caught holding."

Both nevertheless stood out, with Sington even having a song dedicated in his honor.

But Sington wasn't just any player.

"He was alert, fast, aggressive, and, in addition, he was capable of many outside duties," sportswriter Grantland Rice said. "Tackles such as Sington rarely come along."

One of the more memorable stories regarding Sington occurred during his freshman year, when the first-year players would serve as the scout team during practice. Roughly 10 days before the varsity squad would face Georgia, the freshman teams met, and a tired-looking Alabama squad could manage only a 7–7 tie at halftime.

When freshman coach Shorty Propst started to lay into the team during the break, Sington asked if the offense could run Georgia's plays since that's what they had been doing in practice. It worked; Alabama blew out the Georgia freshmen in the second half, and Sington got a nice scar on his face for his efforts.

Singston, listed at 6'2", 225 pounds, is somewhat overlooked in Crimson Tide history because of his position and because most of his career was played during 1928 and 1929, when fans who had been spoiled by Rose Bowl trips were disappointed by 6–3 seasons.

In 1928 Alabama traveled to play a Big Ten school for the first time, a 15–0 loss at Wisconsin. The season ended with a 19–0 victory against Georgia and a 13–0 win over LSU. The 1929 season was highlighted by Sington and back Tony Holm being named All-Americans. That same season, Denny Stadium in Tuscaloosa was dedicated by Governor Bibb Graves.

The 1930 season, when Sington was a unanimous All-American selection, was a little different. Alabama shut out eight of its 10 opponents, finished undefeated, and crushed Washington State 24–0 in the Rose Bowl. The victory, in addition to the song "Football Freddie" by Rudy Vallee, helped vault Sington into the national spotlight, even though those who closely followed the game were already quite familiar with him.

"He was the greatest lineman in the country," Notre Dame coach Knute Rockne said.

Normally, Coach Wallace Wade wanted his players to be completely focused on football, but Sington was also a member of the academic honor society Phi Beta Kappa, served as student body president his senior year, and was an All-American baseball player while also a member of the basketball and track teams. After Sington threw a no-hitter, Wade pulled him into his office not to offer congratulations but to say, "Son, I want you to know that football is first."

After graduating, Sington played baseball for the Washington Senators and Brooklyn Dodgers until 1940. During World War II, he rose to the rank of lieutenant commander. Following the war he became a prominent businessman and civic leader in the Birmingham and Tuscaloosa areas.

Meanwhile, they don't get more All-American than Jones… well, at least one would be extremely hard-pressed to find anyone in college football in which the term better applied.

After first starting at right guard he was an unanimous All-American his junior year when he lined up at left tackle, a consensus selection as a senior when he was a center, and all four years as a player earned Academic All-American status, including being named the 2012 Capital One/CoSIDA Academic player of the year from the College Sports Information Directors of America.

That was in addition to being the first player from Alabama to win the William V. Campbell Trophy, which is commonly referred to as the academic Heisman Trophy, in addition to the Rimington Trophy as the nation's top center.

Yeah, there's a lot more to Jones than being a college football player, even though he was the 2011 Outland Trophy winner as the game's best interior lineman—arguably the highest honor an offensive lineman can receive. He became the second player from Alabama to win in four years (Andre Smith, 2008), and third overall (Chris Samuels, 1999).

That year he also won the Wuerffel Trophy, which goes to the player who best combines exemplary community service with athletic and academic achievement (Jones spent two spring breaks helping earthquake victims in Haiti), and the ARA Sportsmanship Award.

"It would take five minutes to read all the accomplishments that Barrett has received as a football player," former Alabama coach Gene Stallings said. "I don't know where Barrett gets all the energy."

He won three national championships, two Southeastern Conference titles and even with the hectic schedule Jones graduated a year early with a 4.0 GPA, earned his master's degree in accounting, and boasted a ridiculously long list of academic accomplishments including the Dean's List, President's List, and a host of honor societies.

Jones was also a team captain, which was one of his biggest goals heading into his senior year.

"I don't think there's enough good things that you can say about Barrett Jones," Nick Saban said. "He's probably about as fine a person as you're ever going to have the opportunity to be around. I wouldn't even say that I've ever coached—I think that would be an understatement. He's I think as fine a person as you're ever going to be around, me or you or anyone else, in terms of his willingness to serve other people.

"I think his teammates think a lot of him. He's a good teammate. He's done a lot of things to really help others. He really has the right stuff when it comes to doing things you need to be successful in whatever you choose to do."

72 Shaun Alexander and Chris Samuels

When it comes to running back Shaun Alexander, there are a lot more numbers to know than the No. 37 on his jersey.

Alexander was not only Alabama's all-time rushing leader with 3,565 career yards, he also set school records with 727 rushing attempts, 15 100-yard games, 41 rushing touchdowns, and 50 total touchdowns.

Overall, he left the Capstone after the 1999 season holding 15 school records and three Southeastern Conference marks.

"I am a better running back every time I step on the field," Alexander said. "I try to get better each game, each summer, each season."

That certainly proved true at Alabama, although as a redshirted freshman in 1996 he ran for 291 yards to set the Crimson Tide single-game rushing record and scored four touchdowns at LSU.

Alexander played in nine games as a reserve during his sophomore season, accounting for 415 yards on 90 carries, but started his junior year with five touchdowns in the opener against Brigham Young. The Tide stumbled through the rest of the schedule, but at 7–4 was invited to play in the inaugural Music City Bowl in Nashville. Despite 1,178 rushing yards and 13 touchdowns during the regular season, Alexander was limited to just 55 in a 38–7 loss to Virginia Tech.

After deciding against declaring early for the NFL Draft, Alexander returned to Tuscaloosa for an outstanding senior year. He was initially given Heisman Trophy consideration, but a sprained ankle against Tennessee ended his candidacy. Nevertheless, Alexander helped lead the Tide to the SEC championship in 1999, highlighted by his game-winning 25-yard touchdown run in overtime at third-ranked Florida in Gainesville, and his dominating fourth quarter against Auburn.

"I didn't come back to win the Heisman Trophy," Alexander said after the 34–7 victory against Florida in the rematch for the Southeastern Conference title. "I came back to play in games like this. The guys on this team wanted this championship so badly."

Running behind All-American lineman Chris Samuels, Alexander was named first-team All-SEC after rushing for 1,383 yards on 302 attempts and 19 touchdowns, voted SEC Offensive Player of the Year by coaches, and was a finalist for the Doak Walker Award. He concluded his collegiate career with 161 yards on 25 carries and three touchdowns versus Michigan in the Orange Bowl.

With the Seattle Seahawks, Alexander turned in one of the finest seasons in National Football League history to earn 2005 MVP honors and helped lead his team to Super Bowl XL. He scored an NFL-record 28 touchdowns, and his 168 points were the second most in league history behind Paul Hornung's 176 in 1960.

Alabama Career Rushing Leaders (Through 2015)

Name	Years	Yards
Derrick Henry	2013-15	3,591
Shaun Alexander	1996-99	3,565
Bobby Humphrey	1985-88	3,420
Kenneth Darby	2003-06	3,324
T.J. Yeldon	2012-14	3,322

Alexander won the NFL's rushing title with a franchise-record 1,880 yards and had a club-record 11 games with 100 or more yards rushing. When he scored touchdowns at home, the stadium speakers blared out "Sweet Home Alabama" in celebration, which also inspired Dustin Blatnik and the 12th Man Band to record the 2005 tribute song "Sweet Shaun Alexander."

"My first day here, just like my first day at Alabama, I went and got the record books and looked it all up," Alexander said. "It was like, 'Okay, how hard is it going to be for me to get this thing?' I started setting goals to get them fast."

Meanwhile, after not giving up a sack or quarterback pressure, Samuels won the Outland Trophy as the nation's top interior lineman and was the third-overall draft pick by the Washington Redskins in 2000. He was named All-Pro in 2001 and to six Pro Bowls before revealing that he played his entire NFL career knowing that he had a spinal condition which put him at risk of paralysis with every hit to the head.

After losing feeling several times during his career doctors told him it was time to hang it up after he banged heads with a defensive player from the Carolina Panthers and his body went limp.

"A lot of people, they've been praying for me to receive a miracle, but they really don't realize that I received my miracle when I got up off the field in North Carolina," Samuels said when announcing his retirement in 2010. "It's going to be hard to walk away from the game I love, but it's the best thing for me and my family."

He subsequently got into coaching.

73 Bart Starr

Even though his name is synonymous with professional football, Bart Starr wasn't known for his quarterbacking prowess at the University of Alabama. Actually, his most notable award while on the Capstone was being selected to the first-ever Academic All-SEC team in 1953, as a sophomore.

Starr was born in Montgomery, but his family moved around a lot before his father's National Guard unit was activated for World War II. He chose Alabama in part to appease his father, but also so he could continue to see his high school sweetheart, Cherry Morton, who would attend Auburn. After his sophomore year, when Starr helped lead the Crimson Tide to the Cotton Bowl, and he ranked second nationally in punting with a 41.1 average, they secretly eloped.

A back strain sidelined Starr for most of his junior season (later revealed to be from a hazing incident), and after new coach J.B. "Ears" Whitworth wanted a more mobile quarterback his senior year, Starr sat through much of an 0–10 season. He hardly even punted because of a severe ankle sprain.

Starr was a 17th-round draft selection of the Green Bay Packers in 1956 and saw limited playing time until the team brought in a new coach, Vince Lombardi. Together, they helped create one of pro football's great dynasties.

"Coach Lombardi showed me that by working hard and using my mind, I could overcome my weakness to the point where I could be one of the best," Starr said.

From 1960 through 1967, Starr's record as a starter was an amazing 62–24–4, and the Packers won six divisional, five National Football League, and the first two Super Bowl titles. Perhaps his most famous play came on a simple dive in the famous Ice Bowl against the Dallas Cowboys in the NFL Championship Game of 1967. Playing in unbelievably cold conditions in Green Bay, the game came down to one play. Instead of handing off, Starr kept the ball and scored the winning touchdown. Two weeks later, the Packers defeated the Oakland Raiders in Super Bowl II, 33–14, in Lombardi's final game.

"Bart Starr stands for what the game of football stands for: courage, stamina, and coordinated efficiency," Lombardi said.

Steve Sloan

Between Joe Namath and Kenny Stabler, Steve Sloan handled the quarterbacking duties at Alabama and not only led the Crimson Tide to the 1965 national championship but placed 10th in Heisman Trophy voting. He completed 97 of 160 passes for 1,453 yards, and his 153.8 passing-efficiency ratio was the nation's best.

After a brief two-year career in the National Football League with the Atlanta Falcons, Sloan turned his attention to coaching. He was named Southeastern Conference Coach of the Year after just his second year at Vanderbilt in 1974. Sloan received a similar conference honor at his next stop, Texas Tech (1975–77) in 1976, and also had coaching stints at Ole Miss and Duke.

Sloan returned to the Capstone and was athletic director from 1987 to 1989, before having the same position at North Texas (1990–93) and Central Florida, where he oversaw the addition of football to the school's athletic program. In 2002 Sloan returned to the state where he played his high school football, Tennessee, to become athletic director at the University of Tennessee at Chattanooga.

"You instill desire by creating a superlative example. The noblest form of leadership is by example and that is what Bart Starr is all about."

Even though Starr is not in the all-time top 50 in any individual statistical category, he was a three-time NFL passing champion and played in four Pro Bowls. He finished his 16-year career with 24,718 passing yards, 152 touchdowns, and 138 interceptions while completing 57.4 percent of his passes.

In addition to 196 games as a player, Starr coached the Packers from 1975 to 1983, and his numerous honors include the NFL Award for Citizenship and the Byron "Whizzer" White Award. In 1977, he was inducted into the Pro Football Hall of Fame.

"Anyone can support a team that is winning, it takes no courage. But to stand behind a team to defend a team when it is down and really needs you, that takes a lot of courage," Starr said.

74 Visit Bear Bryant's Grave

During the 1982 season, Alabama defeated eventual national champion Penn State, 42–21, but those close to the program knew there was something amiss, and not because of uncharacteristic losses to Tennessee, LSU, Southern Miss, and Auburn.

With his health on the decline, Paul W. "Bear" Bryant knew he could no longer continue and called a press conference for December 15 to announce his retirement from coaching. College football's all-time Division I-A (or Bowl Championship Subdivision as it was renamed in 2007) wins leader would have one final sendoff, against Illinois at the Liberty Bowl.

Led by All-American cornerback Jeremiah Castille's three interceptions and a forced fumble, the Bryant era concluded with a 21–15 victory, and for one last time the Tide players carried the coach off the field on their shoulders.

"I am proud they wanted to win this one for me," Bryant said.

Fullbacks Ricky Moore and Craig Turner, and flanker Jesse Bendross scored the touchdowns, all on runs, and a late interception by linebacker Robbie Jones sealed the victory. Castille was named game MVP.

"Let's face it. Alabama just likes to hit you," Illinois quarterback Tony Eason said. "They are the hardest hitting team I've ever played against."

Just 28 days later, on January 26, 1983, Bryant's heart gave out. He was 69.

Statistically, Bryant's career legacy was a 323–85–17 record, 29 bowl appearances, 15 conference championships, and six national championships. In the 1960s and 1970s, no school won more games than Alabama (193–32–5).

On January 28, 1983, his funeral was held in Tuscaloosa, with the burial at Birmingham's Elmwood Cemetery near Legion Field. Eight players (Castille, Paul Ott Carruth, Paul Fields, Walter Lewis, Mike McQueen, Jerrill Sprinkle, Darryl White, and Tommy Wilcox) served as pallbearers. Tens of thousands, if not hundreds of thousands, many in black, others wearing crimson, congregated along the 50-mile stretch of Interstate 59 to watch the procession, which along the way passed by both Bryant-Denny Stadium and

Visit Bryant's Birthplace

Paul W. "Bear" Bryant was born just outside of Fordyce, Arkansas, in the south-central part of the state, approximately 68 miles south of Little Rock and halfway between it and the Louisiana state border. Originally a railroad town, it's now a popular hunting destination with a population near 5,000.

the university practice fields where Bryant had perched above his players in a tower.

It's said that, in the South, Bryant's funeral could only compare in size, scope, and importance, to those of Jefferson Davis, Elvis Presley, and Dr. Martin Luther King Jr. His grave has frequent visitors, and regular gifts of appreciation (including bottles of Coke, Golden Flake potato chips, and whiskey), but the headstone simply has his name and dates of his birth and death.

"He was more than the finest football coach who ever lived," former university president Joab Thomas said. "He was a great teacher, a great man, and a dear personal friend."

Off the field, plans were already under way for the Paul W. Bryant Museum, which would open in 1988, and Bryant had set up a scholarship fund for the children of his former players to attend Alabama (and not just to play football). Nowadays a person can hardly go anywhere in Tuscaloosa without seeing something named in honor of the icon, and even 25 years later a video tribute to the coach was still being played prior to the start of every home football game at Bryant-Denny Stadium.

"He literally coached himself to death," Ohio State coach Woody Hayes said at the funeral. "He was our greatest coach."

75 Dwight Stephenson

Even though he would be regarded as the premier center of the National Football League during his professional career with the Miami Dolphins, Dwight Stephenson didn't leave the University of Alabama with quite the same level of hype.

Stephenson helped the Crimson Tide to consecutive national championships (1978 and 1979), three straight Sugar Bowl victories (1977–79 seasons), and a 21-game winning streak during his junior and senior years. He was also a finalist for the 1979 Lombardi Award, given annually to the nation's top offensive lineman.

"Dwight Stephenson was the best center I ever coached," Alabama coach Paul W. "Bear" Bryant said. "He was a man among children."

But, in part because of his position, Stephenson (6'2", 255 pounds) was only a second-round draft pick and 48th overall selection of the 1980 draft. He spent much of his rookie season playing special teams, and it wasn't until Mark Dennard was injured during the 11th game of the 1981 regular season that Stephenson made his first pro start.

Stephenson played in 107 straight games and started in 80 consecutive games until the 1987 players' strike ended the streak. He earned both All-Pro and All-AFC recognition five straight years from 1983 to 1987 and was named the AFC or NFL Offensive Lineman of the Year in various major polls four times.

Although a knee injury would cut his career short, Stephenson was selected for five straight Pro Bowl games, the first four as a starter (injuries prevented him from playing in the 1987 and 1988 games). He also started in Super Bowls XVII and XIX and in the 1982, 1984, and 1985 AFC Championship Games.

"Dwight Stephenson was a bear," former Dolphins nose tackle Bob Baumhower, who also played for Alabama, once said. "He was the toughest guy I ever played against, and that made it so much easier for me on game day."

In addition to his intensity and explosive charge off the snap, Stephenson was also known for his uncanny speed and ability to quickly make powerful blocks after hiking the ball. As offensive captain for the Dolphins, Stephenson took his place in front of

Vaughn Mancha

One of the most popular players to ever suit up for the Crimson Tide, Vaughn Mancha was a little late reaching the Capstone. Like so many others of his time, he put off college to join the military for World War II, and when concerns about his vision kept him off the front lines he instead spent two years with the Merchant Navy in California repairing destroyers.

In 1944 Mancha returned to Alabama and was part of the famous "War Baby Tiders," composed mainly of players too young for the military or, like him, turned down for active duty.

During his four years lettering at Alabama, the Tide compiled a 30–9–2 record and played in two Sugar Bowls and one Rose Bowl. He played all 60 minutes in the 1945 Sugar Bowl, was later named to the Sugar Bowl all-decade team, and received All-America consideration in 1945.

"Mancha is a brilliant defensive man, fine at diagnosing plays, a great defender against passes, and a sure tackler," Coach Frank Thomas said about the future Florida State athletic director. "On offense he is a fine blocker, and a good, accurate snapper. And he loves football."

quarterback Dan Marino to anchor the line, which allowed the fewest quarterback sacks in the National Football League for six straight years.

Stephenson also had the unique privilege of having Bryant and Don Shula as coaches, and Shula presented him during induction ceremonies for the Pro Football Hall of Fame.

"Those two guys are very similar," Stephenson said. "I think that if Coach Shula coached on the college level that they would be even closer to the way they were, or if Coach Bryant was on the pro level. But, the difference was, Coach Bryant was dealing with people that were really boys becoming young men, who were still being molded, teaching us about life and that sort of thing. Coach Bryant was really good at that and that was what he realized; he was molding young men. And then, when you get to the pros, you are a man more or less, and Coach Shula continued to mold and work, and teach you things about life and about football.

"Things that I learned from Coach Shula as well as Coach Bryant still stick with me today. The difference was that Coach Bryant was dealing with young men, boys trying to become young men. Coach Shula was dealing with men, and he respected us that way. He wanted guys that were responsible and having their job be an important thing."

76 Mal Moore

The smile was unforgettable, much like the game that had just been played, and even though he was deep in the recesses of the Rose Bowl it was easy to tell that no one could have been happier.

Mal Moore had done it. The rejuvenation, if not resurrection of the University of Alabama athletics program was complete, and with the football victory over Texas in the 2009 Bowl Championship Series title game everyone else knew it as well.

Everything had all come together, even better and faster than he had dared imagined, from the stadium renovations to leaving the open spot along the Walk of Champions that would subsequently be filled with a statue of Nick Saban.

"It was put there for this and I will recommend to the president that we go forth," a thrilled Moore said after the 37–21 victory.

"Immediately?" a reporter asked.

"Yeah. Hell yeah," he responded. "It is really difficult to express just how proud I am."

Actually, it probably should be the other way around as there have been few as beloved and cherished among the university's

Mal Moore was a player on the 1961 national championship team and an assistant coach on numerous other title-winning Alabama teams. On November 23, 1999, he was hired as the Crimson Tide's athletic director.

true sons as the one who essentially gave 50 years of his life to the Capstone and did everything in his power to make it a better place.

"Mal Moore is Crimson Tide sports," former university president Dr. Judy Bonner said after Moore passed away March 30, 2013, at the age of 73, and no truer words could have been used about the man who left a legacy that will last decades, if not longer.

In addition to helping change its landscape and cultivating the Capstone as a destination for some of the finest coaches in the nation, he provided the foundation for turning Alabama athletics into the envy of nearly every other school in the nation.

You see, no one was more crimson than Moore, who as a player, coach and athletic director won ten national championships (1961, 1964, 1965, 1973, 1978, 1979, 1992, 2009, 2011, and 2012), along with 16 SEC titles and 39 bowl trips—not to mention national championships in gymnastics, softball and women's golf.

Because no one had a more prestigious collection of landmark rings, watches and pins he was the Tiffany's of college sports. The other part of that comparison is the corresponding high level of quality that in this case certainly applies.

"There is not a more gracious man than Mal, a man with more integrity than Mal, and there is no person who loves the university more than Mal Moore," former gymnastics coach Sarah Patterson said.

And what a mark he made, going back to 1958 when Moore was a backup quarterback and then stuck around to be one of Paul W. "Bear" Bryant's graduate assistants in 1964, defensive backfield coach from 1965 to '70, quarterbacks coach from 1971 to '82, and offensive coordinator from 1975 to '82.

He left to work for other teams, but Alabama always remained home, and on November 23, 1999, he returned to be its Director of Athletics even though the program was largely in disarray. He didn't know it at the time, but things were about to only get worse with a string of scandals and problems with the National Collegiate Athletic Association, culminating with the Committee of Infractions considering issuing the death penalty.

In order to turn things around, he first had to get people to believe in Alabama again, which was not an easy task. Moore instituted a five-year facilities and endowment initiative, the Crimson Tradition Fund, which evolved into a $150 million campaign.

In addition to a major overhaul and expansion of Bryant-Denny Stadium, Coleman Coliseum and nearly every other athletic venue was upgraded, while Bryant Hall was converted into an academic center that Moore considered essential. The project was completed in 2006, and with then-university president Dr. Robert E. Witt making a strong push for expansion and higher academic standards it helped set the stage for Alabama's renaissance.

In appreciation, the Alabama Board of Trustees renamed the new football building, which was one of the major parts of the facilities upgrade, the Mal M. Moore Athletic Facility. Nevertheless, he orchestrated the $65 million expansion of the south end zone of Bryant-Denny Stadium, making it one of the largest and most desirable venues anywhere.

His defining moment, though, was convincing Saban to leave the National Football League's Miami Dolphins to join him at the Capstone.

"The first thing he did was he recruited Terry," Saban said about his wife after Moore flew down to make his pitch. "I called Terry and said I don't think I'm even going to talk to these guys tonight. She said, 'Oh, Mal's already here. We've been talking for an hour.' That was his first step in the right direction."

Actually, it turned out to be the crucial step towards Alabama's dynasty, maybe the greatest the sport had ever seen.

"Thank God he's on our side," Moore said about Saban after the rout against Notre Dame for the 2012 national title.

Mel Allen

Long before he became a radio legend, Mel Allen (born Melvin Allen Israel in Birmingham) was a student at Alabama, where he also earned a law degree and served as the public-address announcer at football games. After graduating, he took a week's vacation in New York City, auditioned at CBS, and was hired for $45 a week. During his first year at CBS, he announced the crash of the Hindenburg and ad-libbed from an airplane for a half hour during auto racing's rain-delayed Vanderbilt Cup. In 1939 he broadcast baseball games for both the New York Yankees and the New York Giants and eventually became known as the "Voice of the Yankees." Allen officially changed his name after entering the Army in 1943, and after returning to the civilian broadcast booth he called 22 World Series on radio and television and 24 All-Star Games. In 1998 the Yankees dedicated a plaque in his memory at Monument Park at Yankee Stadium. It calls him "A Yankee institution, a national treasure" and includes his signature line, "How about that?"

Roughly 10 weeks later, after Moore passed away, six of his friends and colleagues stood on a stage inside Coleman Coliseum for a public memorial, united not only the bond of the person they knew and honored, but also in how they struggled in describing him.

It wasn't that they couldn't come up with anything, just the opposite.

"He was like a father," men's golf coach Jay Seawell said. "I understand he's my boss, he's an athletics director, and we have a job to do, but I think Mal's greatest attribute was he made me almost feel like a son."

So many others felt the same way as the audience ranged from Moore's family and some of the biggest names in Crimson Tide history to every Southeastern Conference athletic director, including his replacement Bill Battle. Mostly they reminisced about things that made Mal the man special, like his late wife Charlotte, upon whom he doted and took care of through her struggles with Alzheimer's.

"Mal was the most selfless person I think I ever met," said Saban, who's happiest moment with Moore wasn't after winning a championship, but occurred just a few months previous when he received the John L. Toner Award as the nation's top athletics director.

With a tear running down his cheek, "Mal said, 'You changed my life when you came here.' I looked at him and said, 'No, Mal, you changed my life. I'm a better coach. I'm a better person. I'm better teacher for the lessons I have learned being in a partnership with you.'"

77 Alabama Is the New Linebacker U

It began with an impromptu press conference hastily called in 2009.

Linebacker Rolando McClain didn't suspect anything major when he received a phone call the Monday following the SEC Championship Game telling him to be at the football building the next morning for a meeting with head coach Nick Saban followed by an interview session with media.

However, his suspicions were slightly aroused when being told to dress up, which was different because when players were on camera they almost always wore something Crimson Tide–related.

"I was thinking, 'Why do I need to wear slacks and a collared shirt?'" McClain said. "We don't do media like that."

He was still completely surprised when Dick Butkus walked into Saban's office carrying his namesake trophy that annually goes to the nation's best linebacker.

"I had no idea," McClain said. "I'm really at a loss for words. I didn't expect it."

"He was really surprised," Saban said. "It was a lot of fun."

Ever since then Crimson Tide reporters have been on high alert in early December as the program has repeatedly had players in the running for the award. The only years Alabama hasn't had a finalist were 2010 and 2014.

When C.J. Mosley won in 2013, Butkus surprised him at the team banquet, and a strong argument could be made that Reggie Ragland was deserving of the honor in 2015.

"Anytime you're a competitor, I always want to win everything," said Ragland, who used his close second-place finish to Notre Dame's Jaylon Smith as motivation for the playoffs. "A good guy won it. I can't be mad. I'll take it with a grain of salt and keep moving forward."

Nevertheless, Alabama has become the standard when it comes to linebackers, which was only reinforced on National Signing Day in 2016 when it landed star in-state recruits Ben Davis and Lyndell Wilson.

They were the fifth and sixth 5-star linebackers to sign with Alabama under Saban, joining Nico Johnson (2009), Trey DePriest (2011), Reuben Foster (2013), and Rashaan Evans (2014).

Meanwhile, in five of the previous seven seasons Alabama had a consensus/unanimous All-American at linebacker, which easily topped the nation. During that time period only Georgia, Notre Dame and Michigan State had two, and for the Spartans it was Greg Jones named twice.

On the flip side of that, during the six NFL drafts between 2010 and 2015 there were 19 linebackers selected in the first round, led by Alabama with three (McClain, Mosley and Dont'a Hightower, while Courtney Upshaw just missed).

Consequently, Alabama had become college football's Linebacker U.

For years Penn State had that designation under head coach Joe Paterno, and rightfully so. Beginning with Dennis Onkotz, a two-time All-American in 1968-69, the Nittany Lions had the reputation for regularly having outstanding players at the position. Others included Jack Ham, John Skorupan, Greg Buttle, Shane Conlan, LaVar Arrington, Brandon Short, and Paul Posluszny, who were all consensus All-Americans.

Nevertheless, Penn State only had the third-most consensus All-Americans at linebacker since 1965, when the NCAA got rid of its rules requiring the use of the one-platoon system that forced players to play on offense and defense. The most recent player to join that club was Dan Connor in 2007, when he finished his career as Penn State's all-time leading tackler with 419.

Yes, that's the same year Saban landed in Tuscaloosa, and when McClain began his collegiate career. One of the holdovers from Mike Shula's recruiting efforts, he started eight of 13 games as a freshman, finishing with 75 tackles, two interceptions, and a sack.

That year, safety Rashad Johnson led the team with 94 tackles, while tied for second with 80 were defensive lineman Wallace Gilberry and linebacker Darren Mustin, a transfer from Middle Tennessee State. (Note: Johnson, a former walk-on at running back, and Gilberry both had successful NFL careers).

Meanwhile, Alabama's history includes Derrick Thomas, Cornelius Bennett, Lee Roy Jordan, and Woodrow Lowe, who will stand up against any four linebackers in history.

All four are in the College Football Hall of Fame, which as of 2016 was one more linebacker than Penn State has had enshrined, and led all programs.

As for Butkus—who played before 1965 and was listed as a unanimous All-American at center in 1963 and a consensus selection in 1964, but was voted into the College Football Hall of Fame as a linebacker—no one would be surprised if he kept making return trips to Tuscaloosa.

"I'm sitting here like, 'Am I supposed to stop the interview, talk to Dick, or am I supposed to act like he's not there?'" McClain said about his immediate reaction. "I had no idea what to do. So I saw coach get up and shake his hand and naturally just got up. I kind of froze.

"It's kind of humbling. You think you're a pretty good linebacker and then Dick Butkus is in the room."

78 Woodrow Lowe

There aren't too many players who can say that destiny may have had a hand in their landing at Alabama, but Woodrow Lowe was an exception in more ways than one.

Lowe grew up in Phenix City, just a few miles from Auburn, and was set to attend a game there and check out the Tigers with a friend, but fate intervened with a flat tire. He never made it.

"It's not just one thing; It's not one single thing," Lowe said about playing for the Crimson Tide. "It's more of a temperament, a mindset. You have to throw words like tradition and legacy into that equation. When you are a member of the University of Alabama football team, I don't care where you are, people know you. I've been in California, Mexico, and Japan, you'd be surprised at the people that know about the Crimson Tide.

"We have a tradition here in the state of Alabama, I think, for the most part, that if you are a Crimson Tider or you played for the University of Alabama, you pretty much know what football is all about. That association is an honorable thing to be tied to. I don't

First-Team All-Americans (through 2015)

W.T. "Bully" Van de Graaff, T, 1915; A.T.S. "Pooley" Hubert, QB, 1925; Hoyt "Wu" Winslett, DE, 1926; Fred Pickhard, T, 1926; Tony Holm, FB,1929; Fred Sington, OT, 1929–30; John Henry Suther, HB, 1930; Johnny Cain, FB/P, 1931–32; Tom Hupke, G, 1933; Don Hutson, SE, 1934; Bill Lee, DT, 1934; Millard "Dixie" Howell, QB, 1934; Riley Smith, QB, 1935; Arthur "Tarzan" White, G, 1936; James "Bubber" Nesbit, FB, 1936; James Ryba, DT, 1937; Leroy Monsky, G, 1937; Joe Kilgrow, HB, 1937; Carey Cox, C, 1939; Holt Rast, DE, 1941; Don Whitmire, OT, 1942; Joe Domnanovich, C, 1942; Vaughn Mancha, C, 1945; Harry Gilmer, HB, 1945; Ed Salem, HB, 1950; Bobby Marlow, HB, 1952; George Mason, T, 1954; Billy Neighbors, T, 1961; Lee Roy Jordan, LB, 1962; Dan Kearley, DT, 1964; Wayne Freeman, G, 1964; Joe Namath, QB, 1964; David Ray, K, 1964; Paul Crane, C, 1965; Steve Sloan, QB, 1965; Cecil Dowdy, T, 1966; Ray Perkins, SE, 1966; Bobby Johns, DB, 1966–67; Richard Cole, DT, 1996; Dennis Homan, SE, 1967; Bobby Johns, DB, 1967; Kenny Stabler, QB, 1967; Mike Hall, LB, 1968; Sam Gellerstedt, NG, 1968; Alvin Samples, G, 1969; Johnny Musso, HB, 1970–71; John Hannah, G, 1971–72; Jim Krapf, C, 1972; John Mitchell, DE, 1972; Buddy Brown, T, 1973; Woodrow Lowe, LB, 1973–75; Wayne Wheeler, SE, 1973; Leroy Cook, DE, 1974–75; Mike Washington, CB, 1974; Sylvester Croom, C, 1974; Ozzie Newsome, SE, 1977; Marty Lyons, DT, 1978; Barry Krauss, LB, 1978; Jim Bunch, T, 1979; Don

care how old I get or how long I live, it certainly is an honor to have played for the Crimson Tide. It really is."

Lowe is one of only two Crimson Tide players to be a three-time All-American selection, which he earned from 1973 to 1975. Statistically, his best year was as a sophomore, when he had 134 tackles, including six for a loss, and three interceptions to help lead Alabama to the national championship.

"There were a lot of great players on that football team," he said. "We had a lot of great defensive players in Leroy Cook, Mike Christian, Skip Kubelius, Mike Washington, and Tyrone King. We had a great, great offensive team. We only lost one game

McNeal, CB, 1979; Dwight Stephenson, C, 1979; E.J. Junior, DE, 1980; Thomas Boyd, LB, 1980–81; Tommy Wilcox, S, 1981–82; Mike Pitts, DE, 1982; Jeremiah Castille, CB, 1982; Cornelius Bennett, LB, 1984–86; Jon Hand, DT, 1985; Bobby Humphrey, TB, 1986–87; Van Tiffin, K, 1986; Kermit Kendrick, DB, 1988; Derrick Thomas, LB, 1988; Larry Rose, G, 1988; John Mangum, CB, 1989; Keith McCants, LB, 1989; Phillip Doyle, K, 1990; Robert Stewart, NT, 1991; John Copeland, DE, 1992; Eric Curry, DE, 1992; Antonio Langham, CB, 1992–93; David Palmer, WR, 1993; Michael Proctor, K, 1993–94; Jay Barker, QB, 1994; Kevin Jackson, S, 1996; Dwayne Rudd, LB, 1996; Michael Myers, DE, 1996; Chris Samuels, T, 1999; Shaun Alexander, TB, 1999; DeMeco Ryans, LB, 2005; Antoine Caldwell, C, 2008; Terrence Cody, NG, 2008–09; Rashad Johnson, S, 2008; Andre Smith, T, 2008; Javier Arenas, CB, 2009; Mark Ingram, RB, 2009; Mike Johnson, G, 2009; Rolando McClain, LB, 2009; Leigh Tiffin, K, 2009; Mark Barron, S, 2010–11; Dont'a Hightower, LB, 2011; Barrett Jones, T, 2011-12; Dre Kirkpatrick, CB, 2011; DeQuan Menzie, CB, 2011; Trent Richardson, RB, 2011; Courtney Upshaw, LB, 2011; D.J. Fluker T, 2012; Dee Milliner, CB, 2012; C.J. Mosley, LB, 2012-13; Chance Warmack, G, 2012; Ha Ha Clinton-Dix, S, 2013; Cyrus Kouandjio, T, 2013; AJ McCarron, QB, 2013; Amari Cooper, WR, 201; Landon Collins, S, 2014; JK Scott, P, 2014; Derrick Henry, RB, 2015; Reggie Ragland, LB 2015; Ryan Kelly, C, 2015; A'Shawn Robinson, DL, 2015.

that year. For the most part, the best I can reflect upon, there was no individualism. We were a team and we had high expectations. We were never without high expectations. You hear it early, when you first get on campus, what football meant to the great state of Alabama and to this university. That part of it was a given. The expectation level was very high.

"One of the games I remember back then was the game we lost. We lost to Notre Dame in the Sugar Bowl for the national championship. It's ironic. That ballgame was decided by them being able to return a kickoff. I think we dominated pretty much everything else. We split in the national championship, but that right there was the game that I remember the most."

During his four years, Alabama never failed to win the Southeastern Conference championship, and played in two Sugar Bowls, one Orange Bowl, and a Cotton Bowl.

"We had a very prolific offense, running the ball and throwing play-action passes and we were a great defensive team too," Lowe added. "When we went on the field, we just expected to win."

Drafted in the fifth round by the San Diego Chargers, Lowe played 11 years in the National Football League. He started more games for the Chargers than any other defensive player in team history (151 out of a possible 165), and was made a team captain.

But two things in particular about Lowe have stood the test of time. First, although it took a little longer than expected, Lowe was enshrined in the College Football Hall of Fame in 2010. His class included 16 players and coaches John Robinson and Dick MacPherson. Among them were two Heisman Trophy winners, Notre Dame's Tim Brown and Miami's Gino Torretta—whom Alabama beat in the 1993 Sugar Bowl to win a national championship.

"He was consistently excellent throughout his playing career and his induction into the Hall of Fame is very appropriate," said former athletic director Mal Moore, who was an assistant coach during Lowe's career. "He put together a career that set a standard that carries on to this day."

Finally, the 134 tackles still stands as the Alabama single-season record, even though the Crimson Tide plays more games nowadays. No one is more surprised than the former player himself.

"We have some great football players who have attended the University of Alabama for the last 30 to 40 years," Lowe said. "My idol before I got to the university was Lee Roy Jordan. I knew if I could just live up to his expectations, I would be okay and be halfway decent. For that record to stand as long as it has, that means there have been a lot of great defensive players at the University of Alabama in regards to no one single individual player on the team. Even back in 1973, we had a lot of great players on the defensive side of the football.

"I never thought the record would last this long. It's an honor, I must say. The game has changed a lot since then, its more wide open and spread out. They don't run the ball as much as they used to run when I was a player. You also get the opportunity to make a lot of tackles that way. With today's passing game, the spread offense and now the pistol, it's harder for defensive players to rack up that many tackles, or just make big plays. I do know this: the part of the game that has not changed is the impact a good defense can have over the offense. I know you have heard the saying that 'Offense wins games and defense wins championships.' I am believer in that."

79 Alabama vs. Ole Miss' Archie Manning

It was the first nationally televised night game in college football history, and some consider it one of the best ever played. If there had been a Hollywood-type marquee outside of Legion Field on October 4, 1969, it would have read "Ole Miss at Alabama," but the next line could only have been assigned to the starting quarterbacks: "Archie Manning vs. Scott Hunter."

While the Crimson Tide was 2–0, it was coming off back-to-back eight-win seasons that had some fans wondering if the program might be on the decline after challenging to be the first team in major college football history to win three consecutive national titles (1964–66).

Ole Miss was fresh off a 10–9 loss in Lexington to Kentucky, but everyone was already well aware of Manning's capabilities. The previous year as a sophomore, he had a 362-yard game against LSU and helped lead a 7–3–1 season.

In one of the rare true shootouts in Crimson Tide history—during which both teams wore *100* insignias on their helmets to commemorate the 100th anniversary of the start of college football—Hunter completed 22 of 29 passes for 300 yards, while Manning was 33 of 52 for 436 yards and ran for 104 more. The duo combined for 842 yards of total offense, and in the process set numerous school and conference records.

Even though Bryant supposedly told his assistants they were fired numerous times while storming up and down the sideline, Alabama won 33–32 on George Ranager's 14-yard game-winning touchdown reception with 4:32 remaining.

"After the game was over with, I was looking for Archie and found him," Hunter said. "He had tears in his eyes. I didn't even know what to say. I reached out, shook his hand, and he looked me in the eye.

"We didn't have to say a thing to each other. We knew what we had done that night."

Despite the victory, Alabama struggled the rest of the season, beginning with the subsequent Saturday, a 14–10 loss to Vanderbilt. For the first time since 1958, the Tide lost to both Tennessee and Auburn, and closed the year with a 47–33 defeat to Colorado in the

Scott Hunter vs. Pat Sullivan

Hunter is also known for another game during the 1969 season, the Iron Bowl against Auburn and future Heisman Trophy winner Pat Sullivan. Although he passed for a school-record 484 yards by completing 30 of 55 attempts, the Crimson Tide's five-game winning streak in the series was snapped, 49–26. Hunter finished the season completing 157 of 266 passes for 2,188 yards.

Liberty Bowl. The 6–5 finish was the Tide's worst record since the 5–4–1 finish in 1958, Bryant's first season at Alabama.

Ole Miss went the opposite direction. It didn't lose another Southeastern Conference game and defeated Arkansas in the Sugar Bowl, 27–22, to finish 8–3.

Manning was named a first-team All-American and finished fourth in Heisman Trophy voting (he placed third in 1970). His No. 18 was the only number retired by Ole Miss until Chucky Mullins's No. 38 in 2006.

"I have told my boys this," Manning told the *Chattanooga Times Free Press*. "When Eli got to Ole Miss, he was looking through the media guide and called me and said, 'Dad, your numbers weren't very good,' and I said, 'Eli, we didn't throw the ball that much.'

"If you threw for 160 or 170 yards per game in the '60s and the '70s, that was a good day. That night against Alabama was kind of a freak thing."

80 David Palmer

He wore No. 2 and was known simply as "the Deuce."

One would be hard-pressed to find a more dynamic offensive player to ever wear crimson than David Palmer, whose third-place showing in Heisman Trophy voting after his junior season was Alabama's best finish ever at that point.

It was also something Crimson Tide fans saw coming from far away. One of several true freshmen to make an immediate impact during the 11–1 1991 season, Palmer set an Alabama record by returning three punts for touchdowns during the regular season, and another for most punt-return yards (409). Against defending national champion Colorado in the Blockbuster Bowl, which the Tide won 30–25, he opened the scoring with a 52-yard return and was given the Brian Piccolo Award as the game's Most Valuable Player.

Palmer began his sophomore year serving a three-game suspension, but by catching five passes for 101 yards in the first SEC Championship Game, he helped lead a 28–21 victory against Florida. Consequently, No. 2 Alabama was invited to play defending national champion Miami in the Sugar Bowl, where the Hurricanes were considered a sizable favorite.

"Everyone says we can't beat Miami, but we are not just anybody, we are Alabama," Palmer said.

Of course, Alabama won handily, 34–13, to win its 12th national championship.

Palmer was even more of an offensive force his junior season, in part because Coach Gene Stallings moved him all over the field and was always looking for ways to get the ball to him.

As a receiver, Palmer had 61 catches for 1,000 yards, which at the time was a Tide record. But he also took handoffs, lined up at quarterback, handled returns, and helped lead Alabama back to the SEC Championship Game (although it later had to forfeit all but one regular-season victory due to an ineligible player). Overall, he tallied 1,961 all-purpose yards.

Palmer was named an All-American, but he lost out to Florida State quarterback Charlie Ward for the Heisman. Ward's winning margin of 1,622 points over Tennessee quarterback Heath Shuler was second only to O.J. Simpson's 1,750-point difference over Purdue's Leroy Keyes in 1968, when more ballots were distributed. Palmer actually finished with more first-place votes, 16, than Shuler's 10, while Marshall Faulk of San Diego State placed fourth.

A 24–10 victory over North Carolina in the Gator Bowl was Palmer's last game wearing crimson as he decided not to return for his senior season and instead turned pro.

"I've tried to look at all sides, but the bottom line is I have to fulfill the needs of me and my family," Palmer said at a news conference.

The 5'9", 170-pound junior said he had reached his primary goal by helping Alabama win the national championship and called his third-place Heisman finish "one of the highlights of my career."

Notable Records (through 2015)

Rushing yards, game: 291, Shaun Alexander vs. LSU, Nov. 9, 1996 (20 attempts)
Rushing yards, season: 2,219, Derrick Henry, 2015 (395 attempts)
Rushing yards, career: 3,591, Derrick Henry, 2013-15 (602 attempts)
Passing yards, game: 484, Scott Hunter vs. Auburn, Nov. 29, 1969 (30 of 55)
Passing yards, season: 3,487, Blake Sims, 2014 (252 of 391)
Passing yards, career: 9,019, AJ McCarron 2010–13, (686 of 1,026)
Receiving yards, game: 224, Amari Cooper at Tennessee, Oct. 25, 2014 (9 receptions) and vs. Auburn, Nov. 29, 2014 (13)
Receiving yards, season: 1,727, Amari Cooper, 2014 (124 receptions)
Receiving yards, career: 3,463, Amari Cooper, 2012–04 (228 receptions)
Points, game: 30, Santonio Beard vs. Ole Miss, Oct. 19, 2002 (5 touchdowns); Shaun Alexander vs. BYU, Sept. 5, 1998 (5 touchdowns)
Points, season: 168, Derrick Henry 2015 (28 touchdowns)
Points, career: 385, Leigh Tiffin, 2006–09, (83 field goals, 136 point-after-attempts)
Tackles, game: 25, DeMeco Ryans vs. Arkansas, Sept. 27, 2003
Tackles, season: 134, Woodrow Lowe, 1973
Tackles, career: 327, Wayne Davis, 1983–86
Sacks, game: 5, Derrick Thomas at Texas A&M, Dec. 1, 1988
Sacks, season: 27, Derrick Thomas, 1988
Sacks, career: 52, Derrick Thomas, 1985–88
Interceptions, game: 3, five players tied.
Interceptions, season: 10, Hootie Ingram, 1952
Interceptions, career: 19, Antonio Langham, 1990–93

He would be selected in the second round of the subsequent draft by the Minnesota Vikings, and he went on to set numerous franchise special-teams records.

81 Julio Jones

Before the fans, his coaches, and probably even Julio Jones himself had an inkling, Alabama quarterback Greg McElroy knew that the junior wide receiver was going to have a huge night at Tennessee during the 2010 season.

It was the Crimson Tide's second offensive snap of the game and No. 8 lined up to the right, worked his way downfield into a gap, and turned toward the sideline where the pass sailed perfectly over the cornerback and into Jones' hands before the Volunteers' safety could get over to help out.

It wasn't the impressive catch that got McElroy's attention so much, rather the coverage. It told him that the Volunteers were going to try and man-up against Jones, with just one defender, and take their chances he wouldn't torch them.

"It's almost, I don't want to say disrespect, any time they press Julio without a safety over the top it's like *What are you doing?* is kind of what I'm thinking in my head," said McElroy, who proceeded to repeatedly burn the home team by going to his favorite receiver again, and again, and again....

When the cigar smoke eventually cleared from Neyland Stadium that night, Jones had caught 12 passes and set an Alabama single-game receiving record with 221 yards.

"I was waiting for that to happen," said safety Robert Lester, who grew up about a block away from Jones in Foley, Alabama.

What made it even more remarkable was that Jones did it less than two weeks after having surgery to repair a fracture in his left hand.

"That's crazy," center William Vlachos said.

"I'm not surprised [by] anything that Julio does," said junior running back Mark Ingram, who had also seen his teammate endure shoulder, knee, and wrist injuries along with a sports hernia. "He's a warrior. He just goes out and gives his all every time he steps on the field. If he can play, he's going to play. If he hurts little bit, he'll play through the pain."

For every Alabama legend—and Julio may have already been one before he played his first game for the Crimson Tide—there's always that one game that no one ever seems to forget, and for Jones this was clearly it. He punished Tennessee with nearly every kind of reception possible: slants, diving, sideline with only his toes in-bounds, and, of course, deep with completions of 47, 42, and 38 yards.

Yet every time Jones touched the ball he felt the bone-jarring pain, and still tried to make his trademark downfield blocks—albeit scaled down a bit.

"As far as blocking my man and dominating, I had some that were good but I didn't block like the way I want to block," he said, noting that's why he doesn't necessarily consider Tennessee his best game. "I block so they can't get to the runner, but my blocks I want to take them to the sideline, on the ground. I really couldn't do that."

Jones initially sustained the fracture after making his first reception October 9 at South Carolina, when his stiff-arm got caught up in the defender who basically tried to rip his head off.

"I knew after that play because I went to the sideline and my hand started hurting," Jones described. "I pressed down on my hand and it was moving, the bone was moving. I didn't tell the trainers but I told the strength coach, Scott Cochran: 'I think I just broke my hand, don't tell nobody. I'm going to wait until halftime.' I didn't want to make it a big issue."

Somehow, Jones remarkably finished with eight receptions for 118 yards and one touchdown. The only thing that hurt worse than making a catch was trying to open his palms like he would to field a kick, thus the reason he was pulled from special teams. The next day doctors cut into the outer part of his hand below the ring finger.

"There are six screws in there," he said pointing to the scar, in addition to the plate.

Don McNeal

It somehow seems fitting that when people look for help in dealing with difficulty and adversity, they sometimes turn to former Alabama cornerback Don McNeal, who was named both first-team All-American and team co-captain as senior when the Crimson Tide defended the national title in 1979. He subsequently was a first-round draft selection by the Miami Dolphins, and during his nine-year National Football League career made 18 interceptions, returning two for touchdowns.

However, McNeal's pro career had the stigma of one play in particular, during one of his two Super Bowl appearances, when the Dolphins faced the Washington Redskins in January 1983.

Washington was down 17–13 with a little more than 10 minutes remaining and facing fourth-and-one at the Miami 43, with the handoff going to fullback John Riggins. With Miami in its goal-line defense, McNeal was to cover the receiver in motion, only to slip and see his man take out the defensive end. That left McNeal to try and stop Riggins, who ran over the defensive back en route to scoring the game-winning touchdown.

Instead of letting the play overwhelm him emotionally, McNeal's career continued and he later used it as a teaching tool after becoming the children's pastor at New Testament Baptist Church in Miami.

"He was the kind of player Coach Bryant loved because he was first class," former cornerback Jeremiah Castille said about McNeal.

The subsequent week coaches limited him during practices and Jones was yanked near the end of the first quarter against Ole Miss after aggravating the injury while trying to catch a slant pass that bent his finger back.

"My hand had no strength," Jones said. "They had to cut through the muscle in my hand to get to the bone. So the Ole Miss game it was feeling like the South Carolina game, when it broke. But I tried to go out there and see what I could do but my hand didn't have any strength."

Consequently, when he and Saban met the next day, the Sunday before visiting Knoxville, Jones asked that the coaching staff not hold him back during practices, that he fully participate and endure the pain. It was the only way he could be ready to face Tennessee.

"Julio obviously is a special talent," Saban said. "One thing that's great about him, and usually you don't see a lot from the wide receivers position, you see a lot of guys who are selfish 'me' guys, not so much "team" guys and that's not the case with our guys. We are very fortunate and obviously with Julio being the frontrunner of that pack as a leader and with his play.

"We try to learn from what he does and the way he executes. He's definitely a great asset to have not only for us as an offense but for us as a team as well."

Jones followed up the Tennessee game with 10 receptions against LSU and went on to set school single-season records with 78 catches for 1,133 yards and added seven touchdowns.

In 40 games over three seasons he caught 179 passes for 2,653 yards with 15 touchdowns and accumulated 3,084 all-purpose yards. His 179 catches and 2,653 receiving yards were both second in school history.

Consequently, the Atlanta Falcons gave the Cleveland Browns five draft picks—their first- (27th overall), second- (59th), and fourth-round (124th) picks in the 2011 draft and their first- and fourth-round picks in 2012—for the sixth-overall pick to select Jones, who continued to hear "JUUUUULLLIO" from Alabama fans at Falcons games in the Georgia Dome.

"I'm a hands-on kind of guy," Jones said.

82 Dr. Robert Witt

One has to wonder if Dr. Robert E. Witt had any idea what he was getting into when he was hired to be president of the University of Alabama in 2003 after 35 years as a faculty member and administrator in the University of Texas System.

At the time, the school's pride-and-joy football program was in complete disarray. Mike Dubose's reign (1997 to 2000) had ended in disappointment and scandal, and an NCAA investigation had resulted in major sanctions that would plague the program for years.

That was enough for Dennis Franchione to rethink things. After 10–3 season in 2002 he vanished from Tuscaloosa only to show up in College Station as the new head coach at Texas A&M.

So Director of Athletics Mal Moore tried again and settled on Washington State coach Mike Price, who had a career record of 129–122 but badly wanted the job.

Following spring practice, Price attended a celebrity pro-am golf tournament in Pensacola, Florida, where the 56-year-old had a well-publicized night of drinking in a strip club. It was considered a critical moment in Witt's early tenure, and he didn't hesitate, firing Price before he coached a single game.

"To be selected for a leadership position at the University of Alabama is an honor and a responsibility. When you accept the honor, you accept the responsibility," Witt said at the time. "That responsibility includes conducting your professional and personal life in a manner consistent with university policy."

That same year, Witt announced that Alabama would by 2013: become a university of choice for the best and brightest; become a Tier One research university; become an academic community committed to serving the state of Alabama; and increase enrollment to 28,000.

It didn't take that long.

By 2010 enrollment had gone from 19,633 to 30,232 (with plans in place to exceed 35,000 by 2020). Applications rose from 7,322 to 20,112. Among incoming students the average ACT score went from top 25 percent to top 15, the number of students ranked

"No Strike" Joe Sewell

Although most Alabama fans know him from baseball, Joe Sewell was also a standout football player and a halfback for the Crimson Tide from 1917 to 1919.

After graduation in May 1920, he wound up taking over the shortstop position for Cleveland in the World Series when Ray Chapman died after being hit in the head by a pitched ball. Sewell had five hits in 15 at-bats.

Despite using a heavy 40-ounce bat that he called "Black Betsy," Sewell was the toughest player in baseball to strike out, and he had as few as four strikeouts during three different seasons. He finished in the top 10 in American League MVP voting four times, was third in 1925, and in the 1932 World Series with the New York Yankees scored the winning run in the deciding game against Chicago.

In 14 years he had 1,903 games and 7,132 at-bats, and he hit .312 with only 114 strikeouts. Sewell returned to the Capstone in 1964 and coached the baseball team through 1969. He led the 1968 team to a 24–14 record and the SEC Championship, and he compiled a 106–79 (.603) record. The baseball stadium is now known Sewell-Thomas Stadium, or "the Joe."

in the top 10 percent of their class jumped from 15 percent to 44 percent, the number of students with 4.0 GPAs rose from 314 to 1,395, and the National Merit Scholars almost doubled (69 to 128).

Similar to what occurred during Dr. George Hutcheson Denny's tenure, Alabama's academic growth paralleled the school's athletic success, including a massive facilities upgrade and the high-profile hiring of Nick Saban.

"Having a coach of his caliber makes it easier to recruit better students and raise more money," Witt told *Forbes Magazine*, and used the school's $500 million capital campaign as an example. "We have had 100,000 donors in that campaign, and a major reason they support us is football."

On January 21, 2012, roughly six weeks before he was promoted to Chancellor of the UA System, Witt stood on a stage in the middle of Bryant-Denny Stadium, which had been expanded twice since his arrival to make it one of the most desirable home fields in college football, as the Crimson Tide celebrated its second national championship in three years.

Surrounded by dignitaries, trophies, and football players, he made reference to Saban's comment two years previous of "I want everyone here to know this is not the end. This is the beginning," and added that now everyone knows what he meant.

The same could have been said of him.

"We're proud of the way we won the national championship, with class every step of the way," Witt said.

83 Check Out Denny Chimes

It's probably the most recognized and important landmark on the Tuscaloosa campus, and no trip to the Capstone would be considered complete without visiting Denny Chimes.

Shaped like a small lighthouse, the slender tower was dedicated in 1929 and became one of many reminders of the success of the football program, although that wasn't the original intent.

The initial idea for the bell tower was for it to serve as a memorial for Alabama students who died in World War I, but plans were abandoned due to lack of funding.

Shortly after Alabama played in both the 1926 and 1927 Rose Bowls, which essentially put Southern football on the national college football map, rumors began to spread that school president Dr. George Hutcheson Denny was considering leaving the Capstone to return home to his native Virginia. In his honor, students raised the necessary funds, and the structure was built on the south side of the Quad along University Boulevard.

Incidentally, not only was Denny instrumental in making football a high priority at Alabama, which he skillfully used to promote and expand the school, he also coined the term *Capstone* when he referred to the university as the "capstone of the public school system of the state" in 1913.

The tower's 25-bell bronze carillon tolls every quarter hour and plays a daily medley of music at 5 PM along with Christmas music during the holiday.

Beginning in the late 1940s, football team captains were honored by having their names, handprints, and footprints set in slabs of concrete surrounding the tower, on what's now known as the "Walk of Fame." Some names just about anyone would recognize include Crimson Tide legends Joe Namath, Ozzie Newsome, and Kenny Stabler.

Those who are into Alabama football trivia have a smorgasbord of information and possible tidbits from the slabs, including the following:

- Who is the lone person to have been inducted into the Walk of Fame by himself? (Answer: Nick Germanos, 1955)
- Which two notable captains didn't attend his Walk of Fame ceremony? (Answer: Chris Samuels 1999 and Landon Collins 2014.)
- Who has "All-American" and "1961" next to his name? (Answer: Billy Neighbors)
- Who has the words "All-SEC" next to his name? (Answer: Benny Nelson, 1964)
- Who is the only player to have his nickname listed? (Answer: Ken "Snake" Stabler)
- Which two coaches decided not to have the annual Walk Of Fame ceremony at Denny Chimes, but held it at Bryant-Denny Stadium instead? (Answer: Dennis Franchione in 2001 and Mike Price in 2002).
- Which five players have the year of the ceremony and not the season they played listed by their names? (Answer: Steve Allen, Joe Namath, Benny Nelson, Ray Ogden, and Steve Sloan—and anyone who knows that off the top of his or her head needs to write the sequel to this book.)

84 The Tornado

Everything changed on April 27, 2011.

It was an unusually warm day in Tuscaloosa. Most University of Alabama students were dreading their upcoming finals and still basking from the unofficial offseason football holiday known as "A-Day." Less than two weeks after the annual celebration surrounding the final scrimmage of spring practice, this one had been extra special to fans because it had included Nick Saban having his statue unveiled in front of again-expanded Bryant–Denny Stadium, where the other coaches who have won national championships are permanently honored.

Intense weather warnings had been issued for that afternoon, but the sun had come out between the passing storm clusters that are known to frequent the South on a regular basis that time of the year. A particularly nasty one had come though in the early-morning hours, but still the day went on as if it was nothing was out of the ordinary.

That is until about 5:00 PM, when a monster tornado emerged in the southwest corner of Tuscaloosa and quickly began a mile-wide path of carnage.

Words cannot adequately describe what Tuscaloosa experienced and endured, as did many other communities throughout the state and region. Residents witnessed it while looking out of their windows, heard it as it ripped through everything in its way, and felt it as it cut through the heart of the community. Anyone who called Tuscaloosa home knew people who lost their businesses, homes, or lives; their friends, colleagues, and loved ones.

The gash went deeper than any satellite image could show, and after surveying the scene a couple of days later, President Barack

Obama said, "I've never seen devastation like this." To come up with a comparison, one needed to speak with a person who had experienced Hurricanes Andrew or Katrina, or even a war zone.

That's what 15th Street and McFarland Boulevard, perhaps the busiest intersection in town, resembled. The piles of rubble gave no hint to what had been there before, and the path of destruction stretched well beyond what the eye could see. Standing there, one couldn't help but fear the worst.

"I'm just thanking God that I didn't get picked up with it," said linebacker Jerrell Harris, who was in an apartment on 15th Street when it struck. "You never think it'll happen to you. It's mind-blowing."

Nearby, former Crimson Tide football player Javier Arenas was one of the fortunate ones to emerge uninjured after his house disintegrated around him, but two fatalities gave immediate faces to the disaster: Loryn Brown, the well-known daughter of former Alabama football player Shannon Brown, and Ashley Harrison.

"A special young lady," said former defensive tackle Bob Baumhower, who employed Brown at one of his local restaurants. "We went down to the visitation in Wetumpka and it was just amazing the support and the lives that she touched. You talk about making a difference, the short time she was here she made a huge difference."

Harrison was the girlfriend of long snapper Carson Tinker, and the two had taken refuge in a closet along with his roommates and their dogs. When the house took a direct hit, Ashley was ripped from his arms as they were thrown. Tinker sustained a broken wrist, concussion, and ankle injury, while she died almost instantly from a broken neck. Harrison was 22.

Most people first heard about both deaths by word of mouth, not so much because the power was out in most of Tuscaloosa, but due to the sheer volume of people helping their neighbors dig out or salvage what they could. Stories, mostly uplifting, were passed along as volunteers poured into the obliterated neighborhoods and went door to door asking "What do you need?" while passing out whatever supplies they could.

Saban, too, contributed on many levels. Knowing full well that when you're the head of the Crimson Tide football program being the biggest face of the community comes with the job, he embraced the role. He served as a spokesman during Crimson Caravan gatherings, participated in a telethon, helped set up a storm recovery

Peach State Pits

Alabama has a rich history of having to go through the state of Georgia somehow to get to a championship, dating back to even before the 1924 season when it had to defeat both Georgia Tech and Georgia to win its first Southern Conference title. Granted, the Crimson Tide didn't always have such success, but the most disappointing game against either may have been in 1962, when Alabama visited Georgia Tech on November 17. The previous year, linebacker Darwin Holt caught the Yellow Jackets' quarterback with an elbow on a late hit, fracturing his jaw. Georgia Tech didn't forget and pulled out a hard-hitting 7–6 victory after Alabama came inches short of completing a two-point conversion. It cost the Tide a shot at defending its national championship.

Subsequently, in 1963, *The Saturday Evening Post* accused Bryant and Georgia athletic director Wally Butts of fixing their game so they could bet on it. The article also alleged that Bryant had thrown the 1962 loss to the Yellow Jackets. Bryant was already suing the publication regarding an article by an Atlanta-based sportswriter for calling the Crimson Tide a dirty team (from the 1961 Georgia Tech game), and naturally, both Bryant and Butts sued. While investigating, attorneys found that the story had been based on false and fabricated evidence. A court awarded Butts $460,000, and Bryant later settled with Curtis Publishing for $300,000.

In 1964, Bryant wore a helmet on to the field in Atlanta because of all the debris thrown by fans, including bottles, which became a famous college football photograph. Alabama defeated Tech, 24–7, and went on to win the national title.

program through his Nick's Kids Fund, and helped established a program to sponsor a specific neighborhood's recovery.

But just as important as any financial donation—including his wife Terry purchasing hundreds of $50 gift cards and handing them out so people could purchase necessities—may have been his visits to shelters and spending time with people.

"Sometimes your presence means something and you just have to listen," he said. "We fed everyone and we gave away a thousand Alabama shirts, which everyone was really excited about. You would have thought we gave everyone an SUV they were so happy to have an Alabama shirt.

"You can watch all this on television and see the devastation, but until you meet the family that lost their home and all their belongings, things that were dear and personal to them, the guy who just lost his business, it was just blown away, but most importantly anyone who lost any loved ones. That's the saddest thing."

The coach also encouraged current and former players to do what they could as well, although little prompting appeared necessary.

For days, John Fulton, Brandon Gibson, Harrison Jones, and Barrett Jones—who spent his previous two spring breaks in Haiti helping with earthquake recovery—were in numerous neighborhoods, and many others contributed.

"It's the same kind of devastation," Jones said. "We all want to show we're part of this community too. We're all affected by it."

James Carpenter, Marcell Dareus, and Cory Reamer raised money at Crimson Caravan events, with Julio Jones, Mark Ingram, and Greg McElroy all coming back to help out. Courtney Upshaw held a special autograph session in his hometown of Eufala (usually considered territory of rival Auburn) that led to thousands in donations and also brought supplies.

Arenas drove back to Kansas City, where he played for the NFL's Chiefs, and did likewise, as did Preston Dial from Mobile.

Justin Smiley bought an SUV for a family. DeMeco Ryans, who was supposed to be recovering from a torn Achilles, volunteered and made a sizable donation. Le'Ron McClain organized truckloads of supplies.

"Tuscaloosa may never be the same, and I think people have to realize that, but I also think that you almost have to look forward and as an opportunity to rebuild," Saban said. "We can all make our community better by what we can all pitch in and do, but it's not something that's going to take two weeks, or two months, it's going to take years."

It took contributions by people like Baumhower, whose efforts with others to feed people in devastated Alberta City evolved into a relief hub.

"It was an amazing thing to watch," said Baumhower, who estimated that between 30,000 and 40,000 meals were dished out.

It continued through the hot summer when linebacker Nico Johnson and some of the other football players, including defensive back Nick Perry and tackle D.J. Fluker, got a mind-blowing look at what was left of Holt while helping rebuild two houses.

But also lending a hand were a number of volunteers from Saban's alma mater Kent State, including some of the players they would soon face in the season opener at Bryant-Denny Stadium.

The trip was organized after Kent State athletic director Joel Nielsen essentially asked Saban, "What can we do to help?"

"Being from Alabama, I definitely wanted to go," said Kent State running back Jacquise Terry, the proud product of Phenix City, Alabama. "I heard through people in Birmingham and Tuscaloosa how bad it was, you know sometimes people can exaggerate, but it was worse than they really explained. It was worse than I thought, so I was very shocked."

The first of 14 Nick's Kids/Habitat for Humanity houses (one for each national championship, and two more were later added) was completed just in time for the Golden Flashes' return in

September, while each and every day the Crimson Tide woke up to the realities of what had happened.

With the return of football, the familiar feel of everyday life began to return, and the bright lights from Bryant-Denny Stadium helped fill the voids as the area made the transition from cleanup to rebuilding. Fans had never been more anxious to see their beloved Crimson Tide play again, and even though coaches were concerned about there being too much pressure on the players to try and win a national championship for the ravaged community, they went on and won the next two titles anyway—and were joined by the Crimson Tide gymnastics, women's golf and softball teams, with men's golf joining in a year later with back-to-back crowns.

"We're going to fight," Tuscaloosa mayor Walter Maddox proclaimed. "We refuse to let April 27 define us. I told this to the president when he came to visit—the real story about Tuscaloosa, Alabama, is going to be its recovery."

85 The 1973 National Title

Few teams had the kind of promise as that of the 1973 Crimson Tide, which began the season ranked sixth in the preseason Associated Press poll but crushed California, which featured quarterback Steve Bartkowski and running back Chuck Muncie, 66–0.

With a roster boasting first-team All-Americans Buddy Brown (tackle), Woodrow Lowe (linebacker), and Wayne Wheeler (split end), along with second-teamers Mike Washington (cornerback), John Croyle (defensive end), and Mike Raines (defensive tackle), Paul W. "Bear" Bryant appeared more than poised to make a run for his fourth national championship.

The wins quickly piled up: 44–0 at Vanderbilt, 28–14 against Georgia, 35–14 at Florida.

Aided by halfback Randy Billingsley's blocks, Alabama had four players—Wilbur Jackson, Richard Todd, Calvin Culliver, and Jimmy Taylor—each reached 100 yards rushing during a 77–6 victory against Virginia Tech.

1973: 11–1, National Champions, SEC Champions

Date	Opponent	Location	W/L	Score
September 15	California	Birmingham, Ala.	W	66–0
September 22	Kentucky	Lexington, Ky.	W	28–14
September 29	Vanderbilt	Nashville, Tenn.	W	44–0
October 6	Georgia	Tuscaloosa	W	28–14
October 13	Florida	Gainesville, Fla.	W	35–14
October 20	Tennessee	Birmingham, Ala.	W	42–21
October 27	Virginia Tech	Tuscaloosa	W	77–6
November 3	Mississippi State	Jackson, Miss.	W	35–0
November 17	Miami	Tuscaloosa	W	43–13
November 22	LSU	Baton Rouge, La.	W	21–7
December 1	Auburn	Birmingham, Ala.	W	35–0
December 31	Notre Dame	Sugar Bowl	L	23–24
				477–113

Coach: Paul W. "Bear" Bryant
Captains: Wilbur Jackson, Chuck Strickland
Ranking (AP): Preseason—No. 6; Postseason—No. 4.
All-American: First team—Buddy Brown, tackle; Woodrow Lowe, linebacker; Wayne Wheeler, split end. Second team—Mike Washington, cornerback; John Croyle, defensive end; Mike Raines, defensive tackle. Academic—Randy Hall, defensive tackle.
All-SEC (first team): Buddy Brown, tackle; Greg Gantt, punter; Wilbur Jackson, halfback; Woodrow Lowe, linebacker; David McMakin, safety; Mike Raines, defensive tackle; Steve Sprayberry, tackle; Mike Washington, cornerback; Wayne Wheeler, split end.
Leaders: Rushing—Wilbur Jackson (752 yards, 95 carries); Passing—Gary Rutledge (33 of 57, 897 yards); Receiving—Wayne Wheeler (19 catches, 530 yards). Woodrow Lowe had a team-record 134 solo tackles.

Against unbeaten Tennessee, quarterback Gary Rutledge connected with wide receiver Wayne Wheeler for an 80-yard touchdown on the first snap of the game, and Jackson capped the 42–21 victory with an 80-yard touchdown run.

On Thanksgiving, Alabama handled another unbeaten rival, LSU, 21–7.

For an encore, the Tide crushed Auburn, 35–0.

Alabama scored a school-record 477 points and averaged 480.7 yards per game.

At the time, the United Press International coaches' poll held its final voting at the end of the regular season (although the Associated Press had already switched and since 1969 had held its final rankings at the end of the postseason), with Alabama named its national champion.

However, the Tide had one more game to play, the extremely hyped first meeting with Notre Dame, which would take place at the Sugar Bowl.

The game lived up to the billing, with the lead changing hands six times and featuring a wild 90-second span with three turnovers at the beginning of the fourth quarter. The deciding points came with 4:26 left on the clock, when Notre Dame's Bob Thomas, who had missed two attempts earlier in the game, kicked a 19-yard field goal.

After the Tide offense stalled on the subsequent possession, Greg Gantt's 69-yard punt gave Notre Dame first down at its own 1-yard line, but Gantt also drew a penalty on the play that would have given Alabama fourth down and five yards to go.

Bryant decided to decline the penalty, putting the game into the defense's hands, only to see Fighting Irish quarterback Tom Clements, who was named the game's most valuable player, complete a key 35-yard third-down pass to tight end Robin Weber to secure the 24–23 victory.

Not surprisingly, Notre Dame was No. 1 in the final Associated Press poll, and soon after the coaches' poll announced that it too would hold its final voting after all bowl games had been played.

A year later, No. 1 Alabama again finished the regular season undefeated and accepted an invitation to the Orange Bowl for a rematch against Notre Dame, which was ranked eighth.

Unfortunately for Crimson Tide fans, the result was the same, as the Fighting Irish won Ara Parseghian's final game, 13–11. Instead of Alabama taking home another national championship, Oklahoma and Southern California split the title honors.

86 Ray Perkins

How's this for an accomplishment? During the three seasons Ray Perkins was a varsity split end for Alabama (1964–66), the team's record was 30–2–1, and ironically the undefeated season was the one the Crimson Tide didn't win the national championship (11–0 in 1966).

As a sophomore, his touchdown reception from Joe Namath, along with Ray Ogden's 108-yard kickoff return, keyed a 21–14 victory against Auburn that, in addition to Notre Dame's loss to Southern California, propelled the Tide to No. 1 in the final polls (which were held before bowl games that year). The following season, with polls holding the final voting at the end of the postseason, Perkins scored two touchdowns to help lead a 39–28 victory against Nebraska in the Orange Bowl as Alabama successfully defended its title.

His senior year, with Kenny Stabler behind center, Perkins had 33 catches for 490 yards and was named an All-American. Against

Nebraska in the Sugar Bowl, a 34–7 rout in Alabama's favor, he set up the Tide's first score and later recorded a 45-yard touchdown.

Perkins went on to play for the Baltimore Colts and caught a 68-yard touchdown pass from Johnny Unitas in the 1970 AFC Championship Game, a 27–17 victory against the Oakland Raiders, for a berth in Super Bowl V.

After his playing days were complete, Perkins turned to coaching and was an assistant with the New England Patriots (1973–77) and San Diego Chargers (1978) before being named the head coach of the New York Giants in 1979. Bill Parcells, who eventually replaced him, and Bill Belichick were two members of his staff.

What prompted his departure was his dream job, coaching the Crimson Tide, which became a reality shortly after Paul W.

Bill Curry

When Ray Perkins left the Capstone following the 1986 season to take over the National Football League's Tampa Bay Buccaneers, Alabama's search committee and university president Joab Thomas decided to hire the football program's first head coach without an Alabama tie since Frank Thomas in 1937—Bill Curry from Georgia Tech, who even with a 9–2–1 finish in 1985 had a career record of 31–43–4.

For the next three years, most accomplishments would be offset by setbacks, and vice versa, leading to growing tensions between the coach and fans. Even though Alabama won the Southeastern Conference championship in 1989, it lost for the third straight time to Auburn, leading to the famous story about the brick thrown through Curry's window.

Unhappy and feeling unwanted despite flirting with a national championship, Curry resigned after a 33–25 loss to Miami in the Sugar Bowl, which clinched the national championship for the Hurricanes, and accepted the job at Kentucky.

"I knew Coach Curry was leaving when he came in the squad room with a blue jacket on and in its lapels were tickets to the Kentucky Derby," center Roger Shultz said.

Curry's record at Alabama was 26–10.

"Bear" Bryant resigned in 1982. Those who didn't understand him, or Alabama football, were shocked when Perkins left New York, especially to undertake the nearly impossible task of attempting to follow Bryant.

But that didn't stop Perkins from trying to distance himself from the Bear's legacy. One of his more controversial moves was to take down Bryant's imposing coaching tower that stood over Thomas Field for practices (it was later returned to its original spot, primarily to serve as a campus monument and daily reminder of his legacy).

His first season resulted in an 8–4 finish. A year later, Alabama's amazing 25-year bowl streak came to a close, and there were murmurs that the coach's job might already be in jeopardy. Perkins brought in every Alabama great he could to help inspire the team for Auburn, and it worked. On fourth-and-goal at the 1-yard line, Tigers coach Pat Dye went for a touchdown instead of a field goal only to see safety Rory Turner drop Brent Fullwood short of the end zone.

"I just waxed the dude," Turner said.

A year later, Alabama won the rematch on Van Tiffin's dramatic 52-yard field goal and beat Southern California 24–3 at the Aloha Bowl after struggling to a 3–3 halftime score, in part due to seven penalties. Perkins called it "the worst first half I have been associated with to play such a great second half."

Near the end of the 1986 season, rumors began to circulate that Perkins might leave to take over the head coaching job with the National Football League's Tampa Bay Buccaneers. He initially denied them, but the scuttlebutt only gained momentum while Alabama headed to the Sun Bowl to handily defeat Washington, 28–6. Sure enough, Perkins resigned after the dominating victory with a 32–15–1 mark over four years.

"I do so with mixed emotions," Perkins said.

87 The Talking Bear

In some places people like to quote Shakespeare or even a great movie line.

In Tuscaloosa perhaps only the Bible is quoted more than Paul W. "Bear" Bryant, but primarily because the churches outnumber Bryant-Denny Stadium by a wide margin.

Among his most famous lines:

- "I ain't never been nothin' but a winner."
- "If you believe in yourself and have dedication and pride, and never quit, you'll be a winner. The price of victory is high but so are the rewards."
- "What matters is not the size of the dog in the fight, but of the fight in the dog."
- "In a crisis, don't hide behind anything or anybody. They're going to find you anyway."
- "I can reach a kid who doesn't have any ability as long as he doesn't know it."
- "Show class, have pride, and display character. If you do, winning takes care of itself."
- "There is a big difference in wanting to and willing to."
- "I don't hire anybody not brighter than I am. If they're not smarter than me, I don't need them."
- "Every time a player goes out there, at least 20 people have some amount of influence on him. His mother has more influence than anyone. I know because I played, and I loved my mama."
- "If anything goes bad, I did it. If anything goes semi-good, we did it. If anything goes real good, you did it. That's all it takes to get people to win football games."

The Bryant Name

If you ever want to go to Paul W. Bryant Museum in Tuscaloosa, it's on Bryant Drive, next to the Bryant Conference Center. You know you're getting close if you've passed Bryant Bank, but if you see Bryant-Denny Stadium or Bryant Drive Apartments, you've gone too far. If you suddenly find yourself at Paul W. Bryant High School, you're in the wrong part of town.

Incidentally, if you go on the tour of the stadium, make sure to see the Bryant statue out front, not to mention the one that stands in front of Legion Field in Birmingham.

- "In life, you'll have your back up against the wall many times. You might as well get used to it."
- "The first time you quit, it's hard. The second time, it gets easier. The third time, you don't even have to think about it."
- "I'll put you through hell, but at the end of it all we'll be champions."
- "There ought to be a special place in heaven for coaches' wives."
- "How many people watch you give a final exam?" (asked of a Texas A&M professor who questioned his salary and emphasis on winning) "Well, I have 50,000 watch me give mine, every Saturday."
- "Sure I'd like to beat Notre Dame, don't get me wrong. But nothing matters more than beating that cow college on the other side of the state."
- "What the hell's the matter with you people down there? Don't y'all take your football seriously?" (after calling Auburn at 6 AM and being told none of the coaches were in yet)
- "I'm just a simple plowhand from Arkansas, but I have learned over the years how to hold a team together. How to lift some men up, how to calm others down, until finally they've got one heartbeat, together, a team."

- "Never quit. It is the easiest cop-out in the world. Set a goal and don't quit until you attain it. When you do attain it, set another goal, and don't quit until you reach it. Never quit."
- "I don't know if I'll ever get tired of football. One time I thought I might.... I was out there on the practice field wondering whether football had passed me by. Then I heard the Million Dollar Band playing over on the practice field. When they started playing 'Yea, Alabama,' I got goosebumps all over me. I looked out there and those young rascals in those crimson jerseys, and I just wanted to thank God for giving me the opportunity to coach and contribute in some small way at my alma mater and be a part of the University of Alabama tradition."
- "I left Texas A&M because my school called me. Mama called, and when Mama calls, then you just have to come running."

88 The War Baby Tiders

The University of Alabama didn't field a football team in 1943 due to World War II, but the following year Coach Frank Thomas had enough players, 20—down from the then-normal 50—to piece together a team, appropriately nicknamed "the War Babies." Most of the Tide was composed of 17-year-old boys too young to be drafted, students medically disqualified from military service, and returning veterans—not to mention the Southeastern Conference waiving its rule against freshman participation. The key player was an all-around talent named Harry Gilmer, who had a unique passing style of leaping as he threw.

Bobby Johns

This two-time All-American defensive back played on teams that compiled a 28–3–2 record and won the 1965 national championship but didn't finish No. 1 in 1966 despite an undefeated season.

"We beat everyone on our schedule," Johns said in the book *The Missing Ring*.

"What else did they want? Did they want us to beat the Green Bay Packers?"

Johns had three interceptions in the 1967 Sugar Bowl, a 34–7 victory against Nebraska, and in 1966 returned two interceptions for a touchdown.

Thomas went from hoping the ragtag collection wouldn't "disgrace the university" to valuing the team as his favorite of all the teams he coached.

With a 5–1–2 record, the War Baby Tiders secured the school's first invitation to the Sugar Bowl in New Orleans, where Gilmer put on a dazzling performance in front of 72,000 fans. Though much-older Duke pulled out a 29–26 victory in the final moments, Gilmer was named the game's most valuable player.

It also set up one of the most impressive seasons in Alabama history. With the conclusion of the war, the Crimson Tide had not only a full roster again in 1945, including All-American center Vaughn Mancha, but an experienced team.

Even with two military opponents on the schedule, Alabama destroyed its competition with Georgia coming closest, 28–14. It outscored opponents 430–80, and among the lopsided games was a 60–19 victory against Kentucky in which Gilmer had 216 rushing yards—the first time in school history the 200-yard mark had been eclipsed—on just six carries thanks to touchdown runs of 95 and 59 yards, in addition to more than 100 yards passing.

The perfect regular season and Southeastern Conference title resulted in the sixth invitation to the Rose Bowl, and, as usual,

Alabama was considered the underdog, this time to Southern California, which had won eight straight games in Pasadena.

At halftime USC had minus-24 yards of offense on 21 plays while Alabama led 20–0. The Trojans didn't get a first down until the third quarter, when they trailed 27–0, but Thomas held back in the second half. Lowell Tew, who had had a broken jaw that had been taped and wired shut, started, and even Nick Terlizzi hobbled onto the field with a broken leg just so he could say he played in a Rose Bowl.

Alabama won 34–14.

"'Bama just took off and ran where she pleased—through tackle, through center, or around the ends, it made little difference where the plays were directed," Braven Dyer of the *Los Angeles Times* wrote. "The Trojans? Well, let's be charitable and say they just didn't have it."

Despite the perfect 10–0 record, it didn't result in another national title, and the final poll was really never in doubt. Although the National Championship Foundation, the Cliff Morgan Foundation, and the Ray Byrne Foundation all had Alabama at No. 1, it finished second in the rest of the polls to Army, which was still enjoying the benefits of essentially being able to recruit players off other teams. Thus, 1945 is not one of the national championships the Crimson Tide claims.

89 Trent Richardson

As far as running back Trent Richardson was concerned the worst part of summer in Tuscaloosa wasn't the countless repetitions in the weight room, all the times running up the stairs, or the monotony of doing things over and over again during the weeks leading up to the opening of fall camp.

Rather, it was the alarm clock consistently going off before sunrise.

"Oh man," he said at 6:00 AM one day while on his way to work out with teammates. "It's more tough because you have get up early morning and get it going. [Strength and conditioning director Scott] Cochran isn't going to lay back and we're not going to let Coach Cochran lay back or we're not going to reach our full potential."

This is when Richardson and the rest of the Crimson Tide put in the base work and conditioning that could make-or-break the team during the upcoming season. Granted, everyone knew that he was a weight-room junkie who posted the kind of numbers that even the biggest and best lineman could be envious of, but his final offseason at the Capstone in 2011 was no different for the Pensacola, Florida native.

To begin with, there's the leadership factor. Richardson had become not only the elder statesman of the running backs, but the entire backfield, quarterbacks included.

"Trent's always been a good leader for us, he really has," Coach Nick Saban said. "I think lot of players respect him. He's always been a competitor here, [in the] group leadership program here, he's been a leader on the field by the way he competes, the kind of person that he is, the way he practices every day, he's a really good person so he affects the people around him in a positive way.

"I think his role is going to be more significant now that he's sort of the lead back for us. I think his leadership will have a great impact. I don't think we're going to ask him to be anything that he hasn't been, because he has been very good in all those regards."

In general, Saban doesn't just look for players to take ownership of their position group, but have an overall regard for the team's well-being. That, in addition to leading by example.

Richardson played through a number of injuries as a sophomore in 2010, including torn ligaments in his ankle/foot, a knee sprain that caused him to miss the Mississippi State and Georgia State games, and a torn abdominal muscle.

He still finished with 700 rushing yards on 112 carries and six touchdowns, and was fifth in team receiving with 23 receptions for 266 yards and four touchdowns. The rushing yards were actually a bit down from his freshman year when he had 751 on 145 carries and eight touchdowns along with 126 receiving yards on 16 catches (no touchdowns), but Richardson averaged 6.3 yards per carry and was second only to Kentucky's Randall Cobb in SEC all-purpose yards.

"There hasn't been a day that I haven't seen Trent not take a play off," said sophomore right tackle D.J. Fluker. "He always comes in to work because that's the kind of guy he is. He always has that go-go attitude.

"That's what you want to see as a player. He's showing us that he's dedicated to the team. He's bought into it."

Not only did that rub off on other players, so did things like showing up on time, being accountable, and taking others under his wing. As for the rest of the team, he liked what he saw during those early morning workouts.

"Attitude, leadership, everybody is just coming together and trusting one another right now," Richardson said. "Last year we were a team, but we weren't a complete team. We used to practice and we used to work hard, but after that we went our separate ways. Now after practice we hang out, we get to know each other. We have that bond. We have that trust. We regained that and respect each other."

Second, Richardson was taking over as Alabama's primary ball carrier, replacing former Heisman Trophy winner Mark Ingram. If he hadn't been reminded enough of that by the media and fans, Ingram himself kept saying things like, "Stay on top of everything," and "You're the man now," while waiting to start his career with the New Orleans Saints.

"I have big shoes that I have to fill," Richardson said. "Mark was an amazing guy, he was able to do some things than no one was able to do. People that compare me to him, it's just an honor.

"He taught me all of his knowledge of the game. I'm just trying to take what he had, on top of what I have, what Coach [Burton] Burns and Coach Saban have taught me, all into one. It is a lot of pressure, but at the same time you can't worry about it."

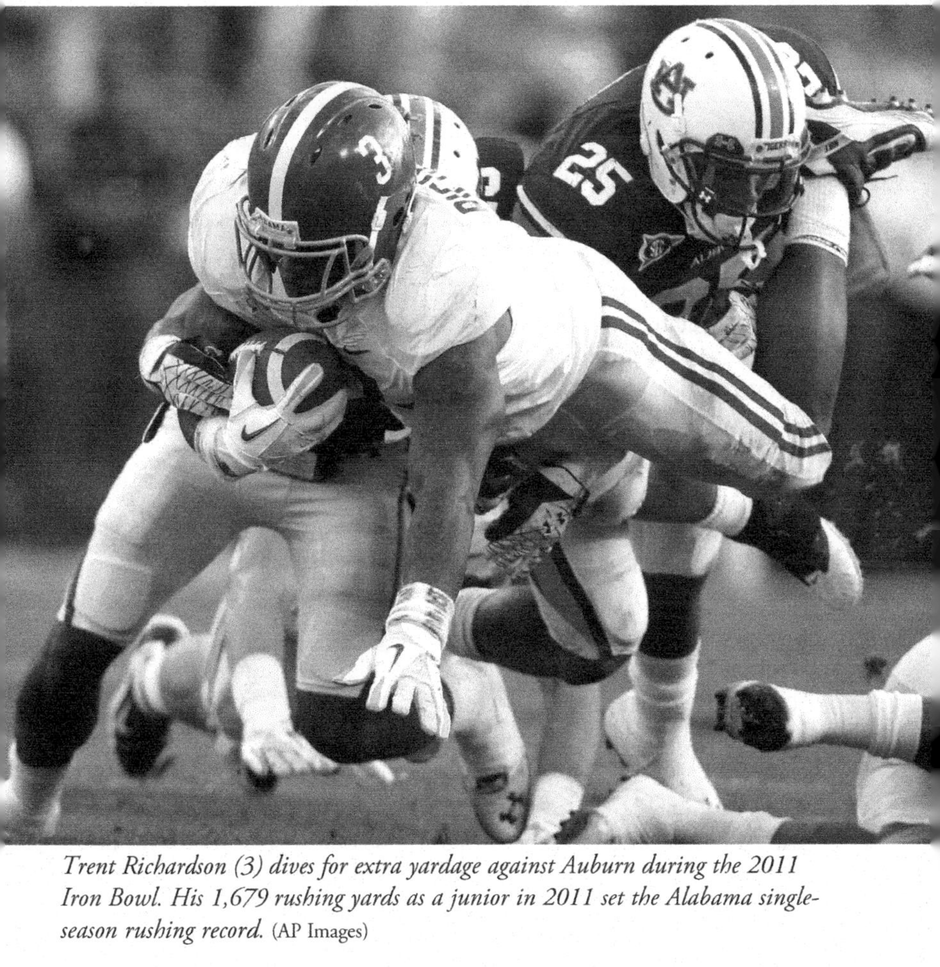

Trent Richardson (3) dives for extra yardage against Auburn during the 2011 Iron Bowl. His 1,679 rushing yards as a junior in 2011 set the Alabama single-season rushing record. (AP Images)

Finally, there was the added pressure everyone on the team felt after Tuscaloosa was devastated by a tornado on April 27.

"We have a lot to play for, we have a lot going on," Richardson said. "If we were to make it [to a championship], this team right here, it would mean so much to so many people. The older guys you don't have to say anything because they know what's going on. Myself? I remind myself all the time, you have so much you're fighting for. It's my family that I'm fighting for. Basically I'm trying to get the team on my back and we're going to ride.

"I just want to go out and dominate every time I get on the field."

Bobby Humphrey

Bobby Humphrey was born on October 11, 1966, in Birmingham, and grew up in the shadows of Legion Field, where he parked cars in yards and sold concessions inside during games. Despite this, his mother didn't want him to play football, and when Humphrey signed up for a youth team at the age of 13 he actually had to keep it from her, which became impossible after winning his first trophy. She had wanted him to be in the band.

In 1986, Ray Perkins' final year at the Capstone, Humphrey accumulated 1,471 rushing yards on 236 carries to become a first-team All-American. With Bill Curry taking the reins, he had 1,255 rushing yards on 238 carries to again earn All-American honors, and against Michigan at the Hall of Fame Bowl tallied 149 yards on 27 carries.

Humphrey finished 10th in voting for the Heisman Trophy voting and seemed poised to make a serious run for the award as a senior, only fate intervened.

During spring practice, the prolific running back sustained a broken left foot, and re-broke it during the regular-season home opener, a 44–10 blowout of Vanderbilt. Instead of risking a repeat, Humphrey decided to turn pro, and left the Capstone owning most of Alabama's rushing records including the career mark of 3,420 yards, which stood until Shaun Alexander came along (1996 to 1999).

Here's how well he did: Alabama won the national championship, his second, and Richardson was a Heisman Trophy finalist and captured the Crimson Tide's first Doak Walker Award as the nation's top running back.

His 1,679 rushing yards set the Alabama single-season rushing record, the 2,083 all-purpose yards established another Crimson Tide record, and the 24 total touchdowns tied the SEC single-season record (Shaun Alexander, 1999). His 144 points scored were significantly more than the Crimson Tide defense allowed all season (106).

90 Hank Crisp

Although he never played for the University of Alabama, nor ever became head coach of the football program, few people left such an indelible mark on the Crimson Tide as Hank Crisp.

Despite losing his right hand at age 13 cutting corn to fill a silo, "Hustlin Hank" became a standout running back at Virginia Tech and captained the 1918 team. In 1921, he was hired to be both an assistant coach for Xen Scott and also coach track. He stayed at the Capstone until 1967.

Not only was Crisp a line coach for Scott, Wallace Wade, Frank Thomas, Red Drew, and J.B. Whitworth, but he also coached the basketball team from 1924 to 1942 and again in 1946. His 19-year run resulted in a 264–133 record that included the Tide's last undefeated season, when it went 20–0 in 1930.

Crisp served as athletic director twice, once for eight years and again for three, but stepped down to make way for the return of Paul W. "Bear" Bryant.

Holt Rast

During his All-American season, Holt Rast made 13 receptions for 207 yards and three touchdowns and had a 10-yard interception return for a touchdown against Texas A&M to be named co-MVP of the 1942 Cotton Bowl (along with Don Whitmire and Jimmy Nelson) as Alabama won a controversial national championship. His other standout performances included a 59-yard touchdown pass from Jimmy Nelson against Georgia in 1941 and blocking a kick and scoring a touchdown against Georgia Tech in 1940.

Bryant had known Crisp since 1930, when as a player he helped lead Fordyce High School to an Arkansas state championship. Crisp was recruiting two of his teammates, but while visiting met Bryant and offered him a scholarship without having seen him play. Because Bryant hadn't completed his coursework, he wasn't academically eligible, yet was allowed by the National Collegiate Athletic Association to complete his courses at Tuscaloosa High School while having his expenses paid by the university (that rule has since been changed).

Crisp looked out for him, but the game that gained Bryant perhaps the most recognition as a player, when as a senior in 1935 he played with a broken leg against Tennessee, was primarily due to Crisp. Bryant recounted in his autobiography what the assistant coach said during a pregame speech:

"I'll tell you gentlemen one thing. I don't know about the rest of you, you or you or you. I don't know what you're going to do. But I know one damn thing. Old 34 will be after 'em, he'll be after their asses.

"In those days they changed the players' numbers almost every week...to sell those quarter programs. So he's up there talking about old 34, and I look down, and I'm 34! I had no idea of playing."

So when Alabama was courting Bryant at Texas A&M, one of the few hurdles to be cleared was Bryant's concern about Crisp,

Hank Crisp was hired as Xen Scott's assistant coach in 1921 and, while he also coached other sports, he stayed at the Capstone until 1967.

whom he did not want to offend. Instead, Crisp flew to Houston, where Tide officials were meeting with Bryant, stood before him, and supposedly said, "Now come on. Get your ass back to Alabama so we can start winnin' some football games."

Crisp's career spanned six Rose Bowls, two Cotton Bowls, an Orange Bowl, 184 wins, 64 losses, and 15 ties. Not only is he enshrined in the Helms Hall of Fame, but he was voted into the Alabama Sports Hall of Fame in the Class of 1970. Approximately an hour before the ceremony, he and his family attended a cocktail party at the Birmingham Museum of Art, where the 75-year-old collapsed and died.

Later that evening, Hank Crisp Jr. accepted the award on his father's behalf and received an emotional standing ovation. He tearfully told the crowd, "This was the happiest day I've ever seen him have."

In 1991 the university dedicated the newly constructed Hank Crisp Indoor Facility in his honor.

91 Hootie Ingram

How could anyone not like a guy called Hootie?

Cecil "Hootie" Ingram was born and raised in Tuscaloosa and became a three-sport standout at Tuscaloosa High School before concentrating on football, and playing some baseball, at the University of Alabama. In addition to being an infielder, Hootie was a standout defensive back and earned All-SEC honors as a sophomore in 1952 after leading the nation with 10 interceptions (which is still a team record) and returning them 173 yards, two for touchdowns.

Ingram also set an Orange Bowl record in the 1953 game, with an 80-yard punt return in Alabama's 61–6 win over Syracuse, and handled kickoffs for the Crimson Tide—developing a reputation for stalling to make sure he got some face time on television.

Ingram later tried his hand at coaching. After serving in the U.S. Army, he coached at the high school level before stints as an assistant coach at Virginia Tech, Georgia, and Arkansas. He was named Clemson's head coach in December 1969.

Following legendary Frank Howard, Ingram tried to give the program a new identity, but his teams only went 12–21.

"When I came to Clemson, then-coach Howard was still athletic director," Ingram recalled in 2000. "He had his office and all of my assistant coaches had an office. The only person who didn't have an office was me. I remember one of the custodial people in Fike [Field House] helped me clean out a storage room. We had some carpet put down and that was my office."

Ingram strongly influenced two Clemson traditions, starting one and nearly derailing the other. The first was the new tiger paw logo.

"I wanted something unique," he said. "The tiger paw was just that."

The other was Clemson's running down the hill to the stadium field. Ingram decided to have the team make its entrance in the west end zone instead, but, after compiling a 6–9 home record, the players came down the hill prior to playing South Carolina in 1972. In a cold, freezing rain, Clemson won 7–6 when Jimmy Williamson knocked down a two-point conversion pass to preserve the win.

But Ingram's best known as an administrator, and for eight years he served on the Southeastern Conference staff before spending nine years as athletic director at Florida State. On September 13, 1989, Ingram returned to the Capstone as director of athletics, which he called "a dream come true."

Ingram's subsequent biggest decision came in 1990, after Bill Curry resigned as head coach. One of the first calls he made was to Bobby Bowden, an Alabama native who would have taken the job when it was instead offered to Curry three years before.

"The timing was bad," Ingram told *The Tuscaloosa News.* "It was just hard to communicate with Bobby in that situation and we had several fine candidates. It wasn't a situation where you wanted to wait that long."

Bowden, who was in Japan to coach an all-star game when Ingram called, considered the proposition, but not for long.

"I thought about it about an hour and decided it was too late," he said. "Gene Stallings evidently was the right guy."

Alabama won the national championship in 1992, but Ingram resigned three years later after the National Collegiate Athletic Association placed the football program on probation, saying he could no longer be an asset to the school.

92 The Heart-Attack Trifecta, the Tuscaloosa Diet

If there's one thing that Tuscaloosa is not particularly known for, it's nutrition.

Healthy proteins and whole grains? Not until they come up with bacon flavor.

Tofu? Can you grill it?

Fruits and vegetables? Do potato salad and coleslaw count?

But that doesn't mean the food isn't worth eating, far from it. In addition to its barbeque huts and college dives, T-town has plenty of places that are must visits for Crimson Tide fans, beginning with Bob Baumhower's restaurants.

The former defensive lineman was a first-team All-SEC and second-team All-American selection in both 1975 and 1976, and obviously a key part of the Crimson Tide defense that yielded just six points per game his junior year and 11.6 his senior season. Baumhower was selected 40th overall in the NFL Draft by the Miami Dolphins, named the NFL Defensive Rookie of the Year, and played in five Pro Bowls.

Baumhower opened his first restaurant in Tuscaloosa in 1981 and has since expanded to other Alabama cities including Birmingham, Huntsville, Daphne, Mobile, and Montgomery. Although they originally specialized in wings, his menus have become more diverse over the years and so have the establishments. He now has two locations just a quick drive from the Capstone: Baumhower's Wings of Tuscaloosa (4251 Courtney Drive) and Bob's Victory Grille in Midtown Village. Both are popular pre- and postgame destinations for fans.

Here are some other key food and drink destinations:

Breakfast: The Waysider (1512 Greensboro Avenue) is in a converted house, which is fitting because it serves homemade food that will probably remind you of your mother or grandmother. The menu features Southern staples like country ham with eggs, red-eye gravy, grits, and warm buttery biscuits.

It's also where Paul W. "Bear" Bryant used to have breakfast, and now the walls help the restaurant serve as a food-related shrine to the coach and Crimson Tide. The numerous regulars add to the local color, but can also make it difficult to get in the door without arriving early.

Lunch: For those in the mood for a good cheeseburger, Rama Jama's (1000 Bryant Drive), across the street from Bryant-Denny Stadium, is essentially a temple to the Crimson Tide. It's full of Alabama memorabilia and owner Gary Lewis looks like he could be Nick Saban's brother. Among its Southern staples are the fried bologna sandwich, which comes in regular and freakishly big sizes, fried onion rings, and breakfast items are served all day. If you're really, really hungry some items include a slice of bacon for each title.

Another local staple is across the Black Warrior River in downtown Northport at City Café (408 Main Avenue), which opens at 4 AM and closes at 3:30 PM. Chances are you'll probably stand in line for a bit, especially near the lunch hour, and the menu changes daily. A typical meal would be something like chicken fried steak, fried green tomatoes, and fried okra. Also, don't even think about getting a drink other than sweet tea.

Dinner: People literally drive from all over to eat at Dreamland, though newcomers are highly encouraged to first visit the original location (5535 15th Ave E) in an area south of town known as Jerusalem Heights. Like numerous other places, its walls honor the Crimson Tide, but if you go be prepared to have ribs, because that's pretty much all that's served. The newer franchise locations, including in Northport, offer more diverse menus.

Although Dreamland is considered *the* T-town delicacy, many locals prefer the sauce and ambiance at Archibald's in Northport (1211 Martin Luther King Jr. Blvd.), but don't act surprised if you see the owner apply water to the cooking ribs with a garden hose. If you're wondering "Is that it?" after driving into a small neighborhood the answer is yes.

Tuscaloosa has numerous other restaurants but on the nicer side is Chuck's Fish (508 Greensboro Avenue), which has some of the best sushi in town, just across the street from Epiphany (519 Greensboro Avenue). Chuck's is where the football coaches take recruits for dinner and the same group owns Five Bar just around the corner. It offers five main entrees every night, five appetizers, etc.

For the truly adventurous, Nick's in the Sticks (4018 Culver Road) is located on the outskirts of town and for years didn't have a sign marking its location. A word of warning, though, if you try the house concoction, a Nickodemus, make sure someone else drives.

Bars: Midway between downtown and the Strip is Innisfree Irish Pub (1925 University Blvd.), a popular destination for both diehard fans and former players. Before moving to its new location and adding a kitchen it was where many people went to try to avoid college students (except on weekend nights, that's impossible). Now the opposite is true. One thing that hasn't changed is when there's no major live sporting event the televisions frequently show a Crimson Tide classic. Except for live games, Alabama has a perfect record at Innisfree, with no losses and no ties.

For those looking for something a little more non-collegiate, the Alcove International Tavern is located a little off the beaten path on 22nd Avenue, between 7th and 8th Street. Billed as the area's first upscale neighborhood pub, it not only offers everything from a vast beer selection to top-dollar drinks, but for a long while was the only bar in Tuscaloosa that didn't allow smoking inside.

With the craft beer movement finally taking hold in Tuscaloosa, Loosa Brews is a popular destination for locals, located across the street from Innisfree, along with the Druid City, Black Warrior and Band of Brothers brewing companies.

Houndstooth Sports Bar (1300 University Blvd.) remains a popular destination on game days, but most other bars along "The Strip," the collection of stores and restaurants within walking distance of Bryant-Denny Stadium (and considered the primary place for Alabama students to celebrate after games), have left or closed. One that has stayed is Gallette's. Some fans have the signature Yellowhammer drink as part of their gameday ritual—along with some Big Bad Wolves' barbecue nachos across the street—but the bar is very much geared to college students.

Some of the staples in, or around, Temerson Square near downtown include Copper Top, Top Shelf Tavern, Catch 22, Avenue Pub and Wilhagan's, which all have very different styles. There's also The Gray Lady, named after Legion Field in Birmingham, and actually has some of the stadium's field turf on display.

93 Xen Scott

There's a story that Joe Sewell, who played football at Alabama but was better known for his success in baseball, used to tell about Xen Scott, who went 29–9–3 from 1919 to 1922 and is considered by many to be Alabama's first great football coach.

The team was in the middle of practice and Scott, who was ill at the time, walked off the field. Not sure what to do, and fearful of making the wrong decision, the players kept practicing until it was dark out. Hours later, someone was able to contact Scott's wife, who told them the coach was resting. Finally, they went home.

Because of World War I, Alabama didn't sport a team in 1918 and had finished 5–2–1 the year before in Thomas Kelly's final season with the Crimson Tide. So naturally, school president Dr. George Hutcheson Denny, a huge football fan, hired a horse racing writer from Cleveland, who had never played the game at a high level, to coach the team.

If anyone was laughing, they certainly weren't after Alabama crushed its first five opponents by a combined score of 225–0, including 49–0 against Ole Miss and 40–0 vs. Sewanee. Led by

Richard Todd

Richard Todd is not listed among Alabama's all-time passing leaders (he completed 101 of 189 passes for 1,642 yards), but from 1973 to 1975 he never lost a conference game as Alabama won three of five straight Southeastern Conference titles.

For his collegiate career Todd passed for 16 touchdowns and ran for 16 more and had a knack for winning. He was named the Most Valuable Player of the 1976 Sugar Bowl, a 13–6 victory against Penn State, and was MVP of the South Team at the subsequent Senior Bowl.

After being the sixth-overall selection in the 1976 NFL Draft, Todd led the New York Jets to their first winning record since 1969, 10–5–1 in 1981, and to the AFC Championship Game the following year.

After 10 years with the Jets and New Orleans Saints, Todd retired having completed 1,610 of 2,967 passes for 20,610 yards and 124 touchdowns, with 161 interceptions. He also rushed for 932 yards and 14 touchdowns. In a 1980 game against San Francisco, he set a National Football League record with 42 completions. The record stood until Drew Bledsoe completed 45 in 1994.

players like Mulley Lenoir, Ike Rogers, and Riggs Stephenson, the Tide posted a then-program-best eight victories, with only a 16–12 loss to Vanderbilt in Nashville preventing a perfect season and first Southern Conference title.

Scott's team managed to top that mark in 1920, the first 10-win season in Alabama history. It outscored its opponents 377–35 with eight shutouts, and crossed the Mason-Dixon Line for the first time, pounding Case College in Cleveland, Ohio, 40–0. The Tide defeated Sewanee again, 21–0, and also avenged its loss to Vanderbilt, even though the Commodores were the only opponent to score during Alabama's first eight games.

However, similar to 1919, the Tide had one stumble, a 21–14 road loss to Georgia, after the Bulldogs returned two blocked kicks and a fumble for touchdowns.

After compiling an 18–2 record over two years, Scott had to rebuild in 1921, and following a 4–0 start, the Tide went into a 0–4–2 tailspin beginning with a 17–0 loss to Sewanee in Birmingham. Only a controversial 14–7 victory over Tulane in New Orleans secured a winning season at 5–4–2, but Scott had laid the groundwork for an impressive run that would propel Alabama into football glory.

It began with a 111–0 victory against Marion Institute, and although Alabama lost 33–7 to Georgia Tech, 19–10 at Texas, and tied Sewanee 7–7, the Crimson Tide's schedule included a November 4 showdown with highly regarded Penn in Philadelphia, where the home team was considered a sizable favorite, especially since Northeast football was still thought to be vastly superior to that played in the South.

A field goal by Bull Wesley and the recovery of teammate Pooley Hubert's fumble in the end zone by center Shorty Propst was all Alabama needed to pull off a remarkable 9–7 upset in front of 25,000 fans. The Tide celebrated the program's biggest victory to date by parading through the city, but due to health reasons Scott had already turned in his letter of resignation. Alabama finished 6–3–1 after a 59–0 victory against Mississippi State. Scott died soon after from throat cancer.

94 Jay Barker

He was 10 years old and had it all worked out: go to Alabama and play for Paul W. "Bear" Bryant.

When Jay Barker's father, Jerome, asked him how success happens, he said, "It isn't so much the will to win but the will to prepare to win."

"In a way it was kind of shocking to some degree," Jerome Barker told *The New York Times* in 1994. "I had always heard in the business world, or athletics, about the will to win.

"I thought to myself, 'This kid has got it together.'"

Although Jay Barker didn't play for Bryant, he did make it to the Capstone despite not playing quarterback until his senior year at Hewitt-Trussville High School in Trussville, Alabama. At Alabama he compiled an amazing record of 35–2–1 as a starter (although Alabama was later forced to forfeit all its regular-season wins from 1993 due to an ineligible player).

The first loss came his junior year to Auburn, when Barker had to leave the game with torn ligaments in his left knee that required surgery. The other came in the SEC Championship Game his senior year, when Alabama was edged by Florida, 24–23.

But Barker's long list of accomplishments started well before then.

As a freshman he stepped in when Danny Woodson was suspended for violating team rules and led a 20–17 victory at LSU followed by a tight 13–6 win against Auburn in the Iron Bowl. After defeating defending national champion Colorado in the Blockbuster Bowl, 30–25, Alabama finished the season 11–1.

As a sophomore, Barker helped lead Alabama to the national championship, but 267 rushing yards against Miami in the Sugar Bowl, the Tide never even bothered to establish its passing game, with Barker completing just four passes for a paltry 18 yards.

"He's a totally unselfish player," Coach Gene Stallings once said of Barker. "He's not in it for the credit. He's in it because he loves to play and compete. I love Jay Barker. He knows that. I love what he stands for."

Greg McElroy

He came in known as the player who filled the gap when star recruit Tim Tebow picked Florida over Alabama, but left holding numerous Crimson Tide records—including single-season passing yards with 2,987 in 2009. That year he also led Alabama to a perfect season, the national championship, and was named MVP of the SEC Championship Game after the Crimson Tide knocked off No. 1 Florida and Tebow.

McElroy was a finalist for both a Rhodes Scholarship and *Sports Illustrated's* Sportsman of the Year, and he nearly dethroned Jay Barker as Alabama's winningest quarterback.

"I want people to remember me as just a teammate," he said. "I want them to remember me as caring for the team, caring about winning, putting all individual accomplishment aside and just worrying about success of the football team. If people remember me as a winner, and people remember me as doing everything I possibly can to help the program succeed and the university succeed, then I'll have done my job here.

"Quite frankly, Alabama owes me nothing. I owe everything to Alabama, and the opportunity to play here definitely shaped my life in a way I never could have imagined."

Despite a bad shoulder, Barker completed an undefeated regular season as a senior, including close victories against Georgia, Tennessee, Mississippi State, and Auburn. He closed his career with a touchdown pass to running back Sherman Williams as Alabama defeated talent-laden Ohio State 24–17 in the Florida Citrus Bowl, and was the recipient of the Johnny Unitas Golden Arm Award.

Even though he didn't put up gaudy single-game passing numbers, Barker set Alabama records for passing yards (5,689), completions (402), and attempts (706).

"For me, just to put on the jersey was a dream come true," Barker said. "Then to finally play, and then to start, all these things seem little to a lot of these guys out here, where they don't grow up around it or are from another state, or maybe they would have played anywhere they wanted. I think I appreciated those little things, and when these big things came along, oh, man. This is unreal to me."

95 The Bear Playing on a Broken Leg

If there was one aspect of Coach Paul W. "Bear" Bryant that was never in doubt, it was his toughness. He was towering and intimidating, and when he told his players to do something, they had better darn well do it if they wanted to keep playing football.

Although Bryant may be best remembered in that regard for his rigorous offseason conditioning programs—especially his famous "Junction Boys" training, when he took his first team at Texas A&M to a barren army base and ran a brutal boot camp in 100-degree heat, and less than a third of the 100 players made the return trip—it was a trait that permeated his entire life.

Arthur "Tarzan" White

Guard Arthur "Tarzan" White was named a first-team All-American in 1936 and played in the National Football League after being a second-round selection by the New York Giants in the 1937 draft (actually held on December 12, 1936)—and he also won the belt as the World Heavyweight Wrestling Champion.

"His nickname was Bear. Now imagine a guy that can carry the nickname Bear," Joe Namath said on ESPN's *SportsCentury* series.

Of course, the nickname came after he wrestled a real bear at age 13.

Bryant's football career began as an eighth grader, and he eventually helped lead the Fordyce High School Redbugs to a state championship. From there it was on to Alabama. While practicing with the Crimson Tide in the fall of 1931, he took high school classes to finish his degree. In June 1935, while still a player, Bryant secretly married Mary Harmon. Their first of two children, Mae Martin, was born nine months later. Paul Jr., who would become a prominent businessman, was born in 1944.

After graduating, Bryant was an assistant coach with Alabama for four years under Frank Thomas, and was at Vanderbilt for two. He then served in the Navy before becoming the head coach at Maryland. Bryant resigned after one season, took over Kentucky, guided the Wildcats to a 60–23–5 record and their lone Southeastern Conference championship in 1950, but resigned from there too when it became obvious that school officials would always consider basketball to be a higher priority. From there it was on to Texas A&M.

As a player, one game Bryant is particularly known for was at Tennessee in 1935, even though standout Riley Smith, who would be the second-overall selection in the first NFL draft (three rounds before Bryant) scored two touchdowns.

In addition to catching a touchdown pass, Bryant lateraled to Smith for another score, all while playing on a broken leg. *Atlanta Constitution* reporter Ralph McGill doubted the diagnosis and showed up early for the following week's game against Georgia and asked to see the X-ray. Indeed, it showed a broken fibula sustained against Mississippi State, from which Bryant was quoted as saying, "It was just one little bone."

(Note: For more on why Bryant played in that game, see No. 90, Hank Crisp.)

96 Mike Shula

As a three-year quarterback (1984–86), Mike Shula completed 313 of 578 passes for 4,069 yards, 35 touchdowns, and 30 interceptions, and he compiled a 32–15–1 record.

Although he led victories against Southern California in the 1985 Aloha Bowl and Washington in the 1986 Sun Bowl, he's known for three games in particular:

- The season-opening 20–16 victory at Georgia in 1985. Down three points with just 50 seconds remaining in the game, Shula marched the Tide 71 yards in five plays, topped by a 17-yard touchdown pass to flanker Al Bell.
- At the 1985 Iron Bowl, he led a six-play, 45-yard drive that was topped by Van Tiffin's 52-yard game-winning field goal.
- The 28–10 victory against Notre Dame in 1986, Alabama's first ever win over the Fighting Irish.

On May 9, 2003, Shula returned to the Capstone with the mandate to save, or at least keep afloat, the program, which

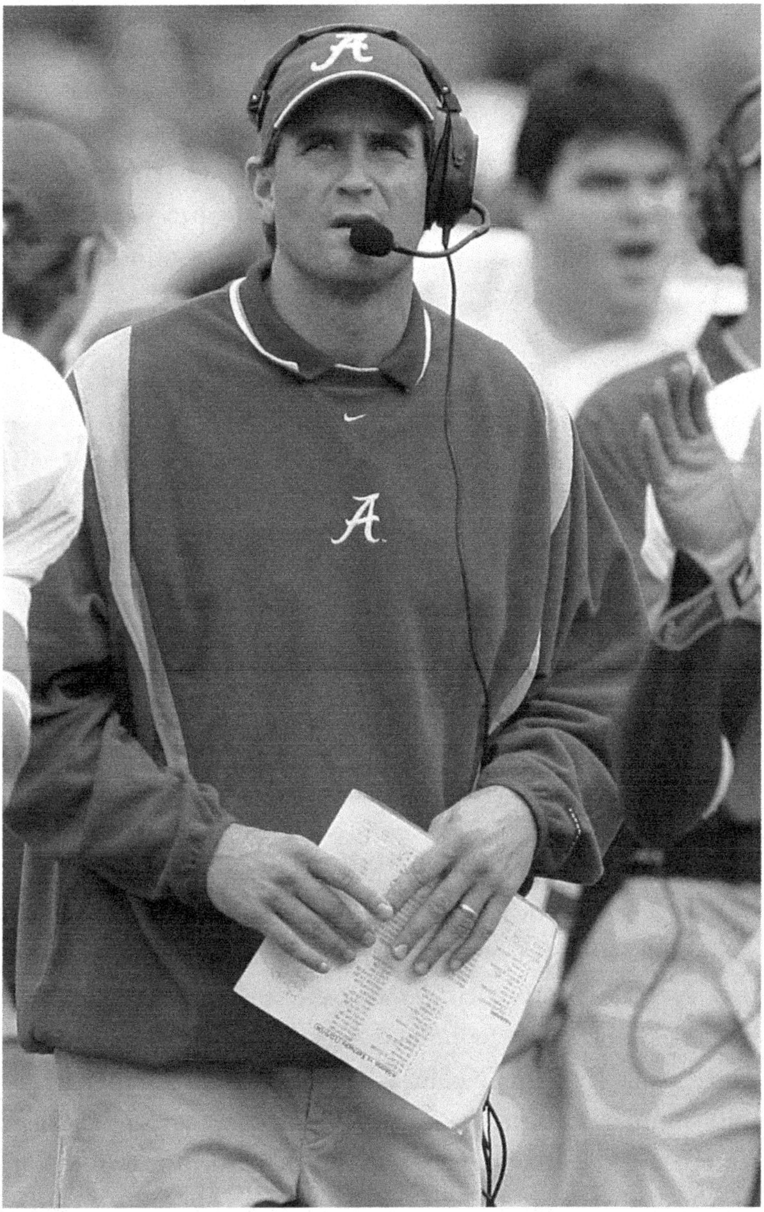

On May 9, 2003, former Alabama quarterback Mike Shula returned to the Capstone after the football program had endured National Collegiate Athletic Association sanctions, Dennis Franchione had skipped town for Texas A&M, and Mike Price had been dismissed before coaching a single game. At age 37, he was the second-youngest head coach in Division I football.

during the previous year had endured National Collegiate Athletic Association sanctions, Dennis Franchione skipping town for Texas A&M, and Mike Price being dismissed before ever coaching a game. At age 37, he was the second-youngest head coach in Division I football (a year and two days older than Greg Schiano of Rutgers), and Alabama's youngest coach since the hiring of 31-year-old Wallace Wade in 1923 and 33-year-old Frank Thomas in 1931.

"I had some unfinished business," said Shula, who never won a Southeastern Conference title as a player.

Signing Day in recruiting and spring practice had already come and gone, leaving just 115 days until the season opener. Despite that, Alabama won 40–17 against South Florida, and then fought No. 1 Oklahoma and Heisman Trophy winner Jason White tooth-and-nail in a 20–13 home loss.

Shula's improbable, if not impossible, first season resulted in a 4–9 record.

"He's paying dues," said former Alabama defensive back Don McNeal, who also played for Shula's father, Don, with the Miami Dolphins. "Coming in like that is going to be tough. Give him some time...please give him some time and he'll be okay."

Alabama was bowl eligible again in 2004, but the season nearly completely unraveled when quarterback Brodie Croyle blew out his right knee against Western Carolina and was lost for the year. He would soon be joined by running back Ray Hudson and fullback Tim Castille, and at one point the Crimson Tide was down to its third-string quarterback, tailback, fullback, and tight end, but still scraped together six wins to play Minnesota in the Music City Bowl.

Shula had Alabama as high as third nationally in 2005 while collecting victories over No. 5 Florida (31–3) and No. 17 Tennessee (6–3). The win over the Gators was the first Tide victory

Joe Kines

To Crimson Tide fans, Joe Kines is thought of as the most popular coach who never won a game at Alabama.

In 1985–86, Kines served as the Tide's defensive coordinator and inside linebackers coach before leaving with Ray Perkins for the National Football League's Tampa Bay Buccaneers. But he returned in 2003 and served as Mike Shula's defensive coordinator for four seasons.

Alabama ended the 2004 campaign ranked second in the nation in total defense (245.5) and in 2005 was in the top nine in all five major statistical categories. The Tide was first in scoring defense, second in total defense, fifth in pass defense and pass efficiency defense, and ninth in rushing defense.

After Shula was fired following the Auburn loss in 2006, Kines was the team's interim coach for the Independence Bowl, but the Tide lost on a last-second field goal.

"I would give anything to be the head coach at Alabama," Kines said. "This isn't an election. I don't know where to go from here. This is the greatest job in America, and I hope to stay in some capacity."

Kines was not retained by incoming coach Nick Saban, but he stayed on at the Capstone for a year as a special assistant to the athletic director and to help with fund-raising before being lured away for a short stint as the Texas A&M defensive coordinator.

over a top-five team at Bryant-Denny Stadium, and the win over Tennessee was the first over the Volunteers in Tuscaloosa since 1930 (they usually played at Legion Field).

With a 13–10 victory against Texas Tech at the Cotton Bowl, Alabama finished 10–2 and ranked eighth in the final Associated Press poll.

"When you go through some tough times together, you find out a lot about each other," Shula said. "There's a lot of different ways you can go, and this team pulled together. And this was the result of it, 10 wins."

However, when the Tide stumbled to 6–6 the following year, including a 24–16 home loss to Mississippi State, and lost its fifth straight game to rival Auburn (four with Shula as coach), he was dismissed with a 26–23 record.

97 The RV Experience

One of the biggest problems many serious Crimson Tide fans have when they purchase a home is that the property must be big enough to also store a mobile home/recreational vehicle.

No joke.

Scores of fans are so into Alabama football that they basically bring their entire lives, and many key and vital possessions, to Tuscaloosa for home games and then go on the road with the team as well. Some all but completely live on the road during the fall, returning home only during bye weeks and after the completion of the regular season (but then take off again for the postseason).

Bowls love the Crimson Tide because the fans travel in droves (RVs or not), and unsuspecting host communities can be caught completely off-guard by the massive volume of traffic clogging the roads days before kickoff.

At the Capstone, RVs will be seen all over town the week of a big game, filling parking lots, lining the sides of roads, and frequently sticking out behind trees in very awkward ways (as though they're playing hide-and-seek but don't seem to quite realize that the tree doesn't offer much protection).

Yes, the recreational vehicle has become as much of a Crimson Tide staple as the elephant (which is smaller) and Denny Chimes (which is less conspicuous).

"You kind of sensed it all week," quarterback Brodie Croyle said about Alabama's crushing defeat of No. 5 Florida at Bryant-Denny Stadium in 2005. "It was the craziest week in the five years I've been there. Me and Coach [Dave] Rader, we always judged how big a game was by how many motor homes were waiting to get into the parking lot [when it opened] on Thursday. That was a record, 19. It was a big game."

The fans also customize their homes on wheels, which open up like giant piñatas, only instead of something like candy and toys spewing out of the exploding carcass, imagine other grown-up goodies, such as a makeshift living room with a large-screen TV (hooked up to a satellite dish), furniture, and a barbeque.

Some even haul behind them an extra car to get around town, or a golf cart, which have also become exceedingly popular in Tuscaloosa.

J.B. "Ears" Whitworth

After Harold "Red" Drew resigned at the end of the 1954 season with a record of 54–28–7, among those mentioned as a possible replacement was former Alabama player and assistant coach Paul W. "Bear" Bryant, who was coming off a 1–9 season in his first year at Texas A&M. Instead, the Board of Trustees athletic committee selected former player J.B. "Ears" Whitworth, who was the head coach at Oklahoma State and had been a tackle on the Crimson Tide's 1931 Rose Bowl team.

The subsequent season was the worst in Alabama history, 0–10 with none of the games even close. Alabama was outscored 256–48. Whitworth didn't get his first victory until his 15th game, 13–12 against Mississippi State, ending a nonwinning streak of 20 that went back to October 16, 1954 (27–0 vs. Tennessee). His second and third seasons resulted in identical 2–7–1 records, for a three-year total of 4–24–2.

Combined with Auburn beating Alabama 40–0 and going on to win its lone national championship, Alabama officials decided it was time for something drastic and went back and hired Bryant.

The RV community, which many say is a must for every true Alabama fan to experience at some point in their lives, grew so much that *The New York Times* writer Warren St. John actually aquired a small motor home and traveled with the Tide for a season. He chronicled his journeys in the very successful book *Rammer Jammer Yellow Hammer.*

St. John also picked a good year to do it, 1999, when Alabama won the Southeastern Conference championship, which helped make the book an essential and popular read for all Tide fans—even those barely old enough to drive.

98 Pat Trammell

One of the most beloved players in Crimson Tide football history was Pat Trammell, who grew up in Scottsboro, Alabama, and was the starting quarterback from 1959 to 1961.

Trammell wasn't your typical college football player, even though he played during the "one-platoon" era when, before unlimited substitutions, players had to line up on both the offensive and defensive sides.

"Well, they're not blocking anyone, so I'd thought I'd see if they could play defense," Trammell once explained to Coach Paul W. "Bear" Bryant on why he quick-kicked on third down.

During his sophomore season, Trammell had the distinction of leading the Tide in both rushing (525 yards, 156 carries), and passing (21 of 49, 293 yards). As a senior, when he was a second-team All-American as well as an Academic All-American, Trammell became the first Alabama player to pass for more than 1,000 yards in a season, while only having two attempts intercepted.

"He can't run, he can't pass, and he can't kick," Bryant once said. "All he can do is beat you."

Trammell's final year with the Crimson Tide was one of the greatest in Alabama history, when the team simply destroyed the competition by going 11–0 and outscored opponents 297–25. It didn't reach No. 1 in the rankings until late November, and then topped the year off with a 10–3 victory against Arkansas in the Sugar Bowl to win Bryant's first national title. Incidentally, Trammell scored the lone touchdown against the Razorbacks.

During his three years taking snaps for Alabama, the Tide compiled an impressive 26–3–4 record, and also played in the Liberty (a 7–0 loss to Penn State in the inaugural game, played in frigid conditions) and Bluebonnet (a 3–3 tie with Texas) bowls.

In 1961 Trammell was named the Southeastern Conference's MVP and finished fifth in voting for the Heisman Trophy.

Alabama Academic All-Americans (Through 2015)

1961: Tommy Brooker, end; Pat Trammell, quarterback
1964: Gaylon McCollough, center
1965: Denis Homan, end; Steve Sloan, quarterback
1967: Bob Childs, linebacker; Steve Davis, kicker
1970: Johnny Musso, tailback
1971: Johnny Musso, tailback
1973: Randy Hall, defensive tackle
1974: Randy Hall, defensive tackle
1975: Danny Ridgeway, kicker
1979: Major Ogilvie, halfback
2002: Kenny King, defensive tackle
2009: Barrett Jones, guard; Colin Peek, tight end
2010: Barrett Jones, guard; Greg McElroy, quarterback
2011: Barrett Jones, tackle
2012: Barrett Jones, center
2014: Arie Kouandjio, guard
2015: Ryan Kelly, center

Additionally, he was inducted into the Alabama Sports Hall of Fame in 1975 (though as of this writing was not eligible for the College Football Hall of Fame because he was only a second-team All-American, and it is required that candidates be first-team).

Trammell also helped set a very high bar for Alabama quarterbacks and was followed by the likes of Joe Namath, Steve Sloan, and Kenny Stabler, who all led impressive runs at national championships over the subsequent five years.

Meanwhile Trammell went back to school and earned his Doctor of Medicine (M.D.) degree at Alabama, only to be diagnosed with testicular cancer. After the 1968 Iron Bowl, a 24–16 victory for the Tide, players presented Trammell with the game ball. He died a week later, on December 10, at the age of 28.

Bryant called it the saddest day of his life.

99 The Million Dollar Band

Before each game, the various sections of the marching band gather in the heart of the campus, the area known as the Quad, go through their pregame warmups, have a little fun with tailgating fans and kids, and then come together as part of the crescendo to kickoff.

The concert begins on the library steps, with the eventual procession, accompanied by more cheerleaders and majorettes than you can twirl a baton at, leading everyone to Bryant-Denny Stadium in time for pregame festivities and to see the team take the field.

It features the first of numerous renditions of the signature song, "Yea Alabama," which mentions early rivalries against

Georgia and Georgia Tech and honors the team's heritage with the line "Remember the Rose Bowl, we'll win then."

When he was coaching the Crimson Tide, Mike Shula would ask boosters to sing the first couple of lines of the song. If they got "drown them Tide," correct, he knew they were real fans.

However, a good Saturday ends with the controversial cheer "Rammer Jammer" to celebrate a victory.

It goes like this (with musical accompaniment from a roaring 400-member marching band and a screaming student section), say after beating a team like Georgia:

"Hey Bulldogs;

"Hey Bulldogs;

"Hey Bulldogs;

Alabama's Most Famous Cheerleader

Although she grew up in Meridian, Mississippi, Sela Ward attended the University of Alabama and graduated in 1977. Along the way, she joined a sorority and became a cheerleader, but she didn't date the starting quarterback. Her best friend did, while Ward dated defensive lineman Bob Baumhower.

Some of her movies include *The Fugitive* and *The Day After Tomorrow*, she appeared in 10 episodes on the TV show *House*, and further endeared herself to Alabama fans when her character on *CSI: NY* openly rooted for the Crimson Tide. The actress won two Emmy Awards and a Golden Globe for her work on *Once and Again* and *Sisters.*

In 2005, Ward returned to the Capstone to address Alabama's spring commencement ceremonies and receive an honorary doctorate of humane letters.

"After several futile attempts to come up with something 'profound' to say to you today, it dawned on me that clearly I was asked to speak to you because I represent an Alabama alum who went on to some modicum of success," she said. "My mission is to encourage and beckon you graduating seniors to the world that awaits you...and inspire you to dream a little."

"We just beat the hell out of you. Rammer Jammer, Yellow Hammer, give 'em hell Alabama!"

Rinse. Repeat if necessary. Repeat again if it was a big game. Repeat all offseason if the opponent was Auburn.

FYI, the yellow hammer is the state bird.

Although the marching band was created in 1913 as a 14–person unit, it picked up the "Million Dollar Band" nickname in 1922 thanks to alumnus W.C. "Champ" Pickens, supposedly in reference to its fund-raising prowess.

The 1948 Alabama football media guide described the name's origins as follows:

"At the time the band was named (1922), it was having a hard struggle. The only way they could get to Georgia Tech for a game was by soliciting funds from the merchants. They usually had to ride all night in a day coach, and we thought it was swell when we finally got a tourist sleeper and put two to a lower and two to an upper berth."

During that Georgia Tech game in 1922, won 33–7 by the Yellow Jackets, an Atlanta sportswriter commented to Pickens, "You don't have much of a team; what do you have at Alabama?" Pickens replied, "A Million Dollar Band."

According to the band's Internet site, there have been seven band directors through 2015: Dr. Gustav Wittig (1913–17); Captain H.H. Turner (1927–34); Colonel Carleton K. Butler (1935–68); Earl Dunn (1969–70); Dr. James Ferguson (1971–83); Ms. Kathryn B. Scott (1984–2002); and Dr. Kenneth Ozzello (2003–15). From 1917 to 1927, the marching band was led by students.

100 1941: The Two-Loss Title

When the Crimson Tide began the 1941 season, it had won only one Southeastern Conference title since the 1934 national championship season, but the program was clearly on an upswing despite a 13–0 loss to Mississippi State to finish the previous season 7–2.

Back Jimmy Nelson and end Holt Rast would lead Alabama, and both were unanimous All-America selections, but another setback against the Bulldogs, this time early in the season, seemed to end any chance of a conference title.

Nevertheless, the Crimson Tide recorded impressive victories against Tennessee (9–2), Georgia (27–14), and Georgia Tech (20–0) to hover near the top of the rankings, even with a late-season 7–0 loss at Vanderbilt.

Alabama concluded the regular season by defeating the Miami Hurricanes 21–7 in the first meeting between the schools (and second-ever night game for the Crimson Tide) and accepted an invitation to play Texas A&M in the Cotton Bowl.

In scouting the Aggies, assistant coach Harold "Red" Drew said they had "the greatest passing team I have ever seen," and head coach Frank Thomas, who almost never slept well the night before a big game, complained that studying the dynamic offense gave him headaches. Fortunately for the Crimson Tide, the game was played in poor weather conditions, making it harder for the Aggies to pass.

Alabama, in its first postseason appearance other than the Rose Bowl, created 12 turnovers, including seven interceptions, in a 29–21 victory that was nowhere near as close as the score indicated. Even though Texas A&M had a 13–1 advantage in first downs, the Tide still scored four touchdowns and attempted just seven passes, and all 41 players who made the trip got into the game (in part leading to two late touchdowns by the Aggies).

Rast returned an interception for a touchdown, halfback Russ Craft twice reached the end zone, and Nelson returned a punt 72 yards for one touchdown and added a second on a 21-yard run. Nelson, Rast, and guard Don Whitmire shared game MVP honors.

"The boys really turned in some defensive work," Thomas told *The Dallas Morning News*. "It was the lifesaver for us. Our boys played a good, aggressive game—the best of the season."

Although the majority of polls had Minnesota No. 1 at season's end, Alabama and Texas, neither of which clinched a conference title, were able to claim a share of the national championship

1941: 9–2, National Champions

Date	Opponent	Location	W/L	Score
September 27	SW Louisiana	Tuscaloosa	W	47–6
October 4	Mississippi State	Tuscaloosa	L	14–0
October 11	Howard	Birmingham, Ala.	W	61–0
October 18	Tennessee	Knoxville, Tenn.	W	9–2
October 25	Georgia	Birmingham, Ala.	W	27–14
November 1	Kentucky	Tuscaloosa	W	30–0
November 8	Tulane	New Orleans, La.	W	19–14
November 15	Georgia Tech	Birmingham, Ala.	W	20–0
November 22	Vanderbilt	Nashville, Tenn.	L	7–0
November 28	Miami (Florida)	Miami, Fla.	W	21–7
January 1, 1942	Texas A&M	Cotton Bowl	W	29–21
				263–85

Coach: Frank Thomas
Captain: John Wyhonic
Ranking (AP): Preseason—no ranking; Postseason—No. 20.
All-American: First team—Holt Rast, end. Second team—Jimmy Nelson, halfback.
All-SEC (first team): Jimmy Nelson, back; Holt Rast, back; John Wyhonic, guard.
Leaders: Rushing—Jimmy Nelson (361 yards, 109 carries); Passing—Jimmy Nelson (25 of 54, 394 yards); Receiving—Holt Rast (13 catches, 207 yards).

thanks to the Houlgate System (1927–58), a mathematical rating system developed by Dale Houlgate of Los Angeles, which was syndicated in newspapers and published in *Illustrated Football* and *Football Thesaurus*.

It wasn't picturesque, but Alabama decided years later to count it. Besides, the Cotton Bowl victory came less than a month after the attack on Pearl Harbor, plunging the country into World War II. It was hardly the time to complain about football. Many players enlisted and eventually headed overseas.

Appendix

To Do:

- See Alabama win a national championship
- Attend an Iron Bowl
- Go to a game at Bryant–Denny Stadium
- Tailgate on the Quad
- See Alabama win an SEC championship
- Smoke a cigar on "The Third Saturday of October"
- Visit the Paul W. Bryant Museum
- Welcome the team at the Walk of Champions
- Go bowling
- Visit Legion Field
- Proudly own and wear crimson and houndstooth
- Attend A-Day
- Visit Bear Bryant's grave
- Have your photo taken with Big Al
- Check out Denny Chimes and the team captain names in concrete
- Go to a game in an RV (or get an autographed copy of Warren St. John's book *Rammer Jammer Yellow Hammer*)
- Get an autograph of your favorite player
- Attend an Alabama game at a rival stadium
- High-five one of the Heisman Trophies
- Visit the College Football Hall of Fame
- Visit the Alabama Sports Hall of Fame
- Attend a neutral-site game
- Check out Mal Moore's ring collection in the lobby of the building bearing his name
- Have breakfast at the table with Bear Bryant's bust on it at Waysider's
- Learn the words to "Yea Alabama"

Sources

The sources for this book are essentially too numerous to list, but most of the accumulated information simply came from years of doing my day job as the Crimson Tide beat writer for Bleacher Report, BamaOnline.com (247Sports) and *The Tuscaloosa News.* That means more media guides, Internet sites, press conferences, interviews, transcripts, and press releases than you could imagine—and from a variety of bowls, conferences, services, and teams. I was also fortunate enough to have access to the minutes from athletics department meetings under the direction of Frank Thomas (although riveting reading it wasn't).

In addition to my thousands of articles, the other sources for this book include:

Books

Brown, Scott, and Will Collier. *The Uncivil War: Alabama vs. Auburn, 1981–1994.* Nashville, TN: Rutledge Hill Press, 1995.

Bryant, Paul "Bear," with John Underwood. *Bear: The Hard Life & Good Times of Alabama's Coach Bryant.* Boston: Little, Brown, 1974.

Dunnavant, Keith. *The Missing Ring: How Bear Bryant and the 1966 Alabama Crimson Tide Were Denied College Football's Most Elusive Prize.* New York: St. Martin's Griffin, 2006.

Groom, Winston. *The Crimson Tide: An Illustrated History of Football at the University of Alabama.* Tuscaloosa, AL: University of Alabama Press, 2000.

Gruensfelder, Melvin Henry. "A History of the Origin and Development of the Southeastern Conference." Thesis, University of Illinois at Urbana-Champaign, 1964.

Hicks, Tommy. *Game of My Life Alabama: Memorable Stories of Crimson Tide Football.* Champaign, IL: Sports Publishing, LLC, 2006.

Maccambridge, Michael. *ESPN College Football Encyclopedia: The Complete History of the Game.* Bristol, CT: ESPN, 2005.

Macmillan. *The Baseball Encyclopedia, 1997 edition.* New York: Macmillan, 1997.

National Collegiate Athletic Association. *The Official 2007 Division I and Division I-AA Football Records Book.* Chicago: Triumph Books, 2007.

Scott, Richard. *Legends of Alabama Football.* Champaign, IL: Sports Publishing, LLC, 2004.

St. John, Warren. *Rammer Jammer Yellow Hammer: A Road Trip into the Heart of Fan Mania.* New York: Three Rivers Press, 2004.

Stone, Naylor. *Coach Tommy of the Crimson Tide.* Vulcan Press, 1954.

Townsend, Steve. *Tales from Alabama Football, 1978–79: A Time of Champions.* Champaign, IL: Sports Publishing, LLC, 2003.

Walsh, Christopher J. *Crimson Storm Surge: Alabama Football Then and Now.* Boulder, CO: Taylor Trade Publications, 2005.

Walsh, Christopher J. Sweet 16: Alabama's Historic Championship Season. Chicago: Triumph Books, 2016.

Walsh, Christopher J. *Where Football Is King: A History of the SEC.* Boulder, CO: Taylor Trade Publications, 2006.

Walsh, Christopher J. *Who's #1?: 100-Plus Years of Controversial National Champions in College Football.* Boulder, CO: Taylor Trade Publications, 2007.

Warner, Chris. *SEC Sports Quotes.* Baton Rouge, LA: C.E.W. Enterprises, 2002.

Warner, Chris. *SEC Sports Quotes II.* Baton Rouge, LA: C.E.W. Enterprises, 2003.

Newspapers, Magazines, and Journals

The [Baton Rouge] *Advocate*
The Atlanta Constitution
The Boston Post
Chattanooga Times Free Press
The Dallas Morning News
Los Angeles Times
The Montgomery Advertiser
The New York Times
San Francisco News
Seattle Post-Intelligencer
Sports Illustrated
The [Nashville] *Tennesseean*
TIME magazine
USA Today

Websites

www.ashof.org
www.auburn.edu
www.baltimoreravens.com
www.bleacherreport.com
www.bryantmuseum.ua.edu
www.clemson.edu
www.collegefootball.org
www.colts.com
www.dallascowboys.com
www.ESPN.com
www.fsu.edu
www.imdb.com
www.kcchiefs.com
www.kenstabler.com
www.miamidolphins.com
www.msu.edu

www.NCAA.com
www.NCAA.org
www.nd.edu
www.NFL.com
www.profootballhof.com
www.seahawks.com
www.SI.com
www.tournamentofroses.com
www.ua.edu
www.unl.edu
www.utexas.edu
www.yankees.mlb.com

Other Sources

1993 Alabama Football Media Guide
2015 SEC Football Media Guide
2011 University of Alabama Media Guide
2015 Alabama Football Record Book
2004 Green Bay Packers Media Guide
Archives at the Paul W. Bryant Museum
International News Service
Professional Football Researchers Association
WHNT, Huntsville, AL
The Associated Press

About the Author

Christopher Walsh has been an award-winning sportswriter since 1990 and currently covers the Southeastern Conference for Bleacher Report. Walsh's recent honors include the First Amendment Award (formerly Freedom of Information Award) by the Associated Press Managing Editors, two Pulitzer Prize nominations, two Herby Kirby Memorial Awards (the Alabama Sports Writers Association's highest honor), and he's a four-time award winner from the Football Writers Association of America. His previous beats include covering the Green Bay Packers, Arizona Cardinals, and Tampa Bay Buccaneers, along with Major League Baseball's Arizona Diamondbacks. Originally from Minnesota and a graduate of the University of New Hampshire, Walsh currently resides in Tuscaloosa, Alabama. He has authored 24 books.